Problem, Risk, and Opportunity Enterprise Management

Problem, Risk, and Opportunity Enterprise Management

*How to use language, data, information, and
analytics that easily align with the ways we think*

by Brian W. Hagen

Probabilistic Publishing

Senior Editor: Paul Wicker
Editor: Brian Solon
Associate Editor: Nancy Winchester

Initial printing: August, 2018

Probabilistic Publishing   www.decisions-books.com
                                e-mail: dave@decisions-books.com
1702 Hodge Lake Ln
Sugar Land, TX 77478
281-277-4006

Written, designed, and printed in the United States of America.

Library of Congress Control Number: 2018952221

ISBN: 978-1-941075-03-6
ISBN: 1-9741075-03-7

To Ron, Amos, and Danny

Reviews

"Thought-provoking book! Weaving in management theory, economics, math, biology and psychology, the author provides a detailed explanation of the influences to the modern-day decision and how to harness for the optimal business decision."

–Patricia Anderson, ERM Director, AMGEN

"The fascinating compilation of wisdom, knowledge, experience, and breakthrough narrative-based analytics shared in this text could not have come at a more crucial time—truly a game changer. Dr. Hagen's upbeat style of communicating difficult material, makes the lessons herein assessable to students, C-suite executives and line managers alike; while providing us all with the most comprehensive guidebook available on the hows and whys of personal and professional decision-making, along with the road map to doing it more effectively."

–Carmen Medina, VP, Technical Services, Parexel International

"*PRO Enterprise Management* is essential reading for anyone trying to improve their critical business decision-making process. PRO EM begins where the subject should begin: with the fundamentals of decision-making psychology. If we don't really want to know the truth we simply don't consider it in ANY decision-making model. After providing a foundation for decision-making, *PRO EM* proceeds to lay out a straightforward approach to complex business decision making based on careful analysis of the three key aspects of any business decision: understanding the problem, identifying the risks, and framing the opportunities."

–Joe Hessmiller, eMarketing Director, Computer Aid, Inc.

"Brian's *PRO Enterprise Management* is one of the most profound and impressive books on risk management practices I have ever read. It's unique insights serve as a practical guide on how to evolve risk management practices to enhance strategic decision support and provide exceptional business value. It went above and beyond my expectations and is a must-read for all decision makers and risk practitioners!"

–Miriam Kraus, Global Senior Vice President, Global GRC, SAP

"Today, working in corporate compliance and risk requires one to overcome the challenge of making a decision in the face of overwhelming data and analytics. *PRO Enterprise Management* shows you what types of questions to ask to make a decision, and the ability to measure the quality of that decision in terms of value creation or erosion. This book explains how to navigate the subtleties between managing problems and managing risk and provides solutions that are as simple as possible (but not simpler) to bridge the gap from Big Data to corporate decision making."

–Neil McCullough, PhD, EVP Quality and Compliance, ICON

"Finally, someone has developed the missing link—a sound methodology that more clearly and directly ties risk management to decision making. Brian Hagen argues successfully that enterprise risk management is primarily a decision-making process that must be integrated into a coherent, repeatable, enterprise-wide method to manage your portfolio of decisions across problems, risks and opportunities. He includes compelling arguments and robust examples that demonstrate how to quantify the alternatives, thereby improving business and financial decisions."

–Jay R. Taylor, Former General Director, Strategic Risk Management, GM

"During the last couple of decades, business leaders have believed that more information could eventually deliver better results. Consequently, we have been inundated by systems, methods and technologies to gather and deliver tsunamis of data and avalanches of information. Like these adjectives, the veritable deluge of data and information has not necessarily been a good thing, because actual, important, real-life decisions are being made on the basis of these out-of-context elements. Now that data acquisition is easier and information can be better constructed from it, leaders of all stripes must learn how to make it actionable. This is a evolutionary discipline which must I contend is prerequisite to success.

"Enter Dr. Brian Hagen and *PRO Enterprise Management*. Dr. Hagen presents a visionary approach to taking a very holistic look at the problems, risks, and opportunities (hence the acronym PRO) of any business situation (or complex life situation event) that ultimately requires a decision. The approach not only helps to establish the typical return-on-investment point of view, but also an analysis of what would happen if you didn't make an investment (sort of an "anti-ROI"). It all sounds so intuitive, but it is actually very complex. Brian and his team take us step by step through the concepts and approach with lots of anecdotes and practical advice along the way. There are some detailed statistical analytics occasionally, but don't be intimidated by the math, everything is well explained (and, frankly, you could really skip the heavy math sections if you are more interested in the concepts). In the end, you will realize that it is not about the data or information, it is all about the decisions. These decisions give life to the information and help knowledge morph into wisdom.

"Reading this book will be the best decision you'll make."

–Dr. Michael Breggar, Managing Partner, Infosys Consulting

"There are many fine books on decision analysis and decision-making that elucidate valuable approaches and tools. But these are not compatible with the way executive, managers, and their analysts think. Brian Hagen's book fills an important gap by demonstrating *how* and *why* a straightforward narrative approach can be used to make these approaches and tools far more effective, efficient, and less biased. After Dr. Hagen shared his narrative approach with me several years ago, the way I approach consulting has been dramatically and forever changed, my clients are happier, and strategy projects lead to higher quality decisions more quickly. Once you read this, it will change your approach to decision making and to analysis of problems, risks, and opportunities as well.

–Paul Papayoanou, Ph.D., Managing Director, Dragonfly,
and author of *Game Theory for Business*

Synopsis

The fundamental responsibility of executives and managers is to deliver value to the bottom line of the company. The primary mechanism for achieving this goal is decision making. To be most effective, decision making must be considered—more specifically primed—from an enterprise perspective first, then other perspectives must follow. In your personal and professional life you make decisions about only three things:

1. How to resolve problems (P),
2. How to mitigate risks (R), and,
3. How to capture opportunities (O).

You own a continuously evolving portfolio of problems, risks, and opportunities. The dilemma you constantly face is, which *problems*, *risks*, and *opportunities* (PRO) should you pursue at this point in time? I refer to this as the "PRO Dilemma." To be an excellent decision maker, you must become a master of resolving this PRO Dilemma. You can achieve that by answering and exploring the five questions of PRO Enterprise Management:

1. "What are your PRO items?"
2. "Which erode the most value if not pursued?"
3. "Which, if pursued, create or protect the most value?"
4. "Which should/will you pursue at this point in time?"
5. "What are the implications to your plan and budget?"

While it sounds straightforward, the challenge is that our natural capabilities in decision making are constrained by the limits of a 100,000 to 200,000 year-old operating system, the human brain.

To overcome this, we need analytics—but not just any logically sound analytics. For the results of analytics to influence our decision making, they must first influence our beliefs. We make decisions based on beliefs, and our beliefs are influenced by the way we think and form judgments. Current normative theories of decision making (decision analysis, Monte Carlo methods, real options, predictive analytics, etc.) insufficiently bridge analytics from the logic and tools to the way we think and form judgments. These methods are also resource intensive in time and cost and therefore cannot be applied to most of the decisions we make. Descriptive theories don't have the analytical rigor to ensure we get the right answer. *PRO Enterprise Management* provides the bridge from thought to decision and action through narrative-based approaches and the language of tipping points.

Our innate system is woefully over-challenged by the vast number and complexity of the personal and professional decisions we make. The notion of a PRO portfolio overwhelms all of us, yet this is precisely the dilemma we all face. Asking the five questions of *PRO Enterprise Management* is the most fundamental job of an executive or manager. Managing both your personal and professional PRO portfolios (coupled with some luck) is the path to a satisfying and accomplished life.

Preface

"Simplicity is the ultimate sophistication."
—Leonardo da Vinci

Throughout history there have been many reminders of da Vinci's insight when it comes to the importance of simplicity in problem solving and the design of systems and processes. The eloquent quote attributed to Albert Einstein, *"Everything should be made as simple as possible, but not simpler"* is one such reminder. Another is the pragmatic *"Keep It Simple, Stupid"* or KISS, which gained popularity in the 1970s as a design principle attributed to Kelly Johnson, a Lockheed aircraft engineer. The initial solutions to problems and the designs of systems and processes are often overly complex. Over time, efficiencies and simplifications are discovered or revealed through use. Corporate and governmental *continuous improvement* programs are based on the natural evolution of understanding and insight that is enabled through use.

As Peter Drucker made clear in the 1950s, *"Whatever a manager does, he does through making decisions."* Decision making is the headwaters from which all value creation and protection flow. However, it is tricky business providing sound and timely decision support that resonates and sticks for executives and managers. Most corporate and governmental decision-making processes are woefully overdue for significant streamlining and improvement, and to further complicate matters, each executive and manager likely has their own way of thinking about specific decisions. If the staff performs a complex analysis that doesn't match the manager's way of thinking, the complex analysis will likely be discarded without effect.

There is good news. Significant emerging theories, understandings, and evidence on the workings of neural pathways in our brains are providing insights into both our innate strengths and the underlying sources of biases in our thinking and judgment. These insights can be integrated into simplified corporate decision-making processes, which can significantly improve our corporate, governmental, and personal decision making.

We can already see hints of these insights, such as the continuous improvement patches on decision making processes that attempt to address our limitations and biases. This is similar to the patchwork the human brain evolved by adding, withering, and overriding neural pathways since homo erectus emerged some 1.3 million years ago with a "ballooned" prefrontal neocortex. The human brain has evolved through evolutionary tinkering to improve our mental processes, flawed as they may be. There is no complete redesign of the brain in our future (*evolution just doesn't work that way*), but we can redesign, improve, and simplify our decision making processes to better account for and integrate the way we think, believe, judge, contemplate, and ultimately decide while minimizing the adverse effects of our innate and acquired mental short-comings.[1]

I am a decision scientist. Improving decision making in corporations, governmental agencies, and people's personal lives is what holds my interest. My laboratory for over thirty years has been organizations within corporations ranging from start-ups to multi-nationals across a variety of industries. This laboratory has afforded me the opportunity to test and observe the broad nature of corporate decision making and to establish a "line-of-sight" on what works and what doesn't. Today's decision scientists must leverage an array of disciplines, including decision analytical methods, information systems and data analytics, neuroscience, cognitive psychology, behavioral economics, social psychology; not to mention foundational business school topics such as finance, accounting, marketing, organizational theory, and organizational behavior. The bridges between these disciplines to effect a comprehensive, holistic corporate decision making theory and practice are improving (but we have a long way to go). Much more understanding and collaboration across these disciplines are needed.

As other fields are providing insights into human thinking and judgment, the quantitative fields supporting decision making and information sciences are busy developing their next generation applications and information systems. Are these disciplines converging toward a generalized solution to corporate decision making? Unfortunately, they are not, and they often add complexity rather than reduce it.

Operations research (OR) emerged during World War II to improve military planning by employing quantitative methods to identify optimized solutions to problems. In the decades following the war, operations research focused on problems in business, industry, and society. There have been points in time when quantitative

---

1 We acknowledge that Intelligent Design is an alternative theory to traditional macro-evolution; however, as we'll discuss in Chapter 6, starting with the premise of Intelligent Design does not change the conclusions we will present as to how our brains work and how our decision making can be improved.

analysts ("quants") like me believed they were on track to a significant breakthrough that would revolutionize organizational decision making. There was great hope that these methods would lead to quantitative methods that could be applied to generalized decision making in corporations and governmental agencies. Operations Research is still a growing discipline with a long history of successes, but as of today, no standard, broadly-applied quantitative method for generalized decision making has emerged.

In the 1950s, artificial intelligence (AI) emerged, and in the late 1970s and 80s, AI became a hot topic with hopes of reaching some generalized decision support solutions. Though the field continues to make important progress, it is deeply divided into subfields of interest and application. Breakthroughs in neuroscience are providing insights into the structure and workings of the human brain, which are enabling the AI community to reconsider their mathematical representations of the brain. Ray Kurzweil, inventor and futurist, predicts that by 2029, machines "will appear to be conscious and that they will be convincing to biological people when they speak."[2] IBM's *Watson*, an artificial intelligence system that can answer questions based on natural language, beat previous human champions on the game show *Jeopardy!* A critical and necessary breakthrough for automated decision making must go beyond just answering the next question but also knowing what the next question should be.

As a doctoral student at Stanford University during the 1980s, I was convinced that my topic of study—decision analysis—would be *that* generalized method and analytical approach that would be applied to decision making throughout organizations across most, if not all, industries. During that time, management consulting firms were emerging that specialized in decision analysis applications and they were commanding top dollars for their services. Corporations such as General Motors and Chevron were training internal staff in these methods and establishing internal organizations specializing in these services for their companies. It seemed like there was momentum and a path to the broader application of these methods to generalized decision making in organizations.

But as I was basking in the glow with my fellow graduate students studying these quantitative methods and eager to take these developments to the next level of innovation and application, there were signs that we might not be on track to such a glorious destination. For me, the most notable signs were the reactions from within

---

2   Ray Kurzweil, *How to Create a Mind: The Secret of Human Thought Revealed* (London: The Penguin Group, 2012), pages 209-210.

the walls of Stanford University among the cognitive psychologists, including the late Amos Tversky and his visiting colleague and future Nobel Laureate, Daniel Kahneman. We had regularly scheduled colloquia in which speakers were invited to present their latest research followed by a panel discussion. The speakers were from both the decision analysis community (*normative* theory of decision making, such as my dissertation advisor, Ron Howard), and from the cognitive psychology community (part of the *descriptive* theory of decision making, some of whom are now considered behavioral economists).

Imprinted in my memory is the polite smile and rolling eyes of Amos Tversky as my normative theorist colleagues would be articulating their latest thinking, offering, or rebuttal. I remember interpreting Amos' expressions to mean, "The normative theory guys just don't get it. It just doesn't work that way for people." His body language and facial expressions were cues that would serve as an intellectual tipping point for me. Since then, I always have been fascinated by the research of individuals such as Amos Tversky, Daniel Kahneman, and many others in the fields of cognition and behavioral economics, and I have attempted to employ their research conclusions into my practice as a decision consultant.

Many years later, I began to understand and realize the profound impact and nature of the brain's *subconscious, involuntary* thought processes that support and at times undermine decision making. How can we even begin to design effective decision analyses, processes, and systems without understanding and leveraging the underlying machinations—both the *voluntary* and *involuntary* decision-influencing systems—that the brain uses in decision making? It seems so obvious, once stated. Or are all the decision support analyses and processes relegated to being at most a psychological *priming effect*[3] on individuals and having to compete with a multitude of influences sorted out in our subconscious mind during the mental exercise of decision making?

While the normative and descriptive decision analysis communities were developing, the business intelligence (BI) community focused on how to codify information and the capabilities of an organization and convert these into knowledge. Their idea is that by

---

3   In simple terms, priming is a subconscious, procedural (implicit) memory effect in which exposure to one stimulus influences a response to another stimulus. See Chapter 7 for a discussion on the different types and stages of human memory.

capturing this knowledge, they can provide historical, current, and predictive views of business operations and beyond. The goal is to improve overall corporate decision making through analytics:

- ◆ Data, text, and process mining,
- ◆ Benchmarking and business performance management, and
- ◆ Predictive and prescriptive analytics.

We do not know the degree to which BI will be successful in supporting generalized corporate decision making. As of the writing of this book, I submit that they are off track and will miss their ultimate goal (with the exception of data-rich recurring decisions like those of a home loan officer). They need to reframe their underlying assumptions and approaches to account for and incorporate the intricate and nuanced human nature of decision making.

In the absence of a comprehensive, holistic corporate decision making theory and practice, we are witnessing an explosion of *specialized* solutions and applications, for *specialized* problems with *specialized* metrics. The hope of corporate decision making on a "level playing field" of comparison across business units and functions, geographies, programs, or products is being buried under the fallout of this explosion. Unfortunately, some of these specialized solutions and offerings—especially the corporate home-grown varieties—are flawed either in their decision framing or their logic, resulting in a loss of decision quality.

For the highly complex and impactful decisions faced by corporations, there are good, proven decision analytic methods available: decision analysis, Monte Carlo methods, game theory, and real options. But these methods require experienced experts and significant time and effort to apply. As a result, these methods are consigned to the most complex situations and are not used for generalized decision making. Moreover, decisions have a shelf life. Delaying a decision can be beneficial or deleterious, but usually time is working against you as options begin to dissipate or the situation is redefined by events. Opportunities can become risks, and risks can become costly problems. Decision timeliness matters.

If we desire to achieve, anytime soon, comprehensive, holistic, practical corporate decision making methods that leverage the insights and capabilities across the many diverse fields, it is time for a course correction. We need to establish some basic principles to enable coherence in future breakthroughs and developments so that the sum of these parts creates simplified, integrated, and valuable corporate decision making.

In the USA, this urgent course correction goes beyond the corporate world as there is a growing sense of urgency and frustration throughout the country with the federal government's decision gridlock in the face of a multitude of globally impactful issues that are crying out for decisive action. Consider this book a clarion call and a first attempt at systematically integrating the current understanding of the many disciplines—including the emerging discipline of neuroeconomics—required to codify the streamlined, comprehensive, holistic, generalized decision making philosophy, theory, practice, and methods.

This is a book that I wish was part of my curriculum back in my university days. I'm grateful to have had the time to write this book, leveraging the contributions of *many* individuals from *many* disciplines and to *pay it forward* for current and future university students so that they may start their careers with a clear vision of a model for effective and efficient corporate decision making across an enterprise. I'm also looking forward to using this book to help internal and external business management consultants and change agents do a consistent and defendable job identifying and measuring the value of the changes they recommend to managers and executives. Most of all, I'm looking forward to enabling high quality decision making throughout the enterprise—something executives and board members should demand. So, let's get started. I hope you enjoy our journey.

PROlogue

Bob Charette
Managing Director, Decision Empowerment Institute

A few years ago, an ex-plant manager acquaintance confided that he often wished his office had two doors. Then at the annual budget review, he would instruct his administrative assistant to line up everyone who wanted his approval of their next-year budget proposal based upon certain criteria. Behind door number one would be those with proposals outlining all the costs involved and their projected benefits.

Behind door number two, he said, his administrative assistant would be instructed to line up all those whose proposal showed not only its costs and benefits, but the quantitative rationale as to why their proposal was a better investment for the plant than any of the others he was likely to review. His assistant would then be instructed to only let those behind this second door enter his office.

My friend smiled wryly as he told me he was sure that there would never be anyone behind his second door.

This story illustrates the quintessential question managers and executives face today, and which is answered in Brian Hagen's book. Every day, managers at every level within an organization are faced with *the* challenging question of how to allocate scarce organizational resources against a myriad of competing and usually worthwhile objectives. Of course, answering the question requires a method for sorting through, in an objective and practical manner, all the competing proposals as well as being able to demonstrate that some are better than others in allocating limited organizational resources.

From a theoretical perspective, the solution is simple: pick those demonstrating the best value, i.e., the ones that generate the best free cash flow. However, from a practical standpoint, how does a manager or executive actually *do* that? How do you create a "level playing field," as it were, where a plant manager, for instance, can compare the value of spending money on such diverse possibilities such as buying new machinery in anticipation of a growing economy, starting a new process quality improvement initiative, or replacing the roof to the main building where the manufacturing occurs? Each may have value, but which has the *most* value?

Picking one out of three choices may not be overly difficult to sort out, but what if there are a dozen or several dozen or more proposals for spending organizational resources (which is the common occurrence)? Which five, or ten, or even thirty proposals create, or alternatively, protect the most value for the organization? And after those are selected, how defensible are they when presented to senior executives and the board of directors? Are the choices explainable not only to senior executive management, but to the constituencies advocating each proposal in a way that they will accept that their proposal wasn't in the best interest of the organization?

The answer to these questions and many more lay in Brian's book. He explains that anyone with a decision—which as Brian says is the allocation of some resource which can't be undone without some cost involved—always chooses to allocate a resource among three competing interests, namely, how to resolve problems (P), how to mitigate risks (R), and how to capture opportunities (O). The "PRO Dilemma" managers face is to select which set of problems, risks, and opportunities create and or protect the most value for the organization. Doing so in an effective and efficient manner requires a decision process that is practical, takes into account how we as humans actually make (biased) decisions involving risk and opportunity, and is mathematically robust enough as well as understandable that anyone in the organization can apply it without difficulty. It is a tall order, but one that Brian's book meets.

As we all know, while organizations claim that they follow rigorous processes when they make decisions (how could they publicly claim differently?), we know the reality is much different. In fact, a recent study of 500 managers and executives showed that "98% failed to apply best practices when making decisions."[1]

While there are "obvious" decisions, which everyone can agree with the resource allocations that must be made, most decision making in organizations is siloed—competing objectives can't be quantitatively evaluated against each other easily or objectively. As a result, too many resource allocation decisions are made based on who can make the most convincing PowerPoint presentation, with the poor future financial returns entirely predictable.[2]

Brian's book shows it doesn't have to be that way. To paraphrase the late management expert Peter Drucker, long-term

---

1   E. Larson. "Don't Fail at Decision Making Like 98% of Managers Do," *Forbes*, 17 May 2017.

2   K. Shariff and J. Davis-Peccoud. "Score your organization to improve decision effectiveness," *Bain*, 28 March 2012.

corporate success is based not on future decisions, but the future of present decisions. One large pharmaceutical corporation has taken this idea to heart and has increased its financial success by applying the PRO decision process described in this book. Like others in their industry that face high risk, high reward resource allocation decisions, this company increasingly found that there was no effective way to quantitatively assess the risks of their decisions either individually, or collectively, or to communicate risk in a meaningful way to senior executives.

Risk was, at best, qualitatively assessed, which meant that the risks among different decisions could not be straightforwardly, if at all, compared. What one manager thought was a "low" risk was viewed as others as being "medium" or even "high" risk, whatever those terms really meant since they were perceived differently by each manager. In no way could a risk, especially its likelihood of occurrence, be quantified in a consistent and measurable manner that showed the financial impact to the corporation if the risk were to occur or how much resource was required to protect the corporation from it occurring through mitigation efforts. Risk, one senior manager at the company told me, "had lost its meaning."

However, by using the process and methods described in Brian's book, managers were finally able to place different types of resource allocation questions all on the same decision plane: problems, risks and opportunities were now able to be assessed in a consistent, understandable, and most importantly, financially measurable manner. Resource allocation decisions were now framed in the same language used by senior executives, and managers could easily explain and defend the rationale behind the decisions.

Interestingly, managers told me that by using the PRO decision approach, they found that they could demonstrate to executives how their investment proposals were giving back resources to the corporation, not just asking for them. In other words, they were able to demonstrate how corporate value was being created and being protected by taking certain decisions and deferring others.

For instance, a decision was made to harden a certain manufacturing site in the event of a natural disaster after using the PRO approach described in this book. In the past, such a decision had been very hard to justify, as the return on investment for that expenditure didn't look worthwhile in comparison to others that were being proposed, managers told me. However, by quantitatively assessing the totality of the risks involved, including within and across the company's supply chain, it was shown that hardening the site would not only protect millions of dollars of corporate value, but protect the corporation's customers and other suppliers from massive disruption. Fortunately, the site was hardened mere months before a natural catastrophe did strike, which would have caused massive financial, reputational, and regulatory costs if the investment had not been taken.

Anyone who has to make a decision and struggles with deciding what needs to be pursued and what doesn't owes it to themselves to read and take the time to understand what's in Brian's book. I think you'll find new ways of thinking about how you (and your organization) can make radically better decisions resulting in improved outcomes with much less effort and cost than you ever expected.

A Note to the Decision Analysis Community

My work as a decision consultant has been split between strategy projects and portfolio projects. My strategy project experience has been quite varied by industry and focus, including corporate strategy, growth strategy, supply chain strategy, manufacturing strategy, acquisition and divestiture strategy, product strategy, and tax strategy. In these projects I have followed a process and analysis that is familiar to many of you, including the use of tools such as influence diagrams, strategy tables, tornado diagrams, and s-curves. In my view the great benefit to clients in these projects is crafting a highly-tailored model that includes all of the key issues, uncertainties, decisions, and value measures that enables crisp insights into the decisions in focus. A significant fraction of the cost of these engagements in time and money is the building, testing, and vetting of the model.

Portfolio projects have been and continue to be a large source of my client engagements. Fundamentally, these projects amount to the dilemma of having many ways to allocate limited resources and thus having to choose which expenditures are best for the organization. These have included portfolios of products, R&D projects, acquisition targets, risks, improvement projects, capital projects, and marketing and sales initiatives. For many years I approached portfolio projects like strategy projects in that I would build a portfolio model from scratch, requiring much time and cost. Over time I learned to reuse portions of the portfolio models and began wondering about a universal approach and model that could be used for most if not all portfolio projects. For me, that universal approach is what I call *PRO Enterprise Management.*

There were several objectives I wanted to achieve in developing a generalized portfolio evaluation method, including:

♦ Scalable level of evaluation from 15 minutes to as complex as deemed necessary by decision makers,

♦ Consistent and logically sound accounting of uncertainty, leveraging subject matter experts, information systems, and predictive analytics,

♦ Standardized structures that are easy to learn, even for individuals without mathematics or finance backgrounds,

♦ Logically sound aggregation within and across portfolios, and

♦ Framing and structuring that better leverages our innate strengths while attempting to mitigate our known biases and thinking limitations.

As indicated in Figure 12.1 of Chapter 12, there is a single tree structure from which all problems, risks, and opportunities can be modeled. The tipping point of a material consequence represents the antecedent to consequences we either don't want, as is the case for problems and risks, or to consequences we desire, as is the case for opportunities. As detailed in Chapter 11, the structure and calculation of the probability of the tipping point occurring can be as complex as we deem necessary or as simple as a direct assessment of the probability by a subject matter expert.

The biggest difference between standard decision analysis practices and PRO Management practices is in the framing, assessing, and modeling of consequences and the creation of the distribution of the outcome variable(s). In effect, PRO Management uses a direct assessment of the outcome distribution given the tipping point has occurred. This is done by performing a 10-50-90 assessment of the outcome variable, not numerically, but as three narratives:

♦ 10th percentile NPV narrative,

♦ 50th percentile NPV narrative, and

♦ 90th percentile NPV narrative.

The narratives then need to be numerically assessed using a net present value of discounted free cash flow model yielding the 10th percentile, 50th percentile, and 90th percentile of the NPV given the tipping point has occurred.

A key benefit of this approach is that all involved parties, especially executive decision makers, can be involved in the definition of the narratives. If there are disagreements in the definition of the narratives it is straightforward to change narratives and determine the impact on the results of the analysis such as the impact to investment productivity. Disagreements on the narratives rarely result in significant changes in investment productivity. As an example, if the investment productivity of a PRO item is about 22 changes to the narratives might move it between something like 17 to 28. But it does not become negative or less than 10 or more than 50. PRO items have a great spread in investment productivity, much more so than what executives and managers realize. In practice I have found that the priorities specified by an investment productivity curve do not change much if at all given extensive sensitivity analyses and assuming the PRO item frames hold up to executive scrutiny.

Another key advantage is modeling on an incremental basis of value to the enterprise. The impact of PRO items to the enterprise can be modeled on an incremental basis if we use the net present value of discounted free cash as the outcome variable. Many in the decision analysis community understand this notion and use it in practice. This means we do not need to calculate the enterprise's entire cash flow when evaluating investments in problems, risks, and opportunities. We only need to model and calculate the incremental changes in sales and costs and their incremental impact to net present value. Mathematically, this can be done because the net present value of discounted free cash flow is a linear operator with respect to delta changes in the income statement line items or after tax cash flow adjustments.

PRO Management methods are new and different from what has been typically practiced in the decision analysis community. You likely have many questions. This book is the result of reducing the content from a much larger draft book that includes all of the mathematical proofs, many example applications, and issues such as addressing dependent PRO items and making a single investment that impacts multiple PRO items. This larger detailed book will be available in the future.

Acknowledgements

In 2005 I was on a business trip visiting a pharmaceutical company near Princeton, New Jersey. I had arrived the afternoon the day before the meeting and decided to take a stroll on the Princeton University campus for a little inspiration regarding a financial mathematics problem I had been thinking about for the past year. It was a beautiful early spring evening. I set out across campus for Fine Hall to stop by the office of one of my academic heroes, Nobel Laureate John Nash. Fine Hall was empty; everyone had left for the day. I scanned the "old school" magnetic directory board and found the name John Nash and his office number. His office was up on the 8th or 9th floor, I don't remember which. I took the elevator on up just to stand outside his office door for probably no more than a minute and then I was off to dinner in Princeton.

The next day I had my meeting and hustled back to the airport in Newark, New Jersey to catch my flight back to Los Angeles. Fortunately, I was upgraded to business class on the flight, which meant a more comfortable seat to do a little work and drink a little wine. With a pen and a yellow legal pad in hand I settled in for the six-hour plus flight back to L.A.

Like a case of *furor poeticus* over the course of the flight I scribbled down the solution and the underlying mathematical proofs to the problem. I remember getting off the plane in L.A. feeling both excited and cautious. The solution to the problem is the foundation of the topic of this book, *PRO Enterprise Management*. And now, thirteen years later, after hundreds of applications across a variety of industries and governmental entities, it is time to acknowledge and thank the many individuals who have contributed to the ideas, applications, product development, and the maturing of PRO Enterprise Management.

Bob Charette has been a friend, colleague, and business partner for over thirty years. He is the cofounder of our company, Decision Empowerment Institute (DEI). His collaboration and contributions to this work have been and continue to be invaluable. I am forever grateful for his support and encouragement.

I would also like to share my sincere appreciation and gratitude to Ali (Naci) Atabek, Terry Chinn, Koray Hagen, and Rajeev C. Sane for their technical contributions in creating the software applications that enable PRO Enterprise Management to be a practical management reality.

My appreciation and gratitude extend to many friends, colleagues, and clients who have contributed by reviewing early versions of the manuscript, adopting the methods and tools within their organizations, developing application templates, and providing support and encouragement over the years. This is a long list of individuals so please accept my apology if I have missed you in this list. The many significant contributors include: David Afzali, Patricia Anderson, Greg Anthos, Suha Ari, Kaan Atilla, Pat Barth, Tarun Bhatia, Michael Breggar, Mark Brodfuehrer, Stacy Brovitz, Dan Cabbell, Dan Cain, Darren Chambers, Steven Cherry, Vijay Chiruvolu, Maisha Cobb, Peg Connelly, Marc Cromer, Marty Dallas, Isabelle Daoust, Marty Deberardinis, Don Finch, Ron Fitzmartin, Coleen Glessner, Conrad Heilman, Lindsay Hernandez, Joe Hessmiller, Eric Horvitz, Rob Johnston, Jeff Keisler, Kim Kerry, Rob Kleinbaum, Miriam Kraus, David Kreutter, Chris Kurtz, Jim Lang, Patty Leuchten, Nancy Liu, Weili Lu, Jim Matheson, Peter McAliney, Scott McCarty, Neil McCullough, Tom McGurk, Chris McKenna, Carmen Medina, Ann Meeker-O'Connell, Kevin Minds, Philip Morin, Luka Mucic, Rick Musser, Greg Nagle, Joe Newell, Waseem Noor, Paul Papayoanou, Lee Partridge, Michelle Priem, Nick Pudar, Brad Repp, David Sandahl, Bill Schmidt, Paul Seaback, Cathryn Shaw-Reid, Sameer Sivammnuaiphorn, Jay R. Taylor, Peter Thompson, Hasan Tureman, Tim Valko, Jaime Velez, Arthur Vermillion, Michelle Wallace, Anne Wesler, Steve Whittaker, Jay Widmyer, Ming Wu, Matt Yedwabnick, and Josh Zimmerman. Once again, my most sincere gratitude to each and every one of you.

When we think about decision theory we must distinguish between a *normative* theory – how decisions *should* be made – and a *descriptive* theory – how decisions *are* made. In the 1980s it was my good fortune to attend Stanford University, the only university at the time where you could study under the thought leaders of both, the yin and yang. My dissertation advisor was Ron Howard, a founder of the *normative* decision theory he named decision analysis (DA). The late Amos Tversky provided invaluable *descriptive* theory tutelage on my research in the realm of subjective estimation. Without their contributions to my thinking and understanding of decision making this book would not have been possible to write. I am forever grateful to them both.

The editing of this book was an extremely difficult and laborious task. The original manuscript was well over 800 pages. Brian Solon took on the Herculean task of restructuring and reducing the book to a readable 380 pages while keeping all of the key concepts and flow intact. At the time I didn't think that was possible but nonetheless Brian prevailed. I am grateful for Brian's timely and critical contribution.

I thank Paul Wicker and Dave and Debbie Charlesworth for their detailed copy editing, numerical error checking, and challenges regarding the contents of the book as all three of them are more than excellent copy editors; they are accomplished decision analysts too. We also appreciate Nancy Winchester's suggestions and corrections.

My final note of gratitude is for my loving family. My wife, Mine, has been on this journey with me for thirty-five years and has always provided her loving and insightful support. My sons, Koray and Altay, and my daughter-in-law, Klodiana, have all provided both encouragement and inspiration.

Thank you all!
Brian W. Hagen, Dana Point, California
July, 2018

Contents

"What is called for is an exquisite balance between two conflicting needs: the most skeptical scrutiny of all hypotheses that are served up to us and at the same time a great openness to new ideas."
– Carl Sagan, Astronomer, Cosmologist, Author

1
A Day in the Life

It's 7:30 Monday morning, and you've just arrived at your office with your Starbucks Venti coffee in hand at a Fortune 200 pharmaceutical company. After a brief "How was your weekend?" discussion with your executive secretary, you slip into your office and behind your desk to check the pile of e-mails that have filled your inbox since you last checked on Sunday evening. With hopes of getting a head start on some critical issues prior to your day of back-to-back meetings, there is a light tap on your door.

"Dave, do you have a quick few minutes?" A staffer's familiar voice and face interject from the doorway. "I'm afraid we got some bad news from the FDA [Federal Drug Administration]. They've put a clinical hold on [fictitious product] Product Crytophan."

"Sure, come on in Chris. Let me guess. They want more toxicity studies?"

Chris remains standing and says, "Yes. We'll need to run more clinical trials for 'tox'. You know, this could push product launch out a couple of years!"

"Ouch!" you say. "There is no way we can delay the product launch that long. You'll have to figure out how to reduce the time of those additional studies. Listen, I have another meeting starting at eight. Get together with the team and put together a plan and budget on how we can fast track these studies and minimize the product launch delay! Okay?"

"Got it," Chris replies as he bolts out of your office.

Your executive secretary pops into your office and reports, "Stephan is here for your 'Tech Transfer' meeting."

[When the location of the manufacturing site for a pharmaceutical product is changed, a formal process must be used called a "Technology Transfer," or "Tech Transfer" for short. Tech Transfers require formal steps for verification and validation prior to FDA approval for U.S. products and ultimately product production.]

"Good morning Dave," Stephan says as he walks into your office.

"Good morning Stephan. Have a seat. So, how's the tech transfer going?"

"Well, mostly on track," Stephan reports. "But we are getting a little nervous about the CMO [Contract Manufacturing Organization] transfer-site meeting the Tech Transfer schedule."

"Do we have enough safety stock [built-up product inventory] to cover any delay?" you ask.

"Well, that's what I'd like to discuss with you. There are a couple of things going on. We have six months of safety stock built up. But there's a chance the delay may eat through all that. The sales organization has also revised their sales forecast that includes an unanticipated uptick in sales, so we are at risk for a stock out. And, you know this product. We'll lose a good chunk of those customers to our competitor if we can't supply product. I brought a few charts for you to review that detail what I think we should do. We'll need another $200,000 to $250,000 but that will be money well spent to protect those sales!"

"Is Susan [Senior Vice President of Global Operations] on-board with your recommendations?" you question.

"Yes," Stephan replies, "I briefly reviewed this with Susan and she has some questions, but she is on board."

"Let me go through your information and get on my calendar for Thursday. I'm on business travel the next two days." You thumb through the document and add, "Hmmm, I'm a little surprised on the cost. Keep Susan in the loop on this."

As Stephan stands up, your executive secretary steps into your doorway and says, "I've got Jennifer [the CEO] on the line."

You punch line 1 on your phone and say, "Good morning Jennifer."

Jennifer asks about the on-going program you are over-seeing that is focusing on switching the company's products from glass-based to plastic-based vials and syringes as has been done in Japan.

In recent years, the FDA and the life sciences industry has recognized that there are issues with small glass fragments getting into small vials due to the interaction of the product with the interior of the glass vial. Several drugs have recently been recalled due to this potentially hazardous interaction though no adverse events [any unfavorable and unintended sign including an abnormal laboratory finding, symptom, or disease associated with the use of a medical treatment or procedure] have been reported. Based on discussions the CEO has had with other executives in the industry, the CEO is questioning the pace of the program and whether the program should be accelerated.

"Well Jennifer, the 'Glass-to-Plastic' Program could be accelerated," you reply. "We've considered that, but we're pretty tapped out on resources. Adding some consulting support could expedite some of the work. We'll take another look at it and I'll get back to you a.s.a.p. ...yeah, no problem...okay, goodbye."

Your executive secretary taps on your door. "Your nine o'clock appointment is here. Would you like to see Jim now?" she asks.

"Sure, send him in," you reply as you take a long drink of your lukewarm coffee.

"Hey Dave, how are you?" Jim [Team Leader of your Six Sigma / Continuous Improvement Organization] says as he walks into your office and sits down at your conference table.

"I'm fine," you reply as you join him at the table. Jim lays a presentation down in front of you.

"Here is an executive summary of our prioritized project recommendations based on the cost-benefit analysis you requested. The first slide is an overview of recommendations on implementation projects," Jim reports.

You quickly glance through the presentation and then return to the recommendation summary slide. You focus on what strikes you as being the "best" opportunity of the bunch, a project to improve clinical trial supply forecasting.

The Six Sigma program has identified an opportunity to improve clinical supplies planning, tracking, and reconciliation processes. The gist of the opportunity is to reduce the time and effort needed to develop, evaluate, and update clinical supply plans. Currently up to fifty percent of each CSO [Contract Sales Organization] resource is expended creating or updating planning and tracking spreadsheets with associated e-mail. It is difficult to maintain version control and a single reliable source of information.

By purchasing and implementing a clinical trials supply forecasting and simulation software application, the team has determined they could reduce clinical trial costs by about $5 million per year by reducing supply overages, expired kits, and time needed to evaluate protocol and participant recruitment plan changes. The presentation Jim reviews with you breaks down the $5 million annual cost savings. The total cost of implementing this software solution is about $515,000.

"Jim, for now, I'd like to focus on the clinical trial supply forecasting opportunity. Have your team complete the capital request form and get that into Finance. I'd like to get that funded this year. I'll sign it given what you have on these slides. Okay?"

"Let's revisit the rest of your list after the start of next year. The budget is really tight for the rest of the year," you add.

"Thanks, Dave. I'll have the capital request back to you tomorrow for your signature," Jim replies with obvious relief at getting *something* approved this year.

You walk out of your office with Jim and head down the hall to the kitchen area to microwave your cold coffee. Before you reach the kitchen, you hear Quinn, the Vice President of Research and Development (R&D) call out to you.

"Hey Dave!" Quinn says.

You stop and greet the approaching R&D executive, and you notice the urgency in Quinn's eyes. Without pausing, Quinn jumps right to his immediate concern.

"Did you hear about our NDA [New Drug Application] Safety Database issues?" he asks. [During the clinical trials of a drug being studied and analyzed prior to FDA approval and subsequent U.S. product commercialization, a database must be maintained with a consistent process and format that documents any adverse events participants report from drug usage during the clinical trial.]

Before you can respond, Quinn continues, "I can't believe it, but you know the medical coding [formal documentation] responsibility for [fictitious product] Zeebach was given to the doctors and other clinical scientists involved in the trials. There were no standardized coding guidelines for language and terms! The lack of standards could result in a delayed product approval and product launch if we have inconsistencies in coding in the database. I think we should stop these trials now and restart them using our CRO [Contract Research Organization, an outsourcing solution]. It's going to cost us, but we should bite the bullet on this one. This is just an FYI for now; I'm going to discuss this with Frank [the CFO] this afternoon. But we're going to need a financial justification for this and I'm going to need your help with that."

"No problem Quinn," you reply to Quinn's back as he continues down the hall. As you duck into the kitchen to microwave your cold coffee, your thoughts are swimming in the morning's issues.

You head back to your office for a 10:00 am meeting, but you can't seem to remember who it was with. Jessica, one of the U.S. sales leaders, is already sitting at your conference table with a few pages of spreadsheets as you walk in.

"Good morning Jessica. How is it going?" you say with a smile.

"Good morning Dave," she replies. "Things are good."

"Remind me, what are we talking about this morning?"

"We need to talk about [fictitious product] Gapcash sales. Gapcash is still trending well below our sales forecast for the year. We've put together a multi-channel marketing campaign to get some sales lift before year's end. But this is a new campaign and it is beyond this year's marketing budget. We'll still miss this year's sales target for Gapcash, but we think we can significantly shrink the sales gap with a new program," Jessica explains as she points to sales forecast data in the spreadsheets. "The multi-channel campaign will cost about $750,000, and we think it will generate up to two million dollars in sales before year's end."

"Wow, that sounds pretty costly. But we have great margins on Gapcash. Are those new sales or are you just pulling forward next year's sales?"

"No, these projected sales are new sales; we are not targeting our existing customers," Jessica responds.

"So ... I see your sales lift and campaign costs. Did you calculate an ROI [return on investment] for this?" you question.

"No, but I can get you that number," she says with confidence.

"Yes, get the ROI on that before we take that up to Frank [the CFO]. He's not going to be happy with this. I know we consider this product strategic, but we just asked for some budget relief on some other products last week and he complained about the lack of supporting justification. So, put together your best case on this. I'd like to see this one more time before we take it to Frank."

"Thanks Dave," Jessica replies as she gathers her documents and leaves your office.

Welcome to a day in the life of a corporate decision maker. Actually, we have just made it through to 10:30 on Monday morning! It is a fast-paced, dynamic environment with a seemingly never-ending stream of unresolved, poorly resolved, recurring, or emerging issues. Behind most of these issues are requests for additional resources or the reallocation of existing resources. These requests arrive to decision makers in a variety of formats, analyses, and language. They all appear worthy of resources—but at what cost? What exactly will they get in return for these additional expenditures? You can bet Dave will get to all the issues given his "problem solver" reputation. But what will be the quality of the decisions he will make or influence? He must address questions like: "How much value will be created or protected by the implementation of the decisions?" and "To what degree will the risks be mitigated given the recommended expenditures?"

Given the information that typically reaches an executive's desk or computer screen, how can he/she consistently comprehend, compare, and ultimately compete these requests for resources based on the "best" value for the enterprise to ensure that he or she makes the "best" decisions for the enterprise? The information the executives use may come from the corporation's enterprise resource planning (ERP) system in the form of a standard or customized report or dashboard. Or the information and analysis may come from a specialty sales software application and database or from a homegrown spreadsheet application that somebody in the supply chain organization created. Chances are that each of these analyses resulted in insights from different perspectives, but they are likely to have similar yet different value measures, consider different time frames, have substantially different treatments of underlying uncertainties from quantitative to qualitative to not at all. They also may have varying degrees of use of subject matter experts and possibly conflicting conclusions. How do executives and managers sort through this?

"That's what the executive or manager gets paid for," you say. Unfortunately in today's hyper-competitive environment, this is no longer the correct answer. In this fast-paced, data intensive, globally interconnected business world, executives and managers need more than gut instinct and intuition to reach the correct conclusions ("to connect the dots") and to make high quality decisions.

How can decision makers achieve the "exquisite balance" of skeptical scrutiny of the many requests for additional resources while remaining open to the new ideas and better solutions? Whatever the decision support remedy may be to improve the current situation, it will need to fit into the current demanding, dynamic environment, or it will face the fate of all the previous decision analytical support solutions—limited use with limited impacts.

The Great Corporate Decision Analytics Gap

Good information and decision analytics are available to support decision making; however, the proven and insightful tools and techniques are relegated to a small percentage of the decisions. Monte Carlo methods,[1] decision analysis,[2] game theory,[3] real options,[4] and a few other types of analyses that rigorously address complex decisions with multiple value measures in the face of multiple, interrelated sources of uncertainty are all proven methods to support corporate decision making. But these methods require too much time and effort to be used on the vast majority of decisions facing corporate decision makers. Moreover, significant skill and experience are required to perform any one of these types of analyses correctly. Hence these methods are reserved for the most strategic decisions of the organization, if they are used at all.

Humans make thousands of decisions every day ranging from changing stride to avoid stepping into a puddle of water to whether to buy that new red sport sedan. Similarly, thousands of decisions are made in organizations each day, and the vast majority of these are made without much or any conscious thought. It is estimated that 90 to 95 percent of the decisions made in corporations require little to no decision analytical methods or analysis; they just require

---

1   A good reference for Monte Carlo Methods is *Handbook of Monte Carlo Methods* by Dirk P. Kroese, Thomas Tamire, and Zdravko I. Botev. Hoboken, New Jersey: Wiley Series in Probability and Statistics, 2011.

2   A good reference for decision analysis is *Foundations of Decision Analysis* by Ronald A. Howard and Ali E. Abbas. Pearson Education, Inc., 2016.

3   A good reference for game theory applications is *Game Theory for Business: A Primer in Strategic Gaming* by Paul Papayoanou. Sugar Land Texas: Probabilistic Publishing, 2010.

4   A good reference for real options theory and applications is *Real Options in Theory and Practice* by Graeme Gutherie. New York: Oxford University Press (Financial Management Association Survey and Synthesis Series), 2009.

good information and data. These decisions are easily made without undue concern about getting them right, because the decisions are considered obvious by the decision maker. Recurring decisions such as the maintenance of equipment, job promotions, or staffing overtime activities to ensure tasks are completed on schedule are examples of these types of decisions. Also included are non-recurring, one-time decisions such as reorganizing staff after a merger or deciding to add a new packaging line to support projected increases in product demand. The other 5 to 10 percent of the decisions, the ones that are not obvious, could be improved with analytics to support getting the correct decision.

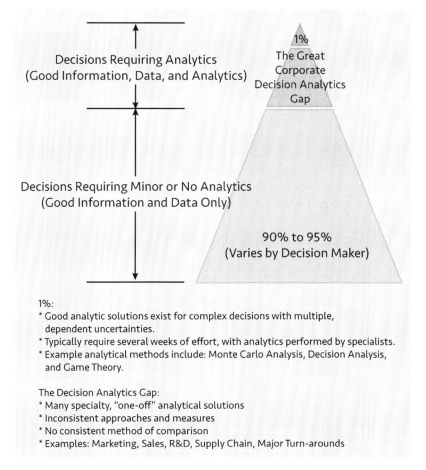

Decisions Requiring Analytics
(Good Information, Data, and Analytics)

1%
The Great Corporate Decision Analytics Gap

Decisions Requiring Minor or No Analytics
(Good Information and Data Only)

90% to 95%
(Varies by Decision Maker)

1%:
* Good analytic solutions exist for complex decisions with multiple, dependent uncertainties.
* Typically require several weeks of effort, with analytics performed by specialists.
* Example analytical methods include: Monte Carlo Analysis, Decision Analysis, and Game Theory.

The Decision Analytics Gap:
* Many specialty, "one-off" analytical solutions
* Inconsistent approaches and measures
* No consistent method of comparison
* Examples: Marketing, Sales, R&D, Supply Chain, Major Turn-arounds

Figure 1.1: The Great Corporate Decision Analytics Gap

Figure 1.1 suggests that roughly one percent of the decisions in a corporation are addressed with rigorous analytics performed by highly trained and experienced analysts (it is probably even less than that in most organizations). The remaining 5% to 10% of decisions that warrant rigorous analytics represent the "Great Corporate Decision Analytics Gap."

This gap is addressed in many ways, with different value measures, using a variety of specialty tools and analytical approaches. There are varying degrees of sophistication for dealing with uncertainty, a wide band of data quality, and multiple ways to incorporate subject matter expertise. These "one-off" decision-supporting analyses are tailored to each class of decision to generate the "believed" most relevant decision-making insight. Highly specialized and unique approaches make it nearly impossible for an executive or manager to consistently compare the enterprise value created or protected and the associated net return across multiple requests for resources.

A primary objective of this book is to fill the "Great Corporate Decision Analytics Gap" with a method and practice that can be applied across all functions of an organization to enable a consistent perspective for corporate decision making.

Key Point:

To maximize long-term enterprise value, corporations need to make decisions on a consistent basis throughout the corporation, based on enterprise-best-value in order to prioritize resource allocation across and within its multitude of customers, products and services, business units, divisions, departments, plants, and functions.

A Vision for Organizational Decision Making

Considering the upper 5 to 10 percent of critical decisions being made today, a vision for organizational decision making would include the following ten capabilities and characteristics:

1. All *decisions* would include, but not be limited to, an enterprise-value perspective balancing short-term with long-term cost and value.

2. All *decisions* would account for all sources and magnitudes of value and cost.

3. All *decisions* would be evaluated on a consistent basis and be compared based on best value for the enterprise.

4. All *decisions* would have sufficient and consistent accounting for uncertainty in information, data, and human judgment.

5. All *decision processes* would be designed to leverage the strengths of human thought processes while attempting to minimize the biases and errors in human judgment.

6. All *decision processes* would ensure the efficient, consistent, and timely use of subject matter expertise.

7. All *decision processes* would build decision quality into the process, not just assess it at the end of the decision process.

8. All *decision processes* would attempt to minimize the number of "must have" expenditures while ensuring all requests for resources compete on a best value basis for the enterprise.

9. *Information systems and predictive analytics* would enable efficient decision making processes through real-time response capability to a broad range of user queries.

10. *Enterprise compensation and incentive systems* would encourage best value decision making for the enterprise.

This book provides methods and approaches to illustrate how these ten corporate decision making capabilities and characteristics can be built into any level of an organization.

The book is built around four main themes:

1. Foundations of Organizational Decision Making

Chapters 2 through 5 focus on the foundations of organizational decision making, including discussions on:

♦ Decision quality and empowerment,
♦ How decision making is about resolving problems (P), mitigating risks (R), and capturing opportunities (O); taken together to create the acronym PRO Management,
♦ The need to embrace and explicitly account for uncertainty, and
♦ The importance of measuring decisions from an enterprise value perspective.

The ultimate management challenge is introduced as the PRO Dilemma: among competing and sometimes conflicting commitments of time and money across problems, risks, and opportunities, how can I determine which commitments should be pursued now to deliver the best value for the enterprise?

2. Belief, Emotion, Cognition, and Judgment in Decision Making

Chapters 6 through 10 focus on the roles of belief, emotion, cognition, and judgment in decision making. These chapters provide a summary of what we have learned from cognitive psychologists, behavioral economists, and neuroscientists regarding the strengths, weaknesses, and biases in human thought and judgment. These learnings underscore the need for simple analytics to improve decision making throughout business and government as well as in our personal lives. They also discuss why a risk-neutral perspective is best for most business and government decisions.

3. PRO Management Constructs and Framework

Chapters 11 through 13 introduce PRO Management constructs and frameworks that enable consistent comparisons of problems, risks, and opportunities throughout the enterprise. The two foundational PRO Management constructs of tipping points and narrative-based analytics are introduced. These improve the speed and quality of decision making. The five questions of PRO Management are introduced to help resolve the PRO Dilemma.

4. PRO Enterprise Management

Chapters 14 through 16 extend the concept of PRO Management to its application throughout the enterprise: PRO Enterprise Management. These chapters explore PRO Management's delegation, escalation, and collaboration within and across organizational structures. Additionally, why capital efficiency requires current Enterprise Risk Management (ERM) practices to be integrated into a PRO Enterprise Management framework is discussed with examples illustrating the benefit of this integration.

The book concludes with an overview on taking the first step to transforming your enterprise into a PRO Enterprise.

"In my house I'm the boss, my wife is just the decision maker."
– Woody Allen, Actor, Writer, Director

2
Decision Quality and Empowerment

Our Decisions Define Our Lives

When we reflect on our past decision making, we tend to focus on the more consequential decisions in our lives. The selection of a university to attend, the field of study to pursue, who to marry, which career path to choose, or which industry or company to work in are all important *crossroads-in-life* decisions, but they are only part of our story. In fact, our lives are probably more the result of the aggregation of smaller day-to-day decisions we made, because those decisions led us to the crossroads in life. Ultimately, the destinations we reach in our personal and professional lives are the results of all the decisions we made, both big and small.

What do you remember from school lessons on decision making during your elementary school years (or your middle or high school years)? Chances are you have no memories of decision-making training because you likely *had* no formal decision-making education. How could something so profound to being human—the skills of considering and making decisions—be absent from our formal educations? You may have had some education in "critical thinking" or "problem solving." Both are important life skills and necessary decision-making elements, but neither is sufficient to enable good decision making. To underscore this void in our educations, ask yourself, "What *is* a decision?" Contemplate this question for a few moments. Chances are you will struggle a bit in coming up with a concise definition. So, let's start there.

What is a Decision?

A *decision* is the commitment of something of value—time or resources—to an explicit course of action. The resources can be money or equipment, and the course of action could be making a purchase or signing a contract. A decision implies that other courses of action are foregone. Often there is a cost to undo a decision. So, we could say a decision is a commitment of something of value to an explicit course of action that is often only revocable at some cost.

Key Point:

A decision is a commitment of something of value to an explicit course of action that is often only revocable at some cost.

Individuals, in both their personal and professional lives, are sometimes involved in conversations about decisions and this can give the incorrect impression that the decisions have already been made. This is a phenomenon I have observed numerous times in many different organizations. It is easy to confuse the notion of *talking* about a decision with that of *making* a decision. Simply stated, a decision is made when there is a commitment of resources.

Good Decisions versus Good Outcomes

A poignant example comes to mind when I consider the distinction between good decisions and good outcomes. It involves my father-in-law. He was a healthy, active man in his mid-seventies when he noticed he was having shortness of breath and seemed to be tiring easily. At the persuasion of his wife and children, he saw a cardiologist for an examination. The cardiologist immediately had my father-in-law admitted into a hospital due to excessive blockage in his arteries. A famous heart surgeon with a stellar success rate recommended immediate surgery based on the seriousness of my father-in-law's condition.

I remember the shock of hearing this news. Given the expert's opinion, did we have any choice in the matter? I remember contemplating this question as my wife and I made plans to go home as quickly as possible. My father-in-law had the heart surgery, but he never regained consciousness after the operation. A few days later, he passed away. Did our family make the *right* decision? That question still haunts some in my family today. The tragic unexpected outcome of my father-in-law's death and our family's loss still stirs emotions even after ten years.

This brings us to the distinction between good decisions and good outcomes. Good decisions attempt to maximize the chances of a good or desired outcome. However, when there is uncertainty involved, good decisions sometimes result in bad or undesired outcomes. I remind myself and my family of this whenever my father-in-law's death comes up. So, what is a good decision? A better question might be: what constitutes a high quality decision?

The Eight Elements of Decision Quality

Since good decisions cannot be defined as those with good outcomes when uncertainty is involved, we must define a good decision by the quality of the process used to make the decision. In other words, we can equate a high quality decision with a high quality decision process. The decision process must result in maximizing our chances of a good or desired outcome while accounting for the resources involved in implementing the decision.

Key Point:

> The quality of a decision with uncertain outcomes should not be measured by its outcome but rather by the quality of the decision process used.

There are at least eight elements to making a high quality decision. The following elements extend previous definitions for decision quality as defined by Manganelli and Hagen[1], and Matheson and Matheson.[2]

1. Incisive Frame

Framing is the work of defining the scope of the decision. Which decisions are in-scope and which are out-of-scope? Framing establishes clearly which decision(s) you are making. In addition, the frame includes the issues, concerns, problems, risks, opportunities, uncertainties, and any other information that needs to be considered while making the decision. An *incisive* frame is one that identifies the motivating factors behind the need to make the decision or decisions. From a decision-making perspective, it is both efficient

---

[1] Raymond L. Manganelli and Brian W. Hagen, *Solving the Corporate Value Enigma: A System to Unlock Shareholder Value* (New York: AMCOM, 2003), pages 43-46.

[2] David Matheson and James Matheson, *The Smart Organization: Creating Value through Strategic R&D* (Boston: Harvard Business School Press, 1998), pages 23-26.

and effective. To paraphrase a favorite quote of mine from Albert Einstein, an incisive frame "makes the decision as simple as possible, but not simpler."

2. Reliable, Material Information

In this era of enterprise resource management systems, data is in high supply. Yet somehow reliable and material (of substantial importance) information to support decision making still seems hard to find. Uncertainty about the future is a major source of concern and difficulty in making decisions today. As an example, past sales performance can be material to future sales performance, but it usually doesn't provide sufficient insight to project future sales. Future sales will be the result of things that you can control and things outside of your control. Market growth or decline, actions taken by competitors, and sales campaign effectiveness are all uncertainties that will impact future sales. As Peter Drucker notes, *decision making is about present decisions influencing future consequences.* Getting reliable, material information provides critical insight for decision quality. Unfortunately, too often the information we wish we had to support the decision frame is specific, nuanced, and ultimately unavailable.

3. Clear Stakeholder Values and Trade-offs

As the old saying goes, value is in the "eye of the beholder." What stakeholders—the beholders—value is a key consideration of a high-quality decision. In most major enterprise decisions, there is a plethora of stakeholders. These include individuals who are making the decision, individuals who influence the decision, and individuals who are impacted (or who think they are impacted) by the decision. What stakeholders consider of highest value will also differ, but most are willing to give up—or trade-off—lower valued items to gain more of what they consider to be of primary importance. Being clear on stakeholders' values and trade-offs means that we can pinpoint the sources and magnitudes of value from each stakeholders' perspective in the process of making the decision. They may agree or be in conflict about what creates value. A good, simple question to ask is, "Who are the stakeholders and what do they want?" As an example, the shareholders of a pharmaceutical company want drugs that will positively impact shareholder value growth, the FDA wants safe and efficacious human and veterinary drugs, while consumers want low-priced prescriptions and over-the-counter drugs that work properly with no adverse side effects.

4. Creative, Compelling Alternatives

Documented or not, well thought out or not, every individual and organization has a current approach, method of operation, or plan of action. Generalizing a term introduced by Mintzberg and Waters[3], *deliberate strategy* or *deliberate plan* will be used to indicate these approaches, methods, or plans even when this overstates the thinking involved. The context of a conversation concerning a decision defines *deliberate strategy* or *deliberate plan*. If the conversation is about dieting, for example, then the *deliberate plan* (though in this case it may not *feel* very deliberate) is your current eating behaviors and exercise routines. If the conversation is about your corporation's product supply chain, then the *deliberate strategy* or *deliberate plan* is defined as the current operational plan, infrastructure, existing initiatives, and relationships your corporation has with respect to the production and distribution of its products.

Formally documented or not, a *deliberate strategy* or *deliberate plan* always exists. This is one alternative for the future, although it may not be an especially compelling alternative if things are not going well. A high-quality decision requires explicit consideration of creative, compelling alternatives—not just a single alternative.

Former Secretary of State Henry Kissinger once unhappily characterized the alternatives his advisors would offer as neither *creative* nor *compelling*. He complained his advisors would bring him three alternatives: one that would lead the United States to thermonuclear warfare, one that would lead to the surrender of the United States, and one that his advisors wanted to pursue.

5. Optimal Timing with Options

Many decisions have what is called a "decision window," i.e., a period of time when particular advantageous alternatives or consequences are available. Examples include the negotiation period of contracts, the time before a competitor introduces a new product, the time before a patent expires, or the period from now until the end of the fiscal year. The timing of decisions is important because the environment and the context of decision making are fluid and changing. Having downstream decision options with well-defined "triggers" is important and valuable whenever the consequences of our decisions significantly change as the result of some uncertain,

---

3   Henry Mintzberg and James A. Waters, "Of Strategies, Deliberate and Emergent," *Strategic Management Journal*, Vol. 6, No. 3 (Jul. - Sep., 1985), pages 257-272.

future event. For example, production capacity decisions under a growth scenario require understanding when and how much capacity should be added. Creating an option for additional capacity in the future given a surprisingly high product demand may drive the company to consider an outsourcing solution with contract option terms regarding additional capacity.

6. Logically Correct Reasoning

Logically correct reasoning means that you have considered each of the alternatives from a structured, logically sound evaluation approach accounting for the stakeholders' values and all the material information—both certain and uncertain. The explicit, quantitative accounting of uncertainty and risk is critical to decision quality. Decades of research by cognitive psychologists and more recently by neuroscientists tells us that humans are usually unable to logically think through complex situations under uncertainty. In fact, human judgment in the realm of risk and uncertainty is often prone to illogical conclusions. Pilots learn to fly from instruments because their judgment under poor weather conditions is impaired. Risk and uncertainty have an analogous impact on decision makers. The "instruments" needed here are logically sound approaches of evaluation that explicitly account for risk and uncertainty.

7. Commitment to Action

Decision making is ultimately the commitment of resources to fulfill an action. Unfortunately, achieving commitment to action is no small feat, especially when the decision involves a change in the *deliberate strategy* or *deliberate plan* that may be perceived as detrimental to the careers or aspirations of those affected by the change. Who among us has not seen an enterprise-wide decision to change a *deliberate plan* quietly die because it was not supported by key stakeholders impacted by the decision? Getting true *commitment* to action requires sufficient involvement of key stakeholders in the decision-making process and sufficiently addressing each of the other seven elements of decision quality.

8. Defensible Choice

Being able to defend a decision made by an executive to a senior leadership team, a board of directors, a regulatory agency, a newspaper, a TV reporter, a court of justice, or even Congress has emerged as another requirement of a high-quality decision process. One might argue that a high-quality decision can be made without the requirement of being able to defend the choices ultimately made, but that is little comfort to the individual who is denied resources for failing to justify or defend the decisions recommended. In today's litigious business environment, being able to state why one choice was made and, as importantly, why other choices were not made is a critical component of a high-quality decision process. The decision alternative(s) chosen should be accompanied by a concise rationale as to why the chosen alternative is preferred to other alternatives not selected.

Measuring the Quality of a Decision

It is possible to measure the quality of a decision by assessing each of the eight elements of decision quality listed above on a scale from 0 to 100 percent, as illustrated below in Figure 2.1. A score near 100 percent for a decision quality element means that additional effort on that element would not improve the quality of the decision. A high-quality decision must score well on all of the eight elements.

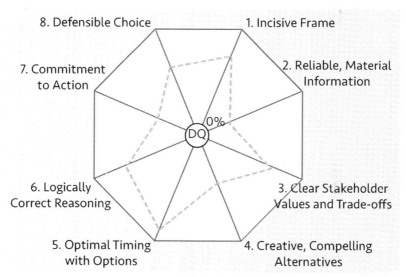

Figure 2.1: Eight Point Decision Quality Assessment

Having the key stakeholders perform a quick decision quality assessment is an effective way to identify points of disagreement and concern. This can help to guide the decision process to a successful conclusion, namely a commitment to a defensible action. Notice that all the elements of decision quality are about how we made the decision and not about the consequences of the decision. Usually, when we have regrets about a decision, one or more of the above characteristics were not satisfied. Have you made a "bad" decision lately? A good exercise is to explain why it was a poor decision in terms of the eight elements of decision quality.

What Does it Mean to be Empowered to Make a Decision?

Two things must be true in order to be empowered to make a decision:

♦ You must have the *capability* to make a good decision. This includes the skills and knowledge about making good decisions. This is likely the formal education you did not receive in elementary school, high school, and even college, but are receiving now through learning the contents of this book.

♦ You must have the *authority* to commit the required resources and be responsible for the outcomes resulting from the decision.

You need both the *capability* and *authority* to be truly empowered to make a decision.

Key Point:

To be empowered to make a good decision requires two things: (1) having the *capability* to make a good decision, including the skills and knowledge about good decision making, and, (2) having the *authority* to commit the required resources as well as the responsibility for the outcomes resulting from the decision.

The Emerging Requirement of Decision Process Transparency

There is an increasing call for decision transparency or, more precisely, decision process transparency. From a government perspective, being clear and upfront about how decisions are made is critical to building trust and to ensuring productive participation among stakeholders. Transparency also fosters greater accountability for the decisions that are made. From a corporate perspective, customers, shareholders, regulatory bodies, credit rating agencies, and governments are seeking trustworthy, relevant and understandable information about how and why decisions are made.

Key Point:

There is an increasing need and emerging requirement for corporate decision process transparency to reveal and record how and why decisions are made (or not made).

Decision process transparency includes both *how* and *why* decisions are made. An effective way to address the how question is to use a decision process that is built upon the eight elements of decision quality. The *why* question can be answered by:

♦ Articulating why a decision alternative was chosen *and* why all the other decision alternatives considered were not selected,

♦ Presenting each stakeholder's perspective—what they want and what they don't want, and,

♦ Stating clearly the decision frame, decision alternatives, information and sources, "decision timeline window," understandable analysis, value measurement scheme, and value trade-offs.

Notice that all the answers to *why* the decision was made can be and should be addressed through *how* the decision was made.

Now that we have discussed decision quality and empowerment, we will turn our attention to a useful way to look at decisions: resolving problems, mitigating risks, and capturing opportunities (PRO).

"Again and again, the impossible decision is solved when we see that the problem is only a tough decision waiting to be made."
– Dr. Robert Schuller, Televangelist, Pastor, Speaker, Author

3
Problems, Risks, and Opportunities

Deliberate (Intended) Strategy versus Emergent Strategy

Husband: "I purchased the carpet cleaner chemical, so we can finally clean up that nasty stain on the floor in the family room."

Wife: "You know, I was thinking we should put in hardwood floors throughout the house and get rid of all the carpeting. It would be so much nicer and cleaner."

Husband: "That would cost a lot of money. If we are going to tear up the house, I think we should have the bathrooms remodeled first and then change the flooring. That's the right sequence, otherwise we might screw up the new hardwood floors."

Wife: "We shouldn't do *all* that work if we are going to move in the next few years. I don't think we would get the money back if we sell the house."

Husband: "If we are going to go through *all* the trouble and costs of moving, I'd want to make sure it's a much bigger house in a better neighborhood. So, as we've discussed before, I'm not really thinking about moving until I get promoted to a more senior position with a good bump-up in salary."

Wife: "You've been saying that for the past couple of years. I'm beginning to wonder if you'll ever get that promotion. But I do like those new homes they are building up in the north hills. Maybe we should look at the new home models this weekend and see if we can afford one."

How many potential decisions are in this conversation? It started with the resolution of a problem: cleaning a stain on the family room carpet. Their current *deliberate* strategy appears to be to stay in and maintain their current home until their personal finances improve (at the time of the husband's job promotion), and then to sell their home and buy a bigger house in a more preferred neighborhood. But the carpeting issue has triggered a recurring discussion about timing and what to do with their current home. Similar decision conversations are occurring daily in corporations and governmental entities.

According to Christensen and Donovan: "In every company there are two independent and simultaneous processes through which strategy comes to be defined. The first strategy-making process is conscious and analytical, involving assessments of market structure, competitive strengths and weaknesses, the nature of customer needs, and the drivers of market growth. Strategy in this process typically is formulated in a project with a discrete beginning and end. Top-tier management consultants often manage these projects. The result of this process is an *intended* or *deliberate* strategy. The second strategy-making process has been termed *emergent* strategy. It is the cumulative effect of day-to-day prioritization decisions made by middle managers, engineers, salespeople, and financial staff—decisions that are made despite, or in the absence of, intentions. In fact, managers typically do not frame these decisions as strategic at all, at the time they are being made; they have a decidedly tactical character. For example, Intel's decision to accept an order from Busicom, a second-tier Japanese calculator company, started the company on the path to microprocessors."[1]

Christensen, Allworth, and Dillon characterize the inherent tension between the deliberate strategy and an emergent strategy. "The unanticipated problems [risks] and opportunities then essentially fight the *deliberate* strategy for the attention of capital, and hearts of the management and employees. The company has to decide whether to stick with the original plan, modify it, or even replace it altogether with one of the alternatives that arises. The decision sometimes is an explicit decision; often, however, a modified strategy coalesces from myriad day-to-day decisions to pursue unanticipated opportunities [mitigate risks] and resolve unanticipated

---

1   Clayton M. Christensen and Tara Donovan, "The Process of Strategy Development and Implementation," INNOSIGHT, https://pdfs.semanticscholar.org/c0a4/13dc3f438d21f62904936819fa34df6331b4.pdf, page 2.

problems. When strategy forms in this way, it is known as *emergent strategy.*[2] The actual commitment of resources for both deliberate and emergent strategies takes place "...through a common filter—the resource allocation process."[3]

Figure 3.1: Slightly modified representation of process provided by Christensen and Donovan[4]

The Process of Strategy Development and Implementation

The applications and implications of the process depicted in Figure 3.1 go beyond a top-down corporate-level perspective and cascade throughout a company within its various organizations, departments, and functions. Simply replace "Strategy" with "Plan" and you can recognize this process being executed on an ongoing basis at all levels throughout the company.

Key Point:

In our personal and professional lives we make decisions about only three things: (1) how to resolve problems, (2) how to mitigate risks, and (3) how to capture opportunities.

---

2   Clayton M. Christensen, James Allworth, and Karen Dillon, *How Will You Measure Your Life?* (New York: HarperCollins Publishers, 2012), page 45.

3   Clayton M. Christensen and Tara Donovan, "The Process of Strategy Development and Implementation," INNOSIGHT, http://www.innosight.com/documents/The Processes of Strategy Development and Implementation.pdf, page 3.

4   Ibid., page 4.

To be precise, an organization's actual strategy or plan is ultimately defined by what comes *out* of the resource allocation process and not by what goes *into* it. The resource allocation process occurs every day at every level in a company. Senior managers are selecting, funding, sequencing, prioritizing, and adjusting initiatives. Sales force staff are targeting customers, emphasizing some products while ignoring others. R&D staff are prioritizing their time on some projects and letting other projects lag. Plant managers are allocating their staff's time to maintenance activities, operations, and improvement initiatives. In fact, anyone with a budget (or anyone who influences a budget) is working within a process similar to that defined in Figure 3.1, whether they recognize it or not.

Table 3.1 provides examples of various organizations or functions and their associated deliberate strategies or plans and the documents by which they are codified.

Everyone who manages a budget or influences a budget faces recurring decisions on how to best allocate resources during the regular planning cycles as well as how to best allocate any discretionary budget or management reserve throughout the fiscal or calendar year. As an example, given eight problems ("P"), five risks ("R"), and four opportunities ("O"), which of these seventeen "PRO" items should be invested in from a best value perspective? How do these investments compare with other PRO investments emerging in other parts of the organization? Is investing in marketing and sales PRO items more valuable than investing in manufacturing PRO items?

The *PRO Dilemma* is: Among competing and sometimes conflicting commitments of time and money across problems, risks, and opportunities, how can you determine which commitments should be pursued now to create or protect the *most* value for *best* value? How do you compare an investment in establishing a sales office in Beijing with an investment in a lean project for cost reductions in a manufacturing plant in Mexico? In most organizations, management tends to focus the preponderance of discretionary investments on one type of PRO item (i.e., problem resolution) with marginal investments in opportunities and little or no investment in the mitigation of risk, despite the emergence of enterprise risk management (ERM) and other risk-related movements in recent years.

Part of the imbalance in investment across a set of problems, risks, and opportunities stems from difficulty measuring the return on investment for the risks and opportunities. For example, knowing that a problem is costing an organization $750,000 per month

Organization or Function	Deliberate Strategy or Plan
Corporate	Strategic Plan including Strategic Initiatives and Objectives, Sales & Marketing Plan and Budget, Operational Plan and Budget, Capital Plan and Budget, and Metrics
Business Unit	Strategic Plan including Strategic Initiatives and Objectives, Sales & Marketing Plan and Budget, Operational Plan and Budget, Capital Plan and Budget, and Metrics
Financial Organization	Strategic Plan including Strategic Initiatives and Objectives, Sales & Marketing Plan and Budget by Organization, Operational Plan and Budget by Organization, Capital Plan and Budget by Organization, and Metrics
Sales and Marketing Organization	Sales & Marketing Plan and Budget by Organization, including Role in Strategic Initiatives and Objectives, and Metrics
Mergers and Acquisitions Group	M&A Plan including Targeted Acquisitions & Divestitures, and Metrics
R&D	R&D Plan and Budget by Organization including Role in Strategic Initiatives and Objectives, and Metrics
Plant	Operational Plan and Budget by Organization including Role in Strategic Initiatives and Objectives, Plant Capital Plan and Budget, and Metrics
Initiative, Program, or Project	Initiative, Program or Project Plan & Budget, and Metrics

Table 3.1: Examples of Deliberate Plans by Organization or Function

provides sufficient motivation to invest in resolving the problem. The cost is something tangible that can be seen every month on a financial statement. Risks and opportunities are perceived differently because of the uncertainty in their size or return on investment and the lack of immediate, measurable benefits in the face of immediate cost.

Before we discuss how to resolve the PRO Dilemma, we need to be clear on the definitions of *problem*, *risk*, and *opportunity*. While these words are in our common vernacular, they do not have consistent definitions in use. This can lead to confusion when discussing them. Let's start with the term *risk*.

What is a Risk?

The common use of the term risk connotes the notion of loss. However, some individuals use the term risk as also including opportunities or as something of positive value.[5] The lack of clarity and precision in the language of risk management continues to undermine risk management initiatives and in some cases, has a materially negative impact on businesses.

As I will use the term, *risk* is any issue, situation or event that may result in a significant deviation from a planned goal ultimately resulting in a loss, i.e., an unwanted, negative consequence. The planned goal could be any aspect of the current direction, the *deliberate* strategy or plan of the business. The degree of risk associated with such an issue, situation, or event is determined by the likelihood (uncertainty or probability) of the risk occurring, the magnitude of its associated loss (consequence), and its timing.

The key in this definition is the notion of uncertainty (probability). At the point in time the issue/situation/event and its consequence are identified as a risk, the actual occurrence of the issue/situation/event is uncertain. This means the likelihood (probability) of the issue/situation/event occurring can be represented as a number between zero and one, but not including zero and one. The consequence may or may not be uncertain. In either case, the event *and* its consequence are identified as a risk.

As an example, consider ABC Company, a manufacturer of truck parts. The RRR Company is a major customer of ABC Company and they have been complaining about issues with on-time delivery of truck parts. The Director of Purchasing of the RRR Company told the sales representative of ABC Company that unless the on-time delivery issues are resolved, the contract extension may not be awarded to ABC Company. The uncertain issue or event in this case for ABC Company is the award of the RRR Company contract

---

5   For instance, *risk* in ISO Guide 73-2002 on risk management terminology defines *risk* as: "The combination of the probability of an event and its consequence." However, the guide provides multiple notes that go along with the definition, such as: "The term 'risk' is generally used only when there is at least the possibility of negative consequences," and "In some situations, risk arises from the possibility of deviation from the expected outcome or event." Even the standard on risk terminology is not consistent. The guide does state, however, that it is important to select one definition and apply it consistently.

extension. Since the RRR Company contract extension is *in* the current sales plan, the issue could result in a potential loss.

Key Point:

Of the three classes of decisions, *risk* is the least attended to and worst managed.

Key Point:

Knowledge about risk is only informative, meaningful, and useful if it supports decision making.

What is a Problem?

The problem with *problems* is that they get confused with risks. Anyone who has been involved in a risk assessment has been caught in a discussion of, "Is this situation a problem or a risk?" Organizations often have escalation processes that focus on problem resolution. Sometimes organizations have separate risk management processes for prioritizing and escalating risks. Many times the two separate processes seem to be addressing the same things resulting in duplication of effort and confusion.

Problems and risks are different, but those differences are subtle. Perhaps the simplest way to define a *problem* is in relationship to the definition of risk. Figure 3.2 identifies the two sources of uncertainty when thinking about problems and risks. The issue, situation, or event may be deemed certain or uncertain meaning it may or may not occur. And the magnitude of the consequence may be deemed certain or uncertain. If the occurrence of the issue, situation, or event is certain and the consequence is certain, then we are addressing a *problem* (as identified in the lower-left quadrant of Figure 3.2).

Alternatively, whenever the issue, situation, or event is deemed uncertain then this is a *risk*—as identified by the top two quadrants —regardless of whether the consequence is certain or uncertain. Our language and understanding becomes a little muddled with the lower-right quadrant where the issue, situation, or event is certain to occur, but the degree of consequence (loss) is considered uncertain. Using our definition of risk, we could conclude that this situation could be called a risk. However, many make the argument that the relationship should be considered a problem.

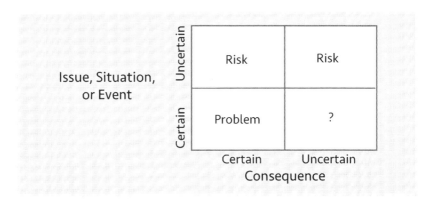

Figure 3.2: The Distinctions between Problems and Risks

In our previous example, for the RRR Company, the non-timely delivery of parts may be seen as a problem (e.g., the parts are always late, and therefore there is always an unwanted cost incurred). However, if the parts are only sometimes late, the RRR Company may see that situation as a risk. Context, as one can see, matters significantly. It can be argued that the situation is still a problem because over a longer period of time, unwanted costs are being incurred. The sharp-eyed reader will note that if the cost is uncertain, are we back into a risk situation or not? You can see how messy the risk versus problem discussion can become.

Since PRO Enterprise Management theory requires that problems and risks be dealt with together, the classification of the lower-right quadrant is only needed for consistency of language in an organization. If, however, you choose to manage problems and risks separately, then the classification of the lower-right quadrant should be done carefully by defining the context of the situation in a consistent manner to ensure internal escalation processes are providing their desired results without duplicative efforts. The PRO Enterprise Management methods defined throughout this book cat-egorize the lower-right quadrant in Figure 3.2 as a problem.

Both problems and risks are associated with loss with respect to the goals of the *deliberate* strategy or plan of the business. The final PRO category of *opportunities* is defined as the *upside* or the expected and desired positive consequences of a plan or goal.

What is an Opportunity?

An *opportunity* is an investment and/or action that can be taken that should result in outcomes that are above and beyond those expected under the *deliberate* strategy or plan of the business.[6] At the point in time that an opportunity is pursued, the degree of positive impact or financial gain may be certain or uncertain. Accordingly, *opportunities* can have a degree of uncertainty like *problems* and *risks*.

Let's return once more to ABC Company, which has been reducing manufacturing costs by applying lean manufacturing principles in the redesign of their manufacturing lines. Unit 42 has not been redesigned and is targeted as a lean manufacturing project opportunity. Since this project is not included in the current capital budget and plan and is expected to produce a positive outcome, it is considered an *opportunity*.

As a final note regarding the categorization of issues, situations and events as problems, risks, or opportunities, the classification should be done from the perspective of before any resources are applied. If not acted upon, is the issue, situation, or event a problem, risk, or opportunity?

Creating a Consistent Basis for Decision Making

Now think about your current personal or professional situation as an executive or manager. Take five minutes and list what you believe are the top problems, risks, and opportunities in your life or in your organization. Don't be surprised if, after some thought, your list is rather long. That is the point! You do not have the resources to address the entire list, at least at this point in time. You will need to prioritize and choose.

How do you identify and prioritize which of these individual PRO items should be pursued based on *best value* for you or for the organization? Are resources being allocated to problems that might better be allocated to addressing risks? Or are there resources allocated to mitigating risks that are better spent pursuing an opportunity? Which combination creates the best value? Answering

---

6   Note that opportunities typically require an action—i.e., an allocation or reallocation of some resource—to bring them to fruition. This is a key difference between an opportunity and a risk, which requires no action to make it happen. Additionally, an opportunity may have some likelihood of resulting in a negative consequence, though this should be less likely than the positive consequences.

these types of questions is the essence of PRO Enterprise Management. We want *all* of the PRO Items (the set of problems, risks, and opportunities) to be compared and judged against one another on a consistent basis.

Pulling the Andon Cord

In manufacturing, the *Andon Cord* is a literal cord that workers can pull at any time should something in the manufacturing process go wrong that would compromise the quality of the product or the safety of people. When the cord is pulled, the manufacturing line stops immediately. At that moment, *everyone's* attention is turned to resolving the problem. The line does not restart until the problem has been fixed, thus ensuring that no scrap or defects are allowed. Pulling the cord is not meant to be a courageous act; rather it is intended to be a normal occurrence once a manufacturing problem is perceived. That said, pulling the proverbial Andon Cord outside the trained manufacturing world requires an act of courage and leadership. When the Andon Cord is pulled, organizations need a repeatable and defendable decision-making process to ensure necessary strategic changes are achieved efficiently and effectively.

As we have already seen, Christensen and Donovan explain that corporate strategy is the result of two simultaneous processes:

◆ the conscious, analytical *deliberate* strategy-making process and

◆ the day-to-day prioritization decisions sometimes revealing components of and motivating a competing *emergent* strategy.

The analogy of pulling the Andon Cord is the point where the decision is made to "stop and focus" on potentially abandoning the *deliberate* strategy to pursue an *emergent* strategy or perhaps step back and create a new *deliberate* strategy altogether. A large or rapidly growing portfolio of problems, risks, and opportunities or potentially any single disruptive event can trigger the need for a change in strategy. In either case, the leadership must decide whether it is time to "pull the Andon Cord."

The term "uncertain" has appeared in each of the definitions of problem, risk, and opportunity. If we are to analyze problems, risks, and opportunities we must account for uncertainty in a consistent manner. How to do this is the topic of the next chapter.

"Every man has a right to his own opinion,
but no man has a right to be wrong in his facts."
– Bernard Baruch, Financier and Presidential Advisor

4
There Are No Facts About The Future

It is a Little Confusing

A friend of mine loves skiing. Every year he anticipates the first snow in the local mountains with great enthusiasm. The process of "tuning" his skis given the first forecast for snow is a celebration. Let's say it is early November and a strong low-pressure weather system from the Gulf of Alaska appears to be headed for the local mountains. If the system dumps snow, my friend has said, "The weekend crowds will be horrendous!" Therefore timing is everything. An early or mid-week dumping would be ideal and allow my friend to enjoy the slopes prior to the arrival of the crowds or worse yet, "those crazy snowboarders."

On Tuesday evening, local meteorologists disagree on whether the jet stream will dip far enough south to enable the weather system to reach the local mountains. My friend's favorite meteorologist forecasts an 80% chance of snow in the local mountains and that the system will be dumping snow on Wednesday through midday Thursday, meaning Friday would be a great day for skiing with hopefully limited crowds. A second meteorologist has a similar forecast with respect to timing, but states that the chance of the jet stream dipping low enough to reach the local mountains is only 30% to 40%.

My friend also has an important report due at work on Friday. If he wants to go skiing on Friday, he will need to work late on

Wednesday so he can complete the report on Thursday. My friend also has a dinner date on Wednesday that he would need to cancel if he works late on the report. What should my friend do?

That week, the jet stream didn't quite dip far enough south to generate snow in the local mountains. What do you think my friend did? You're right—he *loves* to ski. He canceled his dinner date and worked on his report very late Wednesday evening. But with no snow in the local mountains, he went to work on Friday.

Which meteorologist was *right*? The one who predicted an 80% chance of snow or the one who predicted a 30% to 40% chance of snow? Were they both right or both wrong? Can we say that one prediction was more accurate, or more reliable, or better, or more useful than the other?

No, I don't believe we can. What does a forecast of 80% chance of snow in the mountains this Wednesday through midday Thursday mean? According to the U.S.'s National Weather Service, the probability of precipitation is the multiplication product of the confidence that precipitation will occur somewhere in the forecasted area and the percent of the area that will receive measurable precipitation. Does that mean if we had 100 Tuesday evenings with weather conditions similar to today that we can expect 80 of the following Wednesdays through midday Thursdays will result in measurable snow in the local mountains? Or does it mean that the meteorologist is 80% sure that it will snow? And what does "80% sure" mean?

If you are feeling a bit confused, that is good. At this point, you should be. There are no (or few) facts about the future. Yet decision making often requires us to have predictive insights about the future. I will discuss in Chapter 6 how the brain naturally operates in a predictive mode and will point out our innate and learned strengths, limitations, and biases when it comes to forming beliefs and making judgments about the future. Being able to predict is required for our survival as a species, but our innate ability to predict the future is even more limited than we tend to believe. Nevertheless, most decisions are made in the face of uncertainty without facts about the future.

Practical Probability

There are two schools of thought concerning the application of probability theory: "Bayesian or Subjective" and "Classical or Frequentist." The most commonly taught and practiced is the "Classical or Frequentist" approach. This view is largely based on the work of R.

A. Fisher[1] around the turn of the 20th century. In this approach, probability is the measure of frequency in which a specified event occurs. For example, if a "fair" coin is flipped 100 times, you would expect about 50 of the flips would result in "heads" and about 50 of the flips would result in "tails." Consequently, the probability of any one coin flip resulting in "heads" is 0.50, or 50%, based on measurable and repeatable events.

Bayesian or Subjective probability theory (hereafter called Bayesian) was developed (but not originated) by Thomas Bayes.[2] It defines probability based on the personal state of information. In Bayesian probability theory, a probability represents the degree to which an individual, or group, believes a statement to be true based on their current, relevant beliefs at that point in time. From the Bayesian perspective, the notion of *my* probability differing from *your* probability is perfectly acceptable while the Classical perspective would speak in terms of what *is* the probability of an event.

The problems, risks, and opportunities your organization experiences are typically unique in nature, which means there is a lack of identical previous experience or events to measure frequency. Consequently, the definition of the probability of an event cannot be determined using the Classical theory approach. Bayesian theory is the only practical definition of probability and the only probability-based approach that can support generalized decision making with respect to problem resolution, risk management, and opportunistic pursuits.

These distinctions in the definitions of probability are important to understand. Subject Matter Experts (SMEs) need to understand that they are not being asked to provide *the* probability of an event occurring, but rather, their personal informed perspective probability of a future event occurring given their current state of understanding. This would include their beliefs and any relevant information they can glean from reliable sources. Given this back-

---

1   Sir Ronald Aylmer Fisher (1890 – 1962) was an English statistician, biologist, and geneticist who is often referred to as the "father of statistics." He provided a unified and general theory for analysis of data and established the logical foundations for inductive inference.

2   Thomas Bayes (1701 – 1761) was an English mathematician and Presbyterian minister who created the mathematical representation for how a subjective degree of belief should rationally change to account for evidence. This mathematical expression is called Bayes' Theorem and Bayes' Law.

ground the issue becomes: How can we provide the best representation of an individual's or a group's state of understanding regarding an uncertain future?

Key Point:

A probability, from a Bayesian statistics perspective, represents the degree to which an individual, or group, believes a statement to be true based on their current, relevant beliefs at a given point in time.

A probability of an issue, situation, or event occurring is typically represented by a number between zero and one, inclusive. If an expert believes a particular discrete event is certain to occur, then the expert assigns a probability of 1.0 to the event. If an expert believes a particular discrete event is certain not to occur, then the expert assigns a probability of 0.0 to the event. If an expert believes there is a 50/50 chance of a discrete event occurring versus not occurring, then the expert assigns the probability of 0.5 to the discrete event.

Key Point:

The measurement of a probability of a discrete issue, situation, or event occurring is a number between zero and one where zero represents the belief that the event is certain not to occur and one represents the belief that the event is certain to occur.

How likely will our product be first-to-market? What are the chances we will complete the project within schedule and budget? How likely is it that we will have a breach of customer data due to a cyber-attack before year's end? What is the probability a Republican will be elected President of the United States in the next election? These are examples of uncertain discrete events where the concept of probability applies.

Approximations for Estimating Ranges of Outcomes

If the plant is flooded by a hurricane, how long would we be out of stock? If our competitor enters this market, what will happen to our sales over the next three years? If the product launch is delayed by six months, what impact will that have on first and second year sales? If we fund your marketing initiative, how much lift will we get in sales this fiscal year? If we fund this "lean" initiative, how much reduction do we get in labor cost and what will it do to our quality metrics?

Consider the opportunity of funding a marketing initiative and the question of the additional sales we might achieve this fiscal year if the initiative is funded. Figure 4.1 is an example of a continuous probability distribution representing the marketing director's assessment of the uncertainty regarding potential sales. (Bear with me. The marketing director does not have this graph in his head, though he might have a model or a predictive analytics application that generates this curve. I'm just trying to illustrate a point.)

There are three points highlighted in the graph denoted as the 10th, 50th, and 90th percentiles.[3] (Why I've chosen these percentiles will be discussed further in Chapter 9.) In the graph, the 10th percentile value lines up on the horizontal axis at an increase of about $8M in sales. This implies that there is only a 10% chance that the increase in sales would be less than or equal to $8M. The interpretation of the 90th percentile value is that there is only a 10% chance that the increase in sales would be greater than about $48M. The 50th percentile value of about $22M indicates a 50/50 chance that the increase in sales would be less than or equal to $22M.

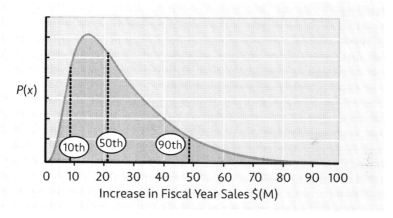

Figure 4.1: Using Percentiles to Measure Uncertainty in Outcomes

Readers with a background in probability and statistics know that the probability distribution illustrated above has an *expected*

3   The curve in Figure 4.1 is the graph of a probability density function. The total area under the curve equals 1.0. The area to the left of the 10th percentile equals 10% of the area or 0.10. The area to the left of the 90th percentile equals 90% of the area or 0.90. The 50th percentile represents the point on the curve in which 50% of the area is to the left of the point and 50% of the area is to the right.

value (also called the *mean*) that is a measure of central tendency and a *variance*, which is a measure of the spread in the distribution.

A continuous probability distribution can be represented by a set of discrete points using a process known as *discretization*. Much has been published on the various methods of discretizing continuous probability distributions. The method used for the PRO Enterprise Management application must be rigorously sound and consistent with our ability to think, comprehend, and judge. Short of this, we won't be able to impact belief generation and consequently impact decision making. Miller and Rice[4] provide a method that meets these requirements. It estimates the continuous probability distribution's expected value by using the 10th, 50th, and 90th percentiles coupled with the discrete probabilities 0.25, 0.50, and 0.25 respectively (see Figure 4.2).

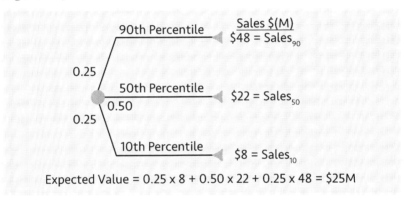

$$\text{Expected Value} = 0.25 \times 8 + 0.50 \times 22 + 0.25 \times 48 = \$25M$$

Figure 4.2: Expected Value

The expected value of the three-branch probability tree shown is calculated as the sum of the sales outcome of each branch multiplied by that branch's probability. For this tree, the estimated expected value is a $25M increase in fiscal year sales. This is obviously a simplified calculation from what would be required to determine the expected value using the entire continuous probability distribution.

This approximation method is applicable to both symmetric and asymmetric distributions.[5] The importance of this approximation

4   Miller, Allen C. III and Rice, Thomas R., "Discrete Approximations of Probability Distributions," Management Science, Vol. 29, No. 3, (1983), pages 352-362.

5   As an example, Miller and Rice have shown that if the underlying distribution is a normal distribution, then the estimated mean of the distribution

method is that instead of attempting to construct the entire continuous probability distribution of an uncertain outcome, we merely need to estimate the 10th, 50th, and 90th percentile outcomes.

Over the years, I've heard managers and executives in organizations make statements like, "I only want to make decisions based upon the facts." If only it were that easy! Facts are mostly about the past, and the past may or may not be a good prognosis of the future. Facts are only one subset of our comprehensive state of understanding about future uncertain outcomes related to issues, situations, or events. We need to account for more than just facts, and high quality decision making requires us to consider our comprehensive beliefs. The key is to do our best in achieving this accounting. PRO Enterprise Management uses the three-point approach based on the 10th–50th–90th percentiles as illustrated here to estimate financial outcomes that have underlying continuous distributions. In Chapter 9, we will discuss our innate cognitive processes, which provide even more reasons for PRO Enterprise Management's selection of this approach.

Now that we have explored how to estimate the uncertainty in the outcomes of our decisions, we must now discuss what should be measured to represent our decision's consequences to the enterprise.

Key Point:

The expected value (and variance) of symmetric and asymmetric unimodal (single hump) continuous probability distributions (such as uniform, normal, and beta distributions) can be well-approximated using a three-point discrete approximation method based on the 10th, 50th, and 90th percentiles of the continuous distribution.

---

as calculated from the three-point discretized distribution will be equal to the mean of the underlying continuous distribution, and the variance (which is equal to the standard deviation squared) as calculated from the three-point discretized distribution will underestimate the variance of the continuous distribution by about 6.5%. Miller and Rice have also shown that for a beta distribution (an asymmetric distribution), the three-point method will result in an estimated mean that is identical to the continuous distribution mean, and the estimated variance will overestimate the continuous distribution variance by only 1.1%.

5

Know Your Decision Value

While executives and managers use many measures to evaluate decisions in their specific domains, I contend that all decisions should first be evaluated using long-term enterprise value as the primary measure. All other relevant measures can be considered thereafter. I refer to this as "priming the decision." The long-term enterprise value measure helps to ensure that expenditures on problems, risks, and opportunities are treated consistently, and the ones selected are best for the enterprise. Net present value (NPV) of discounted free cash flow satisfies all the requirements of being a PRO Enterprise Management measure.

Mired in Measures

Collecting, interpreting, and disseminating data, information, knowledge, and measurements remain areas of ever increasing investment for organizations. Even though information systems produce large quantities of business analysis and reports, they struggle to provide definitive insight when deciding which investments are best from an enterprise perspective, e.g. deciding between improving a product's development process or spending more money on advertising and marketing.

---

1   Peter F. Drucker, *The Practice of Management* (New York: HarperCollins Publisher, Inc., 1986).

I am not suggesting abandoning these business analytic systems. The data and information play an important role in the management of ongoing operations and the execution of the *deliberate strategy and plan* that embody the enterprise's strategic goals. In fact, the performance information from these analytic systems can indicate when a specific business process can be—or needs to be—improved. If this occurs, the subsequent questions should be focused on how much it would cost to effect the change and the potential value to the enterprise.

Current management information systems struggle to provide adequate insights to help with complex decisions, but PRO Enterprise Management is designed to address this type of situation. To create a consistent basis of comparison across problems, risks, and opportunities, we will need to stick to the fundamentals and not get lost in the mire of corporate measures.

What is Your "Priming Measure?"

Most decisions that you make personally or professionally require little to no contemplation; the best answers are obvious. But when you are considering a more complex decision and begin weighing trade-offs, first define your "priming measure or measures." What are your "go-to" measures that immediately come to mind? Cost? Time? Enjoyment? Value-in-Use? Chance of failure? Other people's perceptions? Think about it.

If you use a dashboard in your business, what is the primary measure(s) upon which you focus? Chances are that you ignore most of the metrics on the dashboard anyway. Senior management needs your help and interpretation to wade through all the measures to focus on the most critical. A common one-two punch for project managers is often, "We don't have time for that!" quickly followed by, "We don't have budget for that either." What does *not* come to mind naturally is Drucker's question: "What is right for the enterprise?" Consequently, an enterprise value perspective must be built into corporate decision-making processes. It is not innate to our human nature.

The PRO Enterprise Management perspective is that all decision makers should use the NPV of discounted free cash flow for the enterprise as their priming measure. NPV as the first measure, perhaps coupled with at most one or two others, should be used to define the lead recommendations on decisions. But why focus on cash flow?

Cash Flow is King

The most fundamental element of operating and measuring any business is cash flow: *the net of cash in less cash out*. Every business must bring in more cash than goes out on a consistent basis, otherwise the business will fail (just like your personal checking account). Consequently, cash flow *is* the primary measure of an enterprise, and all other measures become secondary. In other words, cash flow is the ultimate economic measure of success or failure of a business.

Consider cash flow from its accounting components. Receivables are claims that are expected to be collected in cash; however, until they are collected they are only potential cash. When they are not collected, they represent lost cash, the money spent on providing the product or service, e.g. labor and materials, that resulted in the receivable. *Inventory* is tied up cash. The longer it takes to sell your inventory, the longer the cash is tied up and is not productive. Moreover, inventory can age and even lose value so it might become a liability and need to be disposed of, eating yet more cash. On the other hand, if a business does not have enough inventory, it can lose near-term sales opportunities and, worse yet, damage brand reputation resulting in lost long-term sales opportunities.

Capital is cash that a business consumes to either maintain or change its operations. Investors expect a cash return on capital investments. *Debt* and *payables* are cash or products and services already received for which cash payment must be made in the future. Debt is only good if it can generate more cash in profit than the cash value of the debt plus the interest cost of holding the debt. Similarly, payables, cash owed by a business to its suppliers, must serve to generate more cash from sales than their cash cost.

Key Point:

All and any material impacts to corporate enterprise value will impact corporate free cash flow at some point in time.

Cash flow and its timing is the core of an enterprise, regardless of its size. An enterprise must continue to generate sufficient cash from sales to cover all of its payment obligations. That is why Warren Buffet says: "Cash Flow is King."

Intrinsic Value of an Enterprise

The *intrinsic value* of a company or enterprise is the estimated value of a company as determined through fundamental analysis of its future cash flow. This is not to be confused with the stock price or market price of a company (although they should be strongly correlated). When the intrinsic value of a company is inconsistent with stock price, this can create stock market volatility. This happened with the dot.com bubble of the late 1990s.

Key Point:

> The intrinsic value of an enterprise (not to be confused with the stock price nor the market price of a company, although all three should be strongly correlated) is the value of the enterprise as determined through analysis of its future free cash flow over time.

The use of the term "intrinsic" is characterized as the expected cash flow of the company over time. Intrinsic value is defined to be the present value of all expected future net cash flows and is calculated via a discounted cash flow valuation. Warren Buffet is a proponent of using intrinsic value analyses of companies to inform his investment decisions. He buys the stock of companies deemed to be trading at a value less than their intrinsic value.

Key Point:

> The net present value (NPV) of discounted free cash flow over time is a good surrogate measure for shareholder value growth from investments and expenditures.

In for-profit enterprises, what you want is long-term growth as measured in the intrinsic value of the enterprise. PRO Enterprise Management is concerned with how investments and expenditures on problems, risks, and opportunities contribute to the intrinsic value of an enterprise.

Reconsidering the Movement to the "Triple Bottom Line"

The concept of the "Triple Bottom Line" (TBL) was introduced in 1994 by John Elkington, the founder of a consultancy called SustainAbility. The premise of TBL is that companies should measure performance based on three separate and different perspectives sometimes referred to as the three P's - People, Planet and Profit.

The first bottom line is the company's "People account" – attempting to measure how fair and beneficial the company's business practices are with respect to labor, community, and the overall population in the region surrounding the company's operations. The second bottom line is the company's "Planet account"– attempting to measure how environmentally responsible the company has been. This includes how well the company manages its consumption of energy and non-renewables, implementation of practices to reduce manufacturing waste, and practices to ensure waste is less toxic prior to disposal in a safe and legal manner.

The third bottom line measures the economic value or Profit created by the company. This profit is after accounting for the comprehensive costs of the company including the cost of capital investments. It is different from corporate profit defined earlier in this chapter because the TBL profit needs to reflect the real economic impact to the host society's economy.

This means TBL is not as simple as corporate profit plus social and environmental impacts. Robert Kaplan and David Norton said: "What you measure is what you get." TBL, similar to Kaplan's and Norton's Balanced Scorecard approach, implies companies will not meaningfully address social and environmental issues unless they are measured on them and formally report their efforts and measures.

Conceptually, TBL is appealing. On the other hand, the comprehensive measurement of impacts to People and Planet accounts are not simple to define and measure. For example, how would you calculate the comprehensive People and Planet costs of British Petroleum's Deepwater Horizon oil spill in the Gulf of Mexico in 2010? That's a tough question to answer and certainly one that will result in extensive debate for a long time.

Current TBL methods are mired in measures. Corporations interested in implementing a Triple Bottom Line method would be best served by establishing a priming measure for each of the three perspectives: People, Planet, and Profit.

Measuring the Impact of Corporate Decision Making

Net present value (NPV) of discounted free cash flow is the enterprise measure we will use to create a consistent basis of comparison for expenditures on problems, risks, and opportunities. The properties of this measure enable the mathematics we need to answer the five questions of PRO Enterprise Management. Other measures may be added; however, any additional measures should be considered after the discussion and presentation of a decision's value based on its NPV. In short, we want to *prime* the discussion of each decision's value based on enterprise value; all other perspectives and measures should follow.

The reasons for this priming are grounded in our cognitive processes and capabilities that will be discussed in subsequent chapters. This chapter has attempted to make this case by underscoring Peter F. Drucker's profundity expressed in his statement: "The first responsibility of business is to make enough profit to cover the costs for the future. If this social responsibility is not met, no other social [or environmental][2] responsibility can be met."[3]

Thus far we have laid the analytical foundations for PRO Enterprise Management. Now we must understand the strengths and weaknesses of our 100,000 to 200,000 year old operating system, the human brain, so that we can design analytics that will appropriately inform and influence our decision making.

---

2   I have added the phrase "or environmental" to Peter Drucker's quote to directly align his quote with the concept of triple bottom line (TBL).

3   A second enterprise-level perspective that I have found useful, but which is not further developed in this book, is the impact to the quality of life of individuals or groups of individuals. An example of such a measure is Quality-Adjusted Life Years. This will be important for corporate decisions involving hazard and safety of individuals both in the workforce and the consumers of a corporation's products and services. Though hazard and safety have clearly defined economic impacts to corporations that can be assessed and measured, the human impacts, or the "human account," should be and can be isolated, separated, and measured.

6

Beliefs, Emotions, and Cognition

A problem with many business analyses prepared for executives is that they are designed, summarized, and presented by business analysts who fail to connect with the executive's thought framework and perspective on the matters under investigation. Over the years, I've listened to countless presentations given by analysts and witnessed the disconnect between the message and the management audience. This disconnect can be exacerbated when the business analysis is based on probabilistic or statistical methods. Unless the business executive is also a statistician, terms like standard deviation, correlation, statistical independence, covariance, and named probability distributions such as normal, beta, or even triangular are not going to be well received.

Probability and statistics are very subtle and often non-intuitive disciplines. When they are applied, the results are based on underlying assumptions such as independence or dependence of events or situations. These assumptions are material to the insights from the analysis. When there are large relevant data sets to draw upon (think of decisions on home loans), these statistical relationship assumptions can be inferred through statistical analysis and built into predictive models to support decision making. Unfortunately—and much to the chagrin of "Big Data" solution providers—the vast majority of decisions made in corporations have no such relevant databases. Business analysts have no choice but to make assumptions about the statistical nature of issues, situations, and events. When these low-validity assumptions are buried in "black box" statistical models whose output can only be explained with unfamiliar statistical terms, managers and executives naturally become skeptical or at least cautious of the results.

When the results don't match managers' and executives' intuition or can't be explained in intuitive ways, the analyses are often discounted or discarded regardless of their validity. This can be frustrating for the business analyst and other contributors to the analysis. If you want to influence decision making, then the analyses *must be aligned with the way we think* or at least be explained with direct and simple language in ways that are consistent with the ways we think and form beliefs. Short of this, even good business analyses will continue to run the risk of being less influential than they can or should be.

This chapter is devoted to providing an overview of how beliefs, emotions, and cognition influence our thinking and decision making. This foundation will provide the insight required to structure analyses that align with how we think and form beliefs while being mathematically rigorous and sound. Later in the book, I will address the importance of clear and appropriate language when structuring, performing, and explaining probability-based analyses of organizational decisions.

Thinking, Thoughts, and Sensations

"Feelings of knowing, correctness, conviction, and certainty aren't deliberate conclusions and conscious choices.
They are mental sensations that happen to us."
– Dr. Robert Burton, Neurologist and Author

Thinking occurs at both conscious and subconscious (unconscious) levels and results in *thoughts* and *sensations*. We have both conscious and subconscious thoughts while sensations only occur and are perceived at a conscious level. According to Dr. Robert Burton: "Conscious thoughts have the embedded sensation of willful effort and intention; unconscious thoughts lack this sensation. Conscious thoughts feel as if they are being thought; unconscious thoughts don't. Unconscious thoughts that reach consciousness have been pre-screened and assigned a higher likelihood of being worth pursuing than those ideas that do not reach consciousness. Unconscious thoughts with a sufficiently high calculated likelihood of correctness will be consciously expressed as feeling right."[1] Burton concludes that *sensations* are feelings—they are not thoughts nor deliberate conclusions nor conscious choices. *Sensations* include feelings such as certainty, conviction, rightness, wrongness, clarity, and faith. Importantly, he further concludes that we know the nature and quality of our thoughts via sensation, not reason.

There are at least three basic elements that characterize our thinking as it relates to decision making; these include *beliefs, patterns*, and *predictions*.

Key Point:

The human brain performs three functions that are critical to human contemplation and decision making, including:
(1) generating and retaining beliefs,
(2) perceiving, recognizing, generating, and storing patterns, and,
(3) predicting and anticipating future events (which result in expectations).

Beliefs

From a common vernacular perspective, *beliefs* include the notions of truth, trust, and "right and wrong." The following words and terms connote something about our beliefs:

♦ Believe this / Don't believe them / Trust her
♦ True / False / Maybe true / Partially true / Sometimes true
♦ Correct / Not correct
♦ Know / Don't know / Know some

Patterns

Patterns are combinations of qualities, actions, behaviors, and tendencies. The human brain is designed to contemplate types of patterns involving *inter-relationships* among objects and events including:

♦ Order (what comes first, what comes second) / Linearity
♦ Stories / Scenarios / Narratives
♦ Hierarchies

If you are a musician and try to play a piece of music from memory, chances are you might not be able to use any arbitrary starting point in the piece. Rather, you will need to start at a natural beginning

---

1   Robert A. Burton, M.D., *On Being Certain: Believing You Are Right Even When You're Not* (New York: St. Martin's Press, 2008), page 137.

point or transition point to a section of the piece. The musician's *procedural* memory retains segments of music where each segment has a beginning, a middle, and an end.

The physical design of the human brain requires that our thinking and memory operate from the construct of scenarios and narratives. This helps to explain the demand for scenario planning[2] exercises used by executives in corporations and governmental organizations to develop and "pressure test" business strategies and long-term strategic plans. When we create detailed plans for projects, we often first create a detailed work breakdown structure, a hierarchy of higher-level tasks broken down into more detailed sub-tasks. Once the hierarchy of tasks is complete, scheduling the tasks is much simpler than trying to schedule without the work breakdown structure.

Thought Experiment (The Importance of Order to Memory):

Try saying your telephone number in reverse order. Notice the difficulty you have in doing so. Order is an important attribute of human thought and memory.

Key Point:

Individuals think and form beliefs through pattern recognition, stories (narratives), and hierarchies.

A second pattern-based mode of contemplation is making *side-by-side* pair-wise comparisons of two objects or options. The human brain is particularly adept at this form of thinking. As an example, consider shopping for carpeting or other flooring. Most people start by selecting one color and style that they like. Then they use it as a

---

2   According to the *Economist* (see http://www.economist.com/node/12000755), "Scenario planning (sometimes called "scenario and contingency planning") is a structured way for organizations to think about the future. A group of executives sets out to develop a small number of scenarios—stories about how the future might unfold and how this might affect an issue that confronts them. The issue could be a narrow one: whether to make a particular investment, for example. Should a supermarket put millions into more out-of-town megastores and their attendant car parks, or should it invest in secure web sites and a fleet of vans to make door-to-door deliveries? Or it could be much wider: an American education authority, for instance, contemplating the impact of demographic change on the need for new schools. Will the aging of the existing population be counterbalanced by the rising level of immigration?"

reference point to compare other choices, one at a time, until they land on the selection they like best. Examples of side-by-side pair-wise comparisons include:

♦ Cost more versus cost less
♦ More difficult versus less difficult
♦ More valuable versus less valuable
♦ More preferred versus less preferred, and
♦ Status quo versus change to status quo.

Key Point:

Individuals can best perceive differences and distinctions between objects, behaviors, preferences, and performance (including status quo versus change to status quo) when side-by-side, simultaneous comparisons are used.

For comparative relationships, the most impactful to our daily lives is "status quo versus change to status quo" – the driver to *all* decision making. When the human brain perceives a change or potential change to the status quo, it determines whether or not a decision should be made, which results in an action in response to the perceived change. The change to status quo manifests as a problem, risk, or opportunity. As we will learn, the perception of change to status quo occurs at both the conscious and the subconscious level.

As an example, when you walk into your kitchen in the morning after broiling fish the night before, you immediately smell the fish, but a few minutes later, you don't notice it anymore. The brain has subconsciously reassigned it as part of the status quo (uninteresting, not important, not dangerous) and put it in the background of your senses and thoughts. Note that decision making is influenced by both the conscious mind and the subconscious mind.

Predictions

The human brain is also designed to *predict*, which is a critical survival skill. Prediction includes *anticipation* and *expectation*. This includes terms, thoughts, and concepts such as:

♦ Will happen / Won't happen / Might happen,
♦ Chances of occurrence (e.g., What are the chances or what is your assessment of the probability that you will arrive home in time for dinner at 6:30 pm this evening?), and
♦ Causality.

Understanding causality, which enables prediction, is an important contributor to our survival and our progress as a species. But causality can be over applied or over assumed, which leads to erroneous beliefs, incorrect predictions, and ultimately, faulty decision making.

The brain performs three functions that are critical to human contemplation and decision making. The human brain:

1.   Generates and retains *beliefs*;

2.   Perceives, recognizes, generates, and stores *patterns*, and

3.   Predicts and anticipates *future events*, resulting in expectations.

These three brain functions play a fundamental role in decision making and are the result of the evolution of the human brain. A review of the evolution and design of the human brain will help us better understand our innate strengths and weaknesses that influence our judgment and decision making.

The Three Layers of the Human Brain

The core component of our nervous system, and especially our brains, is the *neuron* or *nerve cell*. A *neuron* is an electrically excitable cell that processes and transmits information by electrochemical signaling. Neurons transfer signals to neighboring neurons via a *synapse* and this transfer is known as a *synaptic connection*. According to Joseph LeDoux, professor of neuroscience and psychology at New York University: "Essentially everything that the brain does is accomplished by the process of synaptic transmission."[3]

How we think is largely predetermined. It is the result of millions of years of evolution starting with the evolution of neural nets in jellyfish, then the brain stem in lizards (freeze, fight, or flight), followed by the limbic system in mammals with the inextricable link between emotions and memory, and finally the thinking neocortex in primates.[4] The basic design of the parts of the human brain is

---

3   Joseph LeDoux, *Synaptic Self: How Our Brains Become Who We Are* (Middlesex, England: Penguin Books, 2003).

4   We acknowledge that Intelligent Design is an alternative theory to traditional macro-evolution. Note that starting with the premise of Intelligent Design does not change the conclusions we are discussing in this book as to how our brain works and how our decision making can be improved.

ancient. The three-layer model of the brain is called the *triune brain* and was first proposed by the American physician and neuroscientist, Paul D. MacLean in the 1960s.[5]

As illustrated in Figure 6.1, the triune brain consists of the reptilian complex (reptilian brain), the paleomammalian complex (limbic system), and the neomammalian complex (neocortex). These structures are thought to have been sequentially added to the forebrain during the course of evolution.

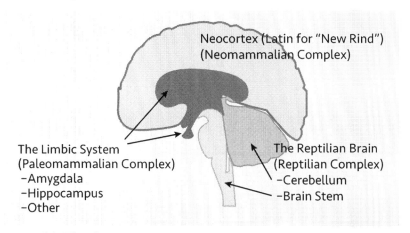

Figure 6.1: The Three Layers of the Human Brain

The *reptilian* layer of our brains includes the main structures found in a reptile's brain, namely the brainstem and the cerebellum. It is genetically encoded, instinctually driven, and controls the body's vital functions such as heart rate, breathing, body temperature, and balance. It also provides instinctive survival skills such as exploration, feeding, aggression, dominance, and sexuality. The reptilian brain, while reliable, works at the subconscious level and tends to be somewhat rigid and compulsive. And it has no learning mechanism. According to David J. Linden, a professor of neuroscience: "The cerebellum is important in distinguishing sensations that are 'expected' from those that are not."[6]

---

5   Paul D MacLean, *The Triune Brain in Evolution: Role in Paleocerbral Functions* (New York: Plenum Press, 1990).

6   David J. Lindon, *The Accidental Mind: How Brain Evolution Has Given Us Love, Memory, Dreams, and God* (Cambridge, Massachusetts: Harvard University Press, 2007), page 9.

Key Point:

> Your three brains include a lizard's, a dog's, and a human's; though interconnected, the three brains are often dissociated and in conflict.

The *limbic* system (paleomammilian complex or "dog brain") contains the center for emotions, and it is also where we make value judgments (mostly subconsciously). The limbic system exerts a strong influence on our behavior. In complex vertebrates, including humans, the *amygdala* [uh-MIG-duh-luh] is the emotional center and plays a primary role in the formation and storage of memories associated with emotional events. A second component is the *hippocampus*, which plays an important role in the consolidation of information from short-term memory to long- term memory. Limbic system functions include: emotions, behaviors, motivations, long term memory, and olfactory (smell). Humans communicate emotion through facial expressions. Control of these expressions lies in the brain stem and amygdala (beyond consciousness).

The *neocortex* (neomammilian complex) is the third and final layer of the human brain. This is the outer layer of the *cerebral cortex,* which includes two large cerebral hemispheres. It is responsible for the development of imagination, abstract thought, contemplation, human language, and consciousness. The neocortex is what enabled human cultures to develop.

The neocortex constitutes the bulk of the human brain accounting for about seventy-six percent of its weight. We also have a frontal lobe where we deal with the more abstract patterns associated with high-level concepts. The neocortex is flexible and is considered to have almost infinite learning abilities derived especially from sight, sound, and touch.

Learning begins before we are born and is even occurring as our prenatal brains are under development. The brain of a one-month old fetus resembles the reptilian brain but then rapidly grows in ways that mirror the human brain's evolutionary path. By the third trimester of pregnancy, the prenatal brain is distinctly human. It has a human neocortex that has begun a lifelong and continuous process of learning by creating new synapses, discarding unneeded synapses, and strengthening or weakening existing synapses based on use.

According to David J. Linden: "The highest functions of our brain, involving conscious awareness and decision making, are located at the very top and front, in the cortex, and the lowest functions, supporting basic subconscious control of our body functions such as breathing rhythm and body temperature, are in the very bottom and rear, in the brainstem. In between are centers that are engaged in higher subconscious functions such as rudimentary sensation (midbrain), homeostasis and biological rhythms (hypothalamus), and motor coordination and sensory modulation (cerebellum). The limbic system, including the amygdala and hippocampus, is the crossroads where the conscious and unconscious parts of the brain meet and initiate the storage of certain types of memory."[7]

Humans' superior abilities to predict, anticipate, and to plan are attributed to specialized regions of the cerebral cortex and to denser interconnections between the prefrontal cortex and the rest of the brain. The prefrontal cortex plays an integral role for the proper functioning of our working memory and interconnectivity is essential. Working memory is the key to many of the cognitive abilities that are so highly developed in humans, such as the ability to perform a task while retaining information about the task, verifying the relevance of the information to the task at hand, and holding the objective of the task in mind—all at the same time. The expansion of the prefrontal cortex seems to be the source of many of our most typically human cognitive abilities.

The Influential Subconscious Brain

According to Dr. Robert A. Burton: "Most neuroscientists believe that conscious thoughts are the mere tip of a cognitive iceberg and that the vast majority of 'thought' occurs outside of awareness."[8] The neural processes by which the unconscious brain decides what should be "dredged up" into the conscious brain is under study and debate. Dr. Burton believes: "We needn't know the exact mechanism to realize that the decision must include a probability calculation ... Unconscious thoughts that reach consciousness have been pre-screened and assigned a higher likelihood of being worth pursuing than those ideas that do not reach consciousness. Unconscious thoughts with a sufficiently high calculated likelihood of correctness will be consciously expressed as feeling right ... We know the nature and quality of our thoughts via feelings, not reason. Feelings such as certainty, conviction, rightness and wrongness, clarity, and faith

---

7   Ibid, page 21.

8   Robert A. Burton, M.D., *On Being Certain: Believing You Are Right Even When You're Not* (New York: St. Martin's Press, 2008), page 130.

arise out of involuntary mental sensory systems that are integral and inseparable components of the thoughts that they qualify."[9]

Because the reptilian and limbic system layers of our brains do not have the capability to deliberate in a conscious way, it is not surprising that we *are largely driven by our subconscious thoughts.* Some scientists estimate that we are conscious of only about five percent of our cognitive processes while the remaining ninety-five percent is outside of our awareness.

This how the human brain works today. A fighter aircraft's Heads-Up Display is a transparent display that presents data without requiring fighter pilots to look away from their visual viewpoints. As the name suggests, the display allows the pilot to view information with their head positioned "up" and looking forward, instead of angled down looking at lower instruments. The role of a Heads-Up Display is analogous to the subconscious brain delivering (dredging) into consciousness information that it has determined should be considered given the current situation. This is based on input from what the sensory systems are perceiving coupled with associated memories.

In Figure 6.2, Burton provides a "skeletal diagram of the interacting components of a thought."[10] This figure illustrates the breadth of the subconscious' considerations and the need for a probability-based weighting system to determine the content delivered into consciousness. Consciousness includes:

- ♦ Mental sensations (cognitive feelings),
- ♦ Thought, and,
- ♦ Action.

It is interesting to note that the diagram lacks any sequence associated with the three outputs, i.e., it does not show mental sensations leading to thought leading to action. It seems that the set is delivered into consciousness as a triplet or possibly with the thought arriving last.

---

9   Ibid, pages 134, 137, and 138.

10 Robert A. Burton, M.D., *A Skeptic's Guide to the Mind: What Neuroscience Can and Cannot Tell Us About Ourselves* (New York: St. Martin's Press, 2013), page 90.

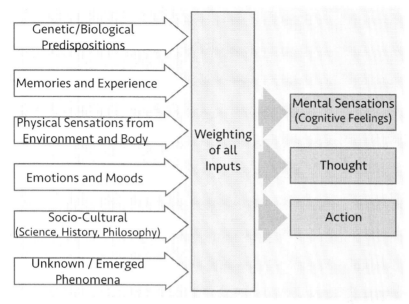

Figure 6.2: Burton's "Hidden Layer and Subliminal Contributions to a Thought" (used by permission).

According to Leonard Mlodinow: "The human sensory system sends the brain about eleven million bits of information each second. The actual amount of information we can handle [consciously] has been estimated to be somewhere between sixteen and fifty bits per second. So if your conscious mind were left to process all that incoming information, your brain would freeze like an overtaxed computer ... Evolution has provided us with an unconscious mind because our unconscious is what allows us to survive in a world requiring such massive information intake and processing. Our sensory perception, our memory recall, our everyday decisions, judgments, and activities all seem effortless—but that is only because the effort they demand is expended mainly in parts of the brain that function outside awareness."[11]

The conscious brain provides a single, linear train of thought. If two people ask you a question at the same time, there is a good chance you won't be able to comprehend either one of them, let alone both. While it has been assumed that the conscious brain is necessary for abstract, symbolic, and logic-based computations, recent research has shown that even "multiple-word verbal expressions

---

11 Leonard Mlodinow, Ph.D., *Subliminal: How Your Unconscious Mind Rules Your Behavior* (New York: Pantheon Books, 2012), page 33.

can be processed outside conscious awareness and that multistep, effortful arithmetic equations can be solved unconsciously."[12]

Priming

Priming is a subconscious, procedural (implicit) memory effect in which exposure to one stimulus influences a response to another stimulus. This social psychological phenomenon of priming occurs at a subconscious level and affects a variety of mental processes including decision making.

For example, have you ever sat in a meeting where a presenter makes a recommendation and as that recommendation is being communicated, all the members of the audience begin nodding in affirmation? In that instance, you have been *primed* for group think.

According to the social psychologist John A. Bargh, priming effects "are ubiquitous and pervasive across the major forms of psychological phenomena: appraisal and evaluation, motivation and goal pursuit, social perception and judgment, and social behavior."[13] Priming is activated through the words we hear, the things we read, and the messages that surround us.

Priming effects can be insidious. Lawrence Williams demonstrated how even *temperature* can influence our judgment, behaviors, and decisions.[14] In an experiment, people were asked to hold either a warm cup of coffee or a cold soft drink with ice and then have a conversation with an individual. After a brief conversation, each participant was asked whether they would recommend the individual to be hired as a project manager. Those holding the warm beverage prior to the conversation were much more likely to recommend the individual for the job than those holding the cold beverage. The simple act of holding the warm beverage primed the activation of feelings of warmth and comfort, which influenced their feelings toward the individual.

---

12 Asael Y. Sklar, Nir Levy, Ariel Goldstein, Roi Mandel, Anat Maril and Ran R. Hasan, "Reading and doing arithmetic nonconsciously", Proceedings of the National Academy of Sciences of the United States, November, 2012.

13 John A. Bargh, "What have we been priming all these years? On the development, mechanisms, and ecology of nonconscious social behavior", *European Journal of Social Psychology*, 2006, Vol. 36(2), pages 147-168.

14 Lawernce E. Williams and John A. Bargh, "Experiencing Physical Warmth Promotes Interpersonal Warmth," *Science*, October 24, 2008, Vol. 322 (5901), pages 606-607.

Most of our decision making is effortless—requiring little contemplation or thought in a state of "cognitive ease" where things *feel* familiar, true, and intuitive. Based on research by Joshua D. Greene and Elinor Amit, responses to difficult decisions compete in the ventromedial prefrontal cortex where "different types of values can be weighed against each other to produce an all-things-considered decision."[15] *Emotional responses tend to override rationalized responses when something triggers vivid imagery in our thoughts* (memory or simulation). This is why it is so important to be sensitive to nonverbal cues and conclusions when discussing and making decisions.

Key Point:

Difficult decisions can result in a battle within our brain between the faster reacting emotionally-driven "right versus wrong" limbic system (specifically the amygdala) response versus the slower reacting rationalized "cost-benefit" (prefrontal neocortex) response.

Greene and Amit explain that some dilemmas produce vivid images in our heads, and we are wired to respond emotionally to imagery and pictures. This may be a variation of "Amygdala Hijack" where the amygdala (in the limbic system) perceives a threat and causes an irrational or destructive reaction. When the hippocampus tells the amygdala that it is a freeze, fight, or flight situation, the amygdala triggers the hypothalmic-pituitary-adrenal (HPA) axis and hijacks the rational brain—literally shutting down the prefrontal cortex. If you take away the pictures, the brain will go into a rational, calculation mode.

"Do you want to be a rational decision maker?" is obviously a rhetorical question. No one wants to make decisions irrationally, but you don't have much choice in the matter regarding rational versus emotional decision making. The three layers of the brain are dissociated and often conflict.

Additionally, there are involuntary overrides that can occur when the reptilian part of the brain supersedes the neocortex. As an example, if you are distraught and decide to commit suicide, you can't execute this by holding your breath. The reptilian brain will override.

---

15 Elinor Amit and Joshua D. Greene, "You See, the Ends Don't Justify the Means: Visual Imagery and Moral Judgment," *Psychological Science*, August, 2012, Vol. 23, pages 861-868.

Truth, Belief, and Knowledge

From the Oxford English Dictionary,[16] we note the following three definitions:

♦ *Truth*: That which is true in accordance with fact or reality,

♦ *Knowledge*: Facts, information, and skills acquired by a person through experience or education, and

♦ *Belief*: Something one accepts as true or real; a firmly held opinion or conviction.

Figure 6-3 illustrates the relationships of truth, knowledge, and belief. Beliefs can be true or not true (which includes partially true and flat-out false). Some of your beliefs are factual and stand up to proof and evidence. These are "knowledge-based beliefs." Some of your beliefs are unknown as to whether they are true or not; these are "faith-based beliefs." Faith-based beliefs are founded on something less than evidence that would stand up to the scientific community's scrutiny; however these boundaries can be fuzzy and debatable.

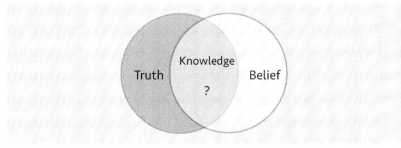

Figure 6.3: The Relationships between Truth, Knowledge, and Belief

To keep it simple (this isn't intended to be a deep philosophical debate), we don't *know* which "faith-based beliefs" are true and which are not—this is denoted by the "?" in Figure 6.3. The strength of your belief does not necessarily correlate with the degree to which something is true. A root cause of poor decision making is the influence of faulty beliefs and their impact on our thought processes and (organizational) decision processes.

Each of us has our own personal mix of knowledge-based and faith-based beliefs. Our decision making is influenced by the comprehensive collection of our beliefs—both faith-based and knowledge-based. We can only speculate as to the degree to which our

---

16 http://www.oxforddictionaries.com/.

personal beliefs are divisible between faith-based and knowledge-based beliefs. This split has great variation from person to person and culture to culture.

Key Point:

Individuals' beliefs (both knowledge-based and faith-based), regardless of their truthfulness, dictate their decision making.

We are all, for the most part, truth-seekers, and we *all* desire to make decisions based on facts and truth. We want truth, knowledge, and belief to be one and the same. We want to know the truth, even when the truth is to our own disadvantage or loss—as in knowledge about end of life, e.g., cancer diagnosis and prognosis. Our decisions and actions will change based on our knowledge of the truth. Our beliefs also heavily influence our internal compass and even rule our lives, regardless of their truthfulness, and our beliefs drive our decision making.

In 2005, the Gallup organization surveyed beliefs held by individuals in the United States.[17]

Belief	*% Believe In*
Extrasensory perception, or ESP	41
That houses can be haunted	37
Ghosts/that spirits of dead people can come back in certain places/situations	32
Telepathy/communication between minds without using traditional senses	31
Clairvoyance/the power of the mind to know the past and predict the future	26
That people can communicate mentally with someone who has died	21
Witches	21
Reincarnation, that is, the rebirth of the soul in a new body after death	20
Channeling/allowing a 'spirit-being' to temporarily assume control of body	9

Table 6.1: Gallup Poll of Beliefs

---

17 Reference: http://www.gallup.com/poll/16915/three-four-americans-believe-paranormal.aspx.

The survey concluded that 73% of Americans believe in at least one of these while 27% believe in none of them. I'm one of the 27%, but this is based on my faith-based beliefs. I don't *know* this—I *believe* this. You may believe that some items on this list do exist, but again, there is likely little or no empirical evidence to support your faith-based belief. If we disagree, *we are unlikely to change our beliefs based on debate.* Beliefs, particularly faith-based beliefs, are not easily changed.

The Human Brain as a Belief-Generating Engine

As we have learned from Dr. Robert A. Burton, we infer "the nature and quality of our thoughts via feelings, not reason." Conviction to our knowledge-based and faith-based beliefs consists of feelings or sensations that "arise out of involuntary mental sensory systems that are integral and inseparable components of the thoughts that they qualify."[18] According to Michael Shermer, author of *The Believing Brain*: "We form beliefs for a variety of subjective, personal, emotional, and psychological reasons in the context of environments created by family, friends, colleagues, culture, and society at large; after forming our beliefs we then defend, justify, and rationalize them with a host of intellectual reasons, cogent arguments, and rational explanations. Beliefs come first, explanations for beliefs follow. I call this process belief-dependent realism, where our perceptions about reality are dependent on the beliefs that we hold about it. Reality exists independent of human minds, but our understanding of it depends upon the beliefs we hold at any given time."[19]

In 1957, Stanford social psychology professor Leon Festinger was the first to characterize how individuals react when issues, situations, or events result in conflicting understandings. Festinger introduced the term cognitive dissonance[20] to describe the feeling of discomfort we experience when simultaneously holding two or more conflicting cognitions: ideas, beliefs, values, or emotional reactions to an issue, situation, or event. Individuals in a state of dissonance may sometimes feel a sense of "disequilibrium" such as frustration,

---

18   Robert A. Burton, M.D., *On Being Certain: Believing You Are Right Even When You're Not* (New York: St. Martin's Press, 2008), page 138.

19   Michael Shermer, *The Believing Brain: From Ghosts and Gods to Politics and Conspiracies—How We Construct Beliefs and Reinforce Them as Truths* (New York: St. Martin's Press, 2011), page 5.

20   Leon Festinger, *A Theory of Cognitive Dissonance* (Stanford, CA.: Stanford University Press 1957).

dread, anxiety, anger, guilt, or embarrassment. From the perspective of beliefs, the theory proposes that people will reduce dissonance by altering existing cognitions, adding new ones to create a consistent belief system, or reducing the importance of any one of the dissonant beliefs. Individuals will avoid situations or information sources that give rise to feelings of uneasiness or dissonance.

Cognitive dissonance plays a critical role in decision making. It emerges when the brain detects the need for change to the status quo. Cognitive dissonance is the brain's "clarion call" for decision and action.

Key Point:

Cognitive dissonance plays a critical role in decision making. It is the brain's "clarion call" for decision and action.

As an example, when someone is coerced to do something they really don't want to do, dissonance is created between their cognition—*I didn't want to do this*—and their behavior—*I did it*. The behavior is a past action and can't be changed, so dissonance is reduced by changing their attitude about what they have done. Individuals who smoke often feel this sense of dissonance right after smoking. Festinger's seminal contribution was the demonstration that such tensions were more often reduced or resolved through changes in personal attitudes than by changing or relinquishing the dissonant belief. Instead of simply acknowledging an error in judgment and abandoning the opinion or belief, individuals tend to develop a new attitude or belief that will justify retaining the older, original belief or justify the past action.

Key Point:

The more committed we are to a belief, the harder it is to relinquish, even in the face of overwhelming contradictory information and evidence.

The Importance of Patterns

Imagine it is late at night. You are alone and walking down a dimly lighted street with no other pedestrians in sight. From the opposite direction, a person approaches you wearing a "hoodie." You become a little nervous and decide to cross the street to walk on the other side. If the person in the "hoodie" has no intention of engaging you in any way, then you have made a Type I error in cognition, also known as a false-positive. You believed the situation was dangerous when it was not. In this case, you have created a non-existent pattern. You connected (A) "person in hoodie at night" to (B) "a dangerous situation." But you improved your chances of not being harmed and living another day.

If, on the other hand, you continue to walk toward the individual with the "hoodie" and you are robbed at gunpoint, you have made a Type II error in cognition, a false-negative, or believing something is not real when in fact it is. You failed to detect the pattern and increased your chances of being harmed. Clearly the safer choice is to cross the street at the potential cost of making an error in judgment. If the individual in the "hoodie" follows you across the street, at least you would have more warning of an imminent threat.

Ray Kurzweil, inventor, author, and futurist, has proposed a model of the neocortex based primarily as a pattern recognition system. "It is my contention that the basic unit is a pattern recognizer and that this constitutes the fundamental component of the neocortex ... These recognizers are capable of wiring themselves to one another throughout the course of a lifetime, so the elaborate connectivity (between modules) that we see in the neocortex is not pre-specified by the genetic code, but rather is created to reflect the patterns we actually learn over time."[21]

According to Kurzweil's calculations, there are about 300 million pattern recognizers in the neocortex. Similar to neuroscientist Robert A. Burton, Kurzweil believes the brain acts as a probability calculator: "What the pattern recognizer module is doing is computing the probability (that is the likelihood based on all previous experience) that the pattern it is responsible for recognizing is in fact currently represented by its active inputs. Each particular input to the module is active if the corresponding lower-level pattern recognizer is firing (meaning that the lower-level pattern was recognized)."[22]

Patterns play the primary role in what we commonly refer to as *intuition*. As we have come to understand, there is no magic regarding the accuracy of intuition. Herbert Simon, Nobel Laureate Economics, had this to say about intuition: "The situation has provided a cue, this cue has given the expert access to information stored

---

21 Ray Kurzweil, *How To Create A Mind: The Secret of Human Thought Revealed* (New York: The Penguin Group, 2012), page 36, 37.

22 Ibid, page 50.

in memory, and the information provides the answer. Intuition is nothing more and nothing less than [pattern] recognition."[23]

Key Point:

Intuition is (to a large extent) perceived pattern recognition.

Daniel Kahneman, Nobel Laureate Economics, provided a stunning summary of the research comparing the use of "Intuitions versus Formulas" in his 2012 book, *Thinking, Fast and Slow.*[24] Kahneman and others have concluded that, in general, simple algorithms outperform human judgment. Several reasons were given why experts tend to have inferior predictive judgment compared to simple algorithms including:

1. Experts sometimes try to be clever, think outside the box, and consider complex combinations of features (low probability events and combinations) in making predictions.

2. Simple combinations of features are more predictive.

3. First order relationships are more informing than second order relationships with respect to prediction.

4. Human decision makers are inferior to prediction formulas even when they are given the value suggested by the formula.

Individuals are incredibly inconsistent in making summary judgments of complex information. Moreover, researchers currently conclude that in order to maximize predictive accuracy, the final decisions should be left to formulas. This is especially true in low-validity environments, i.e., situations where it is difficult to measure or know what is true. This certainly includes the realm of organizational decision making.

Key Point:

Simple mathematical algorithms consistently outperform intuition and human judgment in decision making.

The question is: Under what situations or circumstances can an individual's intuition be trusted? Daniel Kahneman provides the answer: "If subjective confidence is not to be trusted, how can we

---

23 Daniel Kahneman, *Thinking, Fast and Slow* (New York: Farrar, Straus and Giroux, 2011), page 11.

24 Ibid, pages 222-233.

evaluate the probable validity of an intuitive judgment? When do judgments reflect true expertise? When do they display an illusion of validity? The answer comes from the two basic conditions for acquiring a skill:

♦ An environment that is sufficiently regular to be predictable
♦ An opportunity to learn these regularities through prolonged practice

When both conditions are satisfied, intuitions are likely to be skilled."[25]

Professions that meet these two basic conditions include: chess masters, physicians, nurses, athletes, and firefighters. Missing from this list are engineers, scientists, managers, and executives. It all depends on the quality and speed of feedback and the opportunity to have sufficient practice. In general, experts tend not to know the limits of their expertise.

With this basic understanding of the operating system of our triune brain, we can now turn to insights on human judgment in decision making provided by cognitive psychologists over the past several decades.

System 1 versus System 2 Thinking

Daniel Kahneman in his seminal book, *Thinking, Fast and Slow*, summarized and codified over forty years of work with Amos Tversky and others on the psychology of judgment in decision making and what has more recently been called behavioral economics. In his book, Kahneman characterizes two forms of thinking that he distinguishes as System 1 and System 2. Table 6.2 summarizes these two ways of thinking.

According to Kahneman, most of the time we operate under System 1 in a state of cognitive ease. System 2 is the deeper conscious thinking and must be invoked. During conversations, it is easy to pinpoint the awakening of our "lazy" System 2. It happens when something is said that causes us to stop and think about what to say next.

---

25 Ibid, page 240.

System 1: *"Thinking Fast"*	System 2: *"Thinking Slow"*
♦ Intuitive Thought System	♦ Deliberate Thought System
♦ Operates automatically and quickly	♦ Allocates attention to the effortful mental activities that demand it
♦ Takes little or no effort	♦ Must be invoked
♦ No sense of voluntary control	♦ When we think of ourselves, we think of System 2 (the conscious, reasoning self that has beliefs, makes choices, decides what to think about, and what to do).
♦ More influential than your experience tells you	
♦ Uses associative memory to continually construct coherent interpretation of what is going on at every instant	♦ System 2 believes it is in control but it is lazy and often overridden by System 1
♦ Strives for quick coherence of available thoughts	♦ Only System 2 can construct thoughts in an orderly series of steps
♦ Automatic and often unconscious	♦ Associated with "Cognitive Strain"
♦ Generates surprisingly complex patterns of ideas	♦ "Cognitive Strain" is affected by both the current level of effort and the presence of unmet demand.
♦ Can be programmed by System 2 to mobilize attention when a particular pattern is detected	
♦ Associated with "Cognitive Ease"	

Table 6.2: Kahneman's Characterization of "Fast" and "Slow" Thinking

There are several physical indicators when switching from System 1 to System 2. Our eyes dilate, our heart rate increases, we have greater alertness, and our brains burn more glucose. All this results in increased fatigue. Switching from System 1 to System 2 occurs when attention is needed such as:

♦ Bracing for the start gun in a race,

♦ Maintaining a faster walking pace than normal,

♦ Scanning a business "dashboard" and seeing a "red" score or out of bounds metric, or

♦ Disagreeing with something said in a meeting.

Kahneman summarized the causes and consequences of *cognitive ease*[26] as illustrated in Figure 6.5. Notice how much of cognitive ease is associated with *sensations* rather than *thoughts*.

---

26 Ibid, page 60.

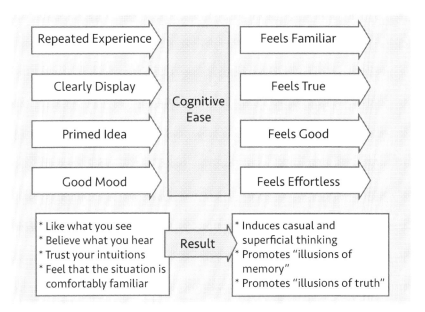

Figure 6.5: Causes and Consequences of Cognitive Ease

From a decision making perspective, the cognitive ease of System 1 thinking results in several undesirable states of thinking and belief.

Associative memory is defined as the ability to learn and re-member the relationship between unrelated items, e.g., the name of someone we have just met or the scent of a perfume. Associative memory is involved when we recall a previously experienced item or situation by thinking of something that is linked with it, thus invoking the association.

System 1 excels at constructing the best possible story, sce-nario, or narrative from the thoughts and ideas that are currently activated. It does not (nor can it) include information that it does not have or access. Kahneman calls this "what you see is all there is" and refers to it by the acronym WYSIATI.[27] Think back to the concept of our subconscious mind providing the Heads Up Display (HUD) for our conscious mind and stream of thought. Associative memory provides the activated ideas and thoughts that are avail-able to the HUD. Information that is not retrieved from memory, consciously or subconsciously, might as well not exist. The measure of success for System 1 is the coherence of the story it creates, not the truthfulness of the story or even its basis in reality.

---

27 Ibid, page 85.

Daniel Kahneman provides a key point: "The combination of a coherence-seeking System 1 with a lazy System 2 implies that System 2 will endorse many intuitive beliefs, which closely reflect the impressions generated by System 1...System 1 is expected to influence even the more careful decisions. Its input never ceases... System 1 is radically insensitive to both the quality and the quantity of the information that gives rise to impressions and intuitions."[28]

WYSIATI facilitates the coherence and the cognitive ease that results in our acceptance of a statement as being true. To maintain cognitive ease, System 1 takes short cuts by replacing tough questions with easier substitute questions (see Table 6.3).[29]

Target Question	*Heuristic Question*
◆ How popular will the President be six months from now?	◆ How popular is the President right now?
◆ This woman is running for the primary. How far will she go in politics?	◆ Does this woman look like a political winner?
◆ Will the project be completed on time and budget?	◆ How do I feel about the project manager?
◆ Should we increase our spending on earthquake preparedness?	◆ How much emotion did I feel watching the news last week on the earthquake in _____?
◆ How likely are we to get a "Warning Letter" for _____?	◆ How much fear did I feel when recently reading in WSJ about our competitor's product recall?

Table 6.3: Target and Heuristic Questions

In a less regular, less familiar, or low-validity environment—a common situation in organizational decision making—the heuristics of judgment are needed. System 1 produces quick answers to difficult questions by substituting simpler questions, creating a sense of coherence where often there is none. The question that is answered is not the one intended; however, the answer may be sufficiently plausible and ultimately slips by the review of the lazy System 2.

---

28 Ibid, page 86.

29 Ibid, pages 97-101.

System 1 creates biases in our judgment and decision making by:

♦ Generating impressions, feelings, and inclinations, and when endorsed by System 2, these become beliefs, attitudes, and intentions,

♦ Linking a sense of "cognitive ease" to illusions of truth, pleasant feelings, and reduced vigilance (everything feels right),

♦ Neglecting ambiguity and suppressing doubt,

♦ Desiring to believe and confirm; jumping to conclusions,

♦ Exaggerating emotional consistency (Halo Effect),

♦ Focusing on existing evidence and ignoring absent information (WYSIATI),

♦ Substituting easier questions in place for harder ones,

♦ Overweighting low probability events,

♦ Showing diminished sensitivity to quantity,

♦ Responding more strongly to losses than to gains (loss aversion),

♦ Framing decision problems narrowly, and

♦ Influencing even the most careful decisions–it never sleeps.

Daniel Kahneman has summarized the role System 2 has in our everyday life as: "System 2 is a minor character who thinks he is the star because in fact most of what goes on in our mind is automatic. It is in the domain that I call System 1."[30] These biases in judgment and decision making will be directly addressed in subsequent chapters when we delve into the mechanics of PRO Enterprise Management.

The Predict-Perceive-Confirm Model of Human Cognition

System 1 has two fundamental and pervasive biases: a *confirmation* bias and a *negativity* bias. They are defined below.

Confirmation Bias: the tendency of individuals to favor information that confirms their beliefs. The bias becomes apparent when

---

30 BBC-Horizon, "How you really make decisions", 2014, http://www.dailymotion.com/video/x1mp2je_bbc-horizon-2014-how-you-really-make-decisions-720p-hdtv-x264-aac-mvgroup-org_news/ min. 21:15 - 21:32.

individuals selectively gather or recall information, or when they interpret information in a biased way. The effect of the bias is stronger for emotionally charged issues and for deeply held beliefs. The bias is also evident as individuals tend to interpret ambiguous evidence as supporting their existing beliefs.

Negativity Bias: the tendency of individuals to pay more attention to and give more weight to negative rather than positive experiences or other kinds of information.

These two biases are part of the way we perceive and interpret all our experiences. Recognition of this alone is an important step toward improving your decision making.

Think of the last time you were in a classroom or a meeting where there was a presenter and an audience of participants. In that group setting, there were many expectations and patterns of behavior that created everyone's perceptions on what would be considered the "status quo" for that situation. As a participant, you are in the "I'm in class" or "I'm at work" story line or narrative with its associated patterns of behavior as opposed to the "I'm at the beach", "I'm on an airplane" or "I'm in an elevator" narratives. As a participant, you sit and face the presenter. The presenter speaks with an appropriate volume. You might raise your hand to ask questions. If the door opens and someone enters the room, you have immediate expectations of who is entering: someone who is late or perhaps an assistant delivering a message. We do not expect to see a clown or your mother or daughter enter the room. If something unexpected occurs, your mind will race to create a story that will make sense of what has happened to resolve the unexpected. The amygdala is constantly on high-alert for bad news, ready with a speedy response to maximize our chances of survival.

There is evidence that the subconscious mind makes decisions well before the conscious mind produces awareness of the decision. An encephalograph is an instrument for measuring and recording the electric activity of the brain. Studies with encephalographs have shown that the brain initiates action before the conscious mind is aware of it. For example, in baseball when swinging at a fast ball, part of your brain decides to swing and another part explains it after the onset of the swinging of the bat. According to research by Chun Siong Soon: "There has been a long controversy as to whether subjectively 'free' decisions are determined by brain activity ahead of time. We found that the outcome of a decision can be encoded in brain activity of prefrontal and parietal cortex up to 10 seconds before it enters awareness. This delay presumably reflects the operation of a network of high-level control areas that begin to prepare an upcoming decision long before it enters awareness."[31] Our ability to predict and anticipate and, at least in some cases, to decide prior to conscious awareness is key to our survival.

Ray Kurzweil says: "We are constantly predicting the future and hypothesizing what we will experience. This expectation influences what we actually perceive. Predicting the future is actually the primary reason that we have a brain ... the neocortex is, therefore, predicting what it expects to encounter. Envisioning the future is one of the primary reasons we have a neocortex. At the highest conceptual level, we are continually making predictions: who is going to walk thought the door next, what someone is likely to say next, what we expect to see when we turn the corner, the likely results of our own actions, and so on. These predictions are constantly occurring at every level of the neocortex hierarchy. We often misrecognize people and things and words because our threshold for confirming an expected pattern is too low."[32]

With this as background, see the *Predict-Perceive-Confirm Model of Human Cognition* as illustrated in Figure 6.6. System 1's standard mode of operation under a sense of cognitive ease is the energy-efficient state in which our brain operates. System 1 cycles through *predict-perceive-confirm* loops until something interrupts the flow and prompts the involvement of System 2.

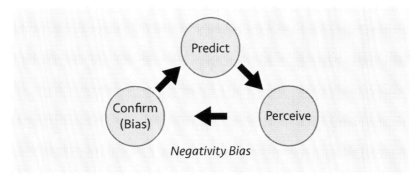

Figure 6.6: The Predict-Perceive-Confirm Model of Human Cognition

31 Chun Siong Soon, Marcel Brass, Hans-Jochen Heinze, and John-Dylan Haynes "Unconscious Determinants of Free Decisions in the Human Brain," *Nature Neuroscience*, Nature Publishing Group, 2008.

32 Ray Kurzweil, *How To Create A Mind: The Secret of Human Thought Revealed* (New York: The Penguin Group, 2012) page 31 and page 52.

The predictive nature of the brain will cue, or perhaps initiate, the subconscious brain's thought-generation algorithm in order to reduce the size of the search for the appropriate thought to be elevated into the conscious stream of thought. In some way, yet to be determined, the human brain has its own probability-based "Google" search engine algorithm. The subconscious brain also qualifies the thought via the sensation of knowing or feelings of certainty, conviction, rightness or wrongness.

The confirmation and negativity biases are built-in features of our thinking and underlie, and sometimes taint, the result of the cognition brought into conscious awareness. As the brain experiences issues, situations, or events through predict-perceive-confirm thought cycles, the confirmation of our learned patterns deepens their associated beliefs (like a river bed deepens from flowing water over time). The physical impact of these thought cycles is the strengthening of the brain's synapses associated with these patterns and beliefs.

Selective attention is the process by which an individual can selectively focus on one input from a mixture of inputs occurring simultaneously. Research shows that people tend to pay more attention to negative issues, and since conscious attention is a limited resource, we tend to selectively focus on the negative messages making them even more profound. Selective attention linked with our natural tendency to pay more attention to negative information results in a negativity bias.

We are always on the lookout for bad news. Bad news stays longer in memory than good news, and unpleasant encounters affect the brain more powerfully than pleasant ones. The brain's supersensitivity to negative emotions resides in the amygdala. Fear, anxiety, and anger prepare the body for freeze, fight, or flight. The fast response of the amygdala has the advantage of preparing the body for the worst-case scenario, while the slower response of the neocortex keeps the body from running away from every shadow. This is key to survival. The negativity bias is a built-in feature of our thinking—an individual's aversion to loss is much greater than their desire for gain.

Key Point:

Our innate negativity bias results in paying more attention to and giving more credence to negative information and experiences rather than positive information and experiences.

System 1 and System 2 both play a role as we observe and communicate. Understanding a statement begins with an attempt to believe it. You must first know what the idea would mean if it were true, only then can you decide to "unbelieve" it. The attempt to believe is performed by System 1. System 2 is only invoked when System 1 fails to confirm. Our bias is that we are more likely to confirm than to reject an idea if System 1 can complete the confirmation in the predict-perceive-confirm cycle of thought.

But negativity has a counter-balance at the time of decision making – Optimism. In fact, Daniel Kahneman believes that optimism may be the most consequential cognitive bias with respect to decision making. He states: "Most of us view the world as more benign than it really is, our own attributes as more favorable than they truly are, and the goals we adopt as more achievable than they are likely to be. We also tend to exaggerate our ability to forecast the future, which fosters optimistic overconfidence. In terms of its consequences for decisions, the optimistic bias may well be the most significant of the cognitive biases. Because optimistic bias can be both a blessing and a risk, you should be both happy and wary if you are temperamentally optimistic."[33]

Key Point:

> Our innate optimistic bias plays a significant role—sometimes the dominant role—in making decisions that involve significant risk. Risk-takers tend to underestimate the odds they face and do not invest sufficient effort to investigate or estimate what the odds are based on experience and informed judgment residing within their organizations.

Because they misread the risks, optimistic managers and executives often believe they are being prudent, even when they are not. Their confidence in personal future success bolsters a positive atmosphere that helps them obtain resources from others, raise the morale of their team, and enhance their prospects for success. Furthermore, as Nassim Taleb, the author of *The Black Swan,* argues: "Inadequate appreciation of the uncertainty of the environment inevitably leads economic agents to take risks they should avoid. However, optimism is highly valued, socially and in the market; people and firms reward the providers of dangerously misleading information more than they reward truth tellers."[34]

---

33 Daniel Kahneman, *Thinking, Fast and Slow* (New York: Farrar, Straus and Giroux, 2011), page 11.

34 Nassim Nicholas Taleb, *The Black Swan: The Impact of the Highly Improbable* (New York: The Random House Publishing Group, 2007).

And so we have pervasive confirmation, negativity, and optimistic biases vying for influence and tainting our thought processes. Does this make us sound conflicted? As we have discussed, our thoughts are largely driven at a subconscious level below our awareness. An unsettling possibility is that the conscious mind makes no decisions at all, and the unconscious mind merely informs the conscious mind of its decisions while being influenced and primed by a variety of subliminal factors and biases. Our brains are often disassociated and in conflict–the limbic system and reptilian complex compete with our more analytical prefrontal cortex when decisions evoke both emotions and rationalized concerns.

Conclusion: Beliefs, Emotions, and Cognition

The human brain is a belief-generating engine. If we are to design processes and analytics to support humans making decisions, we must first understand the operating system of the human brain. Table 6.4 provides a summary of the capabilities, strengths, and vulnerabilities of our triune brain. We make decisions based on our beliefs. Short of influencing our beliefs, decision processes and analytics will not influence our decision making.

Individuals supporting corporate decision makers must learn how to use language, data, information, and analytics to provide systems that leverage the capabilities and strengths of the brain while mitigating the vulnerabilities. In subsequent chapters, we will be designing analytics using scenarios, narratives, and hierarchies. We will leverage side-by-side comparisons to improve our thinking and understanding of an uncertain future.

We have explored in this chapter how the structure of the brain results in vulnerabilities in our thinking and the consequences of those liabilities. In the next two chapters, we will explore specific mistakes we make in thinking and judgment in the face of uncertainty, critical aspects of decision making.

Brain's Capabilities and Strengths	*Brain's Vulnerabilities*

♦ Flexible neocortex considered to have almost infinite learning abilities
♦ Pattern generation and recognition system:
  o order and sequence
  o stories / scenarios / narratives
  o hierarchies
♦ Simultaneous side-by-side comparative judgment
♦ Ability to predict and anticipate, resulting in expectations based on causality
♦ Cognitive dissonance alerts the brain that a decision is required and a change to the status quo is needed
♦ Fast-responding System 1 avoids immediate danger
♦ Slower-responding System 2 useful when contemplation is required
♦ Working memory ensures pursuit of long-term goals and objectives
♦ Makes decisions based on intertwined knowledge-based and faith-based beliefs
	♦ Three layers of the brain are often dissociated and in conflict
	♦ Prefers to operate in System 1's state of cognitive ease, inducing casual and superficial thinking, promoting "illusions of memory" and "illusions of truth"
	♦ Faster-reacting System 1 often precludes deeper contemplation provided by System 2
	♦ Easily influenced by irrelevant subconscious cues (priming)
	♦ Decisions that evoke emotion are overly influenced by the "right versus wrong" limbic system (specifically the amydgala) response versus the slower-reacting rationalized "cost-benefit" (prefontal neocortex) response
	♦ Sensations and intuition (feeling of knowing, correctness, conviction, and certainty) heavily influence decision making and arise with no quality check on truthfulness
	♦ Difficult to make consistent summary judgments of complex information
	♦ Conflicted by three ever-present cognitive biases: confirmation, negativity, and optimism

Table 6.4: Summary of the Capabilities, Strengths, and Vulnerabilities of the Human Brain

"A great many people think they are thinking when they are really rearranging their prejudices."
– William James, American Philosopher and Psychologist

7

The Eight Basic Mistakes

In Chapter 6, we learned that our beliefs shape our perceptions, our perceptions reconfirm our beliefs, and both affect how and what we decide. There has been much published on the heuristics and biases we have in judgment that can undermine our decision making (which will be the topic of Chapter 8). This chapter is devoted to the general errors we make in *thinking*, which are also referred to as "cognitive distortions" and "twisted thinking."[1,2]

The question is: "Where does our thinking and judgment go wrong?" Thomas Kida published an insightful book entitled *Don't Believe Everything You Think: The 6 Basic Mistakes We Make in Thinking*.[3] In his book, Kida makes connections between the basic design and functions of the brain and the implications to the way we think that ultimately can lead to flawed thoughts. I've taken his list of six and added two for a total of eight basic mistakes we make in thinking. Let's review each of these basic errors in thinking.

---

1   David D. Burns, M.D., *The Feeling Good Handbook* (New York: The Penguin Group, 1999), pages 8-9.

2   Dr. Jane Bolton: http://www.dr-jane-bolton.com/support-files/common-thinking-mistakes.pdf.

3   Thomas Kida, *Don't Believe Everything You Think: The 6 Basic Mistakes We Make in Thinking* (Amherst, New York: Prometheus Books, 2006).

1. We Prefer Stories to Statistics[4]

> *"At our core, we are storytellers, not statisticians."*
> – Thomas Kida[5]

We have learned that narratives and stories are innate, fundamental components of thought generation and memory. However, this critical enabler to decision making has a downside.

Rafid Ahmed Alwan al-Janabi, known as *Curveball* by American and German intelligence communities, fabricated stories about Iraq having a secret biological weapons program. Even without substantiated data and evidence of such a program, Rafid's personalized but misleading story became the tipping point for the decision by the United States to invade Iraq in 2003.

On the other hand, investor Warren Buffett famously avoided financial losses resulting from the speculative dot-com bubble collapse of 2000. Buffett ignored the tech stock hype, a narrative that conflicted with historical data and his experience, and continued to base investment decisions on data and simple predictive models. We can't help it; we prefer stories to statistics, especially personalized stories. Stories easily slip by System 1 unchecked by our logical System 2.

Long before there were written language, books, computers, and data storage, information was shared through oral communication and storytelling. It has only been during the last two or three generations that we have been able to store information and knowledge in forms that are accessible without verbal communication. In 1440, Johannes Gutenberg perfected the printing press that enabled publishing of books for the masses. Consequently, storytelling was and remains a primary means by which information is received and stored. We tend to pay close attention to information that comes to us in stories.

We have a neural network in the left cortex of our brain called the "left-hemisphere interpreter" that is always on and works at both subconscious and conscious levels. It is the brain's storytelling system that reconstructs events into a logical sequence that results in a meaningful story. Information and memories need a context to be useful. The left-hemisphere interpreter provides this context as a story, a narrative. As our sensory systems perceive and our subconscious mind retrieves associated memories, the left hemisphere

---

4   Ibid.

5   Ibid, pg 17.

interpreter is hard at work, "24x7," to create critical narratives that give meaning to our thoughts.

The organization of these narratives into memories is believed to be performed during rapid eye movement (REM) sleep. As Robert Stickgold of Harvard Medical School explains: "the unique physiology of sleep and perhaps even more so, of REM sleep, shifts the brain/mind into an altered state in which it pulls together disparate, often emotionally charged and weakly associated memories into a narrative structure ... this process of memory reactivation and association is, in fact, also a process of memory consolidation and integration that enhances our ability to function in the world."[6] In other words, during REM sleep the brain is busy weaving together stories and organizing them into memory storage for future associations and thoughts.

Thought Experiment:

> This Saturday, you are planning on buying a car with great reviews and ratings from Consumer Reports. At a party on Friday night you are told by an old friend that he bought that type of car and it has been a "total lemon".
>
> Would you still buy that type of car?

The bottom line is that even when relevant data and statistical information is available, we still tend to favor personal accounts and stories. Unfortunately, when we form our beliefs, we often give too much credence to the quantity of evidence, e.g., blogs on the internet, and too little credence to its quality. According to Daniel Kahneman and many others (well over 100 studies), we would make better decisions if we relied on statistical and data-based predictions instead of relying on intuition or predictions based solely on our internalized beliefs and stories.

Thought Experiment:

> Consider the sequence of numbers "4-6-8". I created this sequence based on a simple rule.
>
> The question is: "What is the rule?"

---

6   Robert Strickgold, "Sleep-Dependent Memory Consolidation," *Science* 437, pages 1272-1278.

2. We Seek to Confirm, Not to Question, Our Ideas[7]

> *"We like information that confirms our existing beliefs."*
> – Sir Francis Bacon, 16th Century English Philosopher,
> Statesman, Scientist, Author

In the quote above, Sir Francis Bacon succinctly expressed a truth about one of our basic mistakes in thinking. Considering Sir Francis was born over four hundred years ago, this concept is neither a new thought nor a current breakthrough in the understanding about ourselves.

Richard Paul "Dick" Rowe was an influential producer and record executive at Decca Records in the 1950s and early 1960s. In 1960, he believed that guitar groups were on their way out. Nonetheless, the Beatles' manager Brian Epstein secured an audition with Decca Records and Dick Rowe for New Year's Day 1962. Rowe was unimpressed with the Beatles' audition and concluded: "The Beatles have no future in show business." The Beatles, with producer George Martin, went on to sell more than 600 million records, more than any other band in history.

Thought Experiment:

Consider the numerical thought experiment proposed on the previous page. Write down a couple of three-number sequences to test the rule that I used to construct the sequence listed: 4-6-8.

If you presented number sequences to confirm the rule, you would be using a "positive test" strategy. For example, if your proposed rule was "positive even numbers", you might test by offering sequences such as: 8-10-12, 2-4-6 and 40-60-80. In each of these examples, you would be attempting to confirm your proposed rule, not to disprove it by offering sequences like 1-2-3.

In general, we seek to confirm our ideas, not to question or disprove them. This is easily explained by the System 1 model of the predict-perceive-confirm thought process presented in the previous chapter. This same pattern of thinking flows into our judgment and decision making. Our tendency is to use confirming decision strategies. We look for evidence to support what we consider to be the "best choice" in a decision-making situation while minimizing or discarding other information that may conflict with our logic supporting the "best choice."

---

7   Thomas Kida, *Don't Believe Everything You Think: The 6 Basic Mistakes We Make in Thinking* (Amherst, New York: Prometheus Books, 2006).

We focus on and select information from situations, issues, or events that support our existing beliefs, expectations, and desires. We tend to undervalue or discard information that is contrary to our beliefs. So in effect, we are using confirming decision strategies and make decisions based on incomplete or biased information. In *On Being Certain*, Robert A. Burton says, "The brain is only human; it too, relies on established ways. As interneuronal connections increase, they become more difficult to overcome. A hitch in your golf swing, biting your nails, persisting with a faulty idea, not dumping your dot.com stocks in late 1999—habits, whether mental or physical, are exasperating examples of the power of these microscopic linkages."[8]

As previously stated, System 1 has two fundamental and pervasive biases: *confirmation* bias and *negativity* bias. This leads us to the third error in thinking.

3. We Tend to Overreact to Negative Information

> *"I feel that life is divided into the horrible and the miserable...*
> *So you should be thankful that you're miserable."*
> – Woody Allen, (Quote from his 1977 comedy film, Annie Hall)

In the previous chapter, we learned that we naturally have a negativity bias. The question is: "How does this influence our thinking and decision making?" Consider the thought experiment below:

Thought Experiment:

You are considering hiring an individual named Tom who has been recommended to you for managing an important corporate project. A trusted colleague knows Tom and tells you the following:

"I've known Tom for over 15 years. He worked with me at XYZ Company. He is very honest and responsible. He was good at keeping schedules within budget. He garnered a lot of respect from his staff and worked well with cross-functional teams. But, sometimes he made some pretty consequential decisions without consulting me. He is enthusiastic and keeps his teams focused and enthused too. He is very loyal. I really like Tom."

Question: Would you hire Tom?"

After reading your trusted colleague's description of Tom, stop and think about what you remember about Tom. Write this down without

---

8   Robert A. Burton, M.D., *On Being Certain: Believing You Are Right Even When You're Not* (New York: St. Martin's Press, 2008), page 52.

re-reading his description. The question for you is: "Would you hire Tom?" If you would hire Tom, explain to yourself why. Or, if you would not hire Tom, explain to yourself why not.

In 1979, the Three Mile Island Nuclear Generating Station in Pennsylvania had a partial nuclear meltdown that resulted in a leak of significant amounts of nuclear reactor coolant into the environment. This coolant contained known cancer-inducing agents. The Kemeny Commission Report, created under President Jimmy Carter's order, concluded that less than one case of cancer would be expected from the accident. Later it was determined that the average radiation dosage to individuals within a ten-mile radius of the accident was equivalent to a single chest x-ray. However, the accident created a ground swell of public and political opinion that led to no new nuclear plants being built in the United States for thirty years. Ironically, in the years following the accident, coal-fueled and oil-fueled plants were built instead. These generated much greater health hazards than the avoided nuclear facilities.

In March 2011, a magnitude 9.0 earthquake off the coast of Japan resulted in a tsunami that caused three meltdowns within the Fukushima Daiichi nuclear power plant. While over 18,000 people died from the earthquake and tsunami, there have been no short-term deaths due to over exposure to radiation. The current long-term expectation for radiation deaths from the accident range from 100's to as many as 1,800. Before the Fukushima accident, there were 442 nuclear reactors in 30 countries generating 14% of the world's electricity. By 2012, fifteen nuclear reactors were shutdown (primarily in Japan and Germany), reducing output to about 11% of the world's electricity. Though heavily debated, nuclear generated electricity remains a clean and relatively safe source of energy.

This example illustrates how our cognitive biases can combine to support our existing beliefs. If you are not a supporter of nuclear-generated energy, your confirmation bias was triggered by the Fukushima disaster, and you likely disagree with my comment "clean and relatively safe source of energy." Additionally, you probably thought of the other impacts the disaster had and will have to Japan and the surrounding areas. If you are a supporter of nuclear-generated energy, your focus was likely on the failure of the plant operator, Tokyo Electric Power Company (TEPCO), to meet basic safety requirements. After all, if the plant had been run properly, there would not have been a radiation component to the disaster. The question is: "Why do we tend to over react to negative information?"

The amygdala uses about *two-thirds* of its neurons searching for negative experiences. Once the amygdala finds bad news, that information is fast tracked into long-term memory coupled with associated emotions. Conversely, positive experiences must be held in awareness for more than twelve seconds to transfer from short-term to long-term memory. The overall limbic system, which includes the amygdala, can become overloaded with negative information and override the higher-level cognitive processes in the neocortex. Remember, the brain's ancient hyper-sensitivity to negative emotions emerged with the limbic system some 100 million years ago for good reason—it prepares the body for freeze, flight, or fight. It shepherds our survival.

As detailed in the previous chapter, the *negativity bias* is a psychological phenomenon where we tend to pay more attention to and give more credence to negative information and experiences over positive. We can't help it. That is how our brains are designed. This negativity bias, driven by our innate desire to survive, results in strong aversions to loss or even potential loss, that is, *risk*.

Did you want to hire Tom?

4. We Rarely Appreciate the Role of Chance and Coincidence in Shaping Events[9]

> *"Million to one odds happen eight times a day in New York."*
> – Penn Jillette, American Illusionist and Comedian

Leonard Mlodinow provides a telling Wall Street tale in his book *The Drunkard's Walk*[10] that demonstrates our under-appreciation of the role chance plays in shaping events and outcomes in our lives. For 15 straight years, Bill Miller, the portfolio manager of the Legg Mason Value Trust, outperformed the S&P 500. *Money Magazine* called Miller "The Greatest Money Manager of the 1990s." *Morningstar* named Miller "Fund Manager of the Decade." *Smart Money* magazine referred to him as one of the top 30 most influential people in investing from 2001 to 2006. *CNN* ordained Miller the "Greatest Money Manager of Our Time." *CNN* computed the odds of him beating the S&P 500 for fifteen straight years as 372,529 to 1.

Mlodinow asked: "Is this all true, or was Bill Miller just lucky?" After all, there are over 6,000 mutual fund managers. Mlodinow

---

9   Thomas Kida, *Op. cit.*

10   Leonard Mlodinow, Ph.D., *The Drunkard's Walk: How Randomness Rules Our Lives* (New York: Pantheon Books, 2008).

calculated the odds of beating the S&P 500 in a given year for the past 40 years of mutual fund trading using a random stock selection process based on a coin flip. The probability of at least one fund manager beating the market every year for 15 years in a row is about 75%! This is like saying someone will win the lottery—it's just probably not you. So, was Bill Miller a great fund manager or just the lucky lottery winner? Prior to Miller's retirement, his luck apparently ran out as the fund under his management significantly underperformed the S&P 500 five out of his last six years. *Fortune* had this to say: "Legg Mason's superstar is closing out a legendary career. Too bad his investors can't afford to call it quits … the longevity of that streak, which ran from 1991 through 2005, will probably never be matched. It was a fabulous performance."[11]

During the years on my high school basketball team, I can remember the sensation of having a "hot hand"   the belief that for a particular period of time my shooting performance was significantly better than my overall average. Thomas Gilovich, Robert Valone, and Amos Tversky published an article in 1985 entitled "The Hot Hand in Basketball: On the Misperception of Random Sequences." Gilovich, Valone, and Tversky[12] found that 91% of fans agreed that a player has "a better chance of making a shot after having just made his last two or three shots." For free throws, 68% said the same, and 84% of fans believed that "it was important to pass the ball to someone who has just made several (two, three, or four) shots in a row."

Everyone I've met who has played or is a fan of basketball believes in the "hot hand." However, Gilovich, Vallone, and Tversky analyzed basketball players' successive shots and showed that they are statistically independent events—meaning the probability of a player making his or her next shot is independent of whether they made the previous shot. To this day, I struggle with that conclusion. I still feel that I can get into a groove of shooting and, for a while, have a "hot hand." I have to remind myself of the "Hot Hand" study. Beliefs, truthful or not, are hard to shake even in the face of strong counter-evidence.

We want to believe that things happen for a reason. We seek causality as we interpret situations, events, issues, and outcomes.

---

11 http://finance.fortune.cnn.com/2011/12/07/bill-miller-legg-mason-returns/.

12 Thomas Gilovich, Robert Valone, and Amos Tversky (1985), "The Hot Hand in Basketball: On the Misperception of Random Sequences," *Cognitive Psychology* 17, pgs 295-314.

Our brains are wired with a desire to understand the underlying story. In general, we tend to believe that our successes are due to our personal actions, and our failures are due to events beyond our control. Understanding causality was central to our evolution and remains central to our progress as a species—it's just over-applied. Dr. Robert Burton says, "We are further burdened by having a brain that learns by seeking generalizations over ambiguity. This preference prods us by producing its own mental state—the uncomfortable feeling that an ambiguous situation must have an answer."[13]

We shouldn't require nor seek a causal explanation for everything. We need to learn to better appreciate the role of chance in shaping events that impact our lives and others. But this learned, wise perspective is clearly not one we innately have.

5. We Sometimes Misperceive the World Around Us[14]

"The eyes see only what the mind is prepared to comprehend."
– Henri-Louis Bergson, French Philosopher

In 1980, IBM was scrambling to get its first personal computer (PC) to market to compete with upstarts Apple and Commodore. Knowing the importance of time-to-market, IBM outsourced the central processing unit (CPU) to Intel and the operating system to Bill Gates and Microsoft. There was a critical difference in perceptions of the PC market between IBM and Microsoft. IBM believed they could maintain a highly profitable, differentiated product for the long haul. Gates believed that personal computers would rapidly become a commodity, but the operating system they required would not. Microsoft secured the outsourcing agreement by purchasing an operating system from Seattle Computer Products and reselling it to IBM while retaining the right to license the operating system to other PC makers. Within a few years, manufacturers of "PC clones" running Microsoft's operating system were severely eroding IBM's profit and PC market share while Microsoft (and Intel) were building empires. IBM sold their PC business to Lenovo in 2005.

Thought Experiment: PARIS
IN THE
THE SPRING

---

13 Robert A. Burton, M.D., *On Being Certain: Believing You Are Right Even When You're Not*, (New York: St. Martin's Press, 2008), page 187.

14 Thomas Kida, *Op. cit.*

How we perceive the world is greatly influenced by what we expect to see and what we want to see. Read the thought experiment. If you are like many others, you probably did not notice the extra "the" in the third line. That is, you see what you expect to read. Police departments regularly deal with false sightings whenever there is news of a bear or a mountain lion in a community or a fugitive at-large. In 2013, during the Christopher Dorner manhunt, the Los Angeles Police Department (LAPD) had over 700 "sightings" called in. Dorner was wanted for killing a police officer, a husband and wife, and for injuring a second police officer.

Our brains easily fill in missing, often non-existent, information to create a coherent story (memory) consistent with our beliefs. These memory gaps filled in with falsifications are called *confabulations* by psychiatrists. Confabulations consistently are believed to be true. All of this is played out in System 1's predict-perceive-confirm thought process cycle. As we have learned, the neocortex does a good job spinning explanations that are coherent and consistent with a set of sensory inputs and associated memories. We mimic this process when we retell stories or describe past events. We simply fill in details that were either forgotten or might not have even happened. We can only imagine the impact this tendency has had on the retelling of history from generation to generation, especially prior to a written record.

Unfortunately, each of our five senses can easily be tricked resulting in misperceptions that lead to erroneous beliefs. We *trust* our sight the most. About one-third of our brain is devoted to processing vision. The high-resolution images our brain "hallucinates" are created from the optic nerve's ten to twelve output channels, each of which provides a small amount of information. The optic nerve sends the brain a series of edges, outlines, colors, background, and other clues about our visual field. By using memories combined with this visual information, our brains essentially hallucinate the high-resolution images we believe we see. According to neurobiologist Frank Werblin, "Even though we think we see the world so fully, what we are receiving is really just hints, edges in space and time. These twelve pictures of the world constitute all the information we will ever have about what's out there, and from these twelve pictures, which are so sparse, we reconstruct the richness of the visual world."[15]

---

15 Boton Roska and Frank Werblin, "Vertical Interactions Across Ten Parallel, Stacked Representations in the Mammalian Retina," *Nature* 410, no. 6828 (March 29, 2001), pages 583-587.

When it comes to sensing the world around us, humans are pretty mediocre compared to the rest of the animal kingdom. For example, our eyes can only detect a fraction of the colors that birds can see, and our ears can't hear very high frequencies like bats or dogs. Similarly, our noses need to be bombarded with odors before we can detect any scent; moths can detect individual molecules. Our single, critical advantage is that our brains have a large and highly interconnected prefrontal cortex. Our perception of reality can be unreliable, so we should think twice about our thoughts and beliefs that are based solely on our personal experiences, especially if these thoughts and beliefs are the foundation used for making important decisions.

6. We Tend to Oversimplify Our Thinking[16]

> *"Everything should be made as simple as possible,*
> *but not simpler."*
> – Albert Einstein

For the past two decades, China was presumed to be the next great growth opportunity for hundreds of international companies. However, oversimplified and failed marketing strategies by western enterprises in the Chinese market have become the norm. In 2004, eBay entered the Chinese market and was planning to replicate its successful internet-based auction and sales services business model. Alibaba (founded by Jack Ma) was a local Chinese e-commerce firm that enabled small and medium-sized companies to conduct business online. Fearing that eBay might take his customers, Ma launched a new web-site called Taobao which means "digging for treasure".

While executives at eBay were confident their business model should work well in any market, Ma thought differently. Taobao and eBay both provided the same basic service: a means through which individuals and businesses can sell products over the internet. But the platform and methods used by Taobao were tailored for the Chinese market. As in the west, eBay required customers to pay online with a credit card for purchases. Many Chinese prefer not to use credit cards for payment, so Taobao allowed for payment with cash on delivery. eBay also required sellers to pay a transaction fee for the service. Selling goods on Taobao was free. Taobao generated revenue through advertisements, something that was much more acceptable than fees to the Chinese. Due to the Chinese culture of

16 Thomas Kida, *Op. cit.*

bargaining and establishing trust and relationships prior to making purchases, Taobao provided a chat feature to enable buyers and sellers to communicate. eBay had no such chat functionality fearing this would enable buyers and sellers to circumvent eBay's transaction fee. In 2006, eBay terminated its operations in China and Taobao prevailed.

Simplifying things down to their essence is a critical life skill; however, the problem too often is oversimplification. System 1 is radically insensitive to both the quality and quantity of the information that gives rise to impressions and intuitions. System 1 is quick to create a simple, coherent story that often sneaks by the lazy System 2, even when the story has a weak or flawed foundation. Therefore, System 1 is vulnerable to oversimplifying issues, situations, or events.

Thought Experiment:

"Corporal punishment is no longer in public schools. This is why children have no self-discipline and are losing respect for authority."

"People end up in jail because they are lazy or have weak morals."

Do you agree with either of these statements?

Both quotes in the thought experiment are examples of oversimplification. The problems of self-discipline and loss of respect for authority are not new. The ancient Greeks were concerned and debated these same issues. They are very complex and highly unlikely to have a single cause. Tracing the problems regarding children solely to the abandonment of corporal punishment in schools is an oversimplification. Likewise, the statement regarding why people end up in jail ignores the complexities of societal influence, mental illness, and other factors. For these reasons, the conclusions should be rejected. There is not sufficient evidence to support their implicit and crucial premises.

These are examples of the "fallacy of the single cause" or causal oversimplifications. This is where a single, simple cause of an outcome is assumed where in reality there may be a number of jointly sufficient causes. When you think, make, or hear statements that conclude a single cause resulted in a significant situation or event, you need to remind yourself that events are almost always the result of many factors. The causal analysis may be oversimplified if it seems insufficient to account for the event in question or if it overemphasizes the role of one or more specific factors. Point out these problems and request further justification on the analysis. You can help, of course, by suggesting additional factors that you think need to be considered.

Often after a tragedy it is asked, "What was *the* cause of this?" Such statements imply that there was a single cause, when instead there were probably multiple contributing factors. After you produce a list of several contributing factors, it may be worthwhile to look for the strongest of the factors or a single root cause underlying several of them. A need for simplification may be desired to make the explanation of the tragedy straightforward and direct. We prefer simple explanations and simple stories to complex ones. But we should settle for and only believe simple stories when there is evidence that they are true and accurate.

After a school shooting, politicians and editorialists debate whether it was caused by the shooter's parents, violence in the media and video games, stress on students, or the accessibility of guns. In fact, many different contributing factors—including some of the above—may have motivated the shooting. It should be no surprise that System 1 is a master of oversimplifying issues, situations, or events into straightforward, simple, linear logic. And without System 2 being invoked, these oversimplifications can result in erroneous beliefs.

7. We Have Faulty Memories[17]

> *"The palest ink is better than the best memory."*
> – Chinese Proverb

Elizabeth Loftus, a cognitive psychologist and expert on human memory, tells a cautionary and tragic tale of thirty year-old Steve Titus. Steve was arrested in 1980 because he bore some resemblance to a man who had raped a woman nearby. By looking at a lineup of photographs, the victim informed the police that Titus looked "the closest" to her assailant. Months later at the trial, the victim was *certain* that Steve Titus was the rapist. Titus was wrongly convicted of Rape in the First Degree that carried a mandatory prison sentence. Though he was later exonerated, Titus lost his fiancée and his job. He remained unemployed until his death at age 35 from a stress-related heart attack. How did the victim's memory go from some degree of uncertainty to certain by the time of the trial? At

---

17 Ibid.

his second trial, Elizabeth Loftus argued that the victim's recollections had been changed through cues during the court proceedings resulting in a false memory.

Human memory is essentially associative. You will remember a new piece of information better if you associate it with other previously acquired information or knowledge that is already in your memory. The more significant the association is to you personally, the more effectively it will help you to remember. Most of our memories are reconstructions, not memory retrievals like in a computer. Whenever we remember something, it is reconstructed from information scattered throughout various regions of our brains. Remembering is part of an ongoing process of reclassification resulting from continuous changes in our neural pathways and parallel processing of information in our brains.

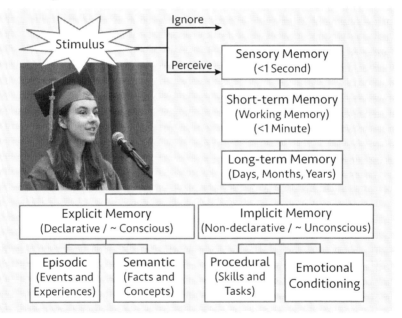

Figure 7.1: The Three Stages of Creating Long-Term Memory and Types of Long-Term Memory

Thought Experiment:

Look at the young woman's graduation picture in Figure 7.1. Close your eyes and try to keep the image of the young woman in mind.

You may notice that the image will remain vivid for less than a second. After that, you will be trying to recreate the image from your short-term memory.

As illustrated in Figure 7.1, stimuli detected by the senses are either ignored by the brain, in which case they disappear almost instantaneously, or perceived by the brain and placed in *sensory memory*. Sensory memory does not require conscious attention; perceived information is stored in sensory memory automatically. When we perceive an object, our eyes jump from point to point (called *saccades*) to examine the details. Our sensory memory is essential as it provides a sense of unity of an object while this occurs.

If you dwell on information, it will continue on into *short-term memory* where limited amounts of information are recorded for periods of less than one minute. With effort, you can retain information in short-term memory for longer periods, such as when you repeat a telephone number over and over until you dial it. Otherwise, the memory will disappear in less than a minute.

Keeping information in short-term memory for a certain amount of time allows for the eventual transfer to long-term-memory for more permanent storage. This process is facilitated by the mental work of repeating the information, which is why the expression *working memory* is commonly used as a synonym for short-term memory. But such repetition seems less effective than giving the memory a meaning by associating it with previously acquired knowledge. Once a piece of information is stored in *long-term memory*, it can remain there for a very long time, sometimes even for the rest of your life. There are, however, several factors that can make these memories hard to recollect, including:

♦ How long has it been since the event occurred?
♦ How long has it been since the last time you remembered it?
♦ How well have you integrated it with your own knowledge-based or faith-based beliefs?
♦ Is it unique?
♦ Does it resemble a current event?

Explicit memory involves the *conscious* recollection of events, concepts, and facts such as "George Washington was the first president of the United States." Conversely, things that are encoded in *implicit memory* can be recalled automatically without conscious effort. Procedural memory, a type of implicit memory, enables you to acquire, retain and gradually improve things such as motor skills, e.g., riding a bicycle. *Procedural memory* is subconscious (unconscious) and composed of automatic sensor and motor behaviors that have become deeply embedded so that you might not be aware of them.

Implicit memory is also where many of your conditioned re- flexes and conditioned emotional responses are stored. These occur very quickly, even before conscious thought. As demonstrated by Ivan Pavlov, a Russian physiologist and Nobel Laureate, a reflex response to a new stimulus can be learned. Pavlov trained dogs to expect food whenever he rang a bell. The dogs eventually produced saliva, the conditioned reflex, when they heard the bell ring. The associative learning that forms the basis for conditioned reflexes and conditioned emotional responses is a very old process from an evolutionary perspective and can take place without the conscious mind. In other words, we form implicit memories without being aware that it is happening.

Episodic memory (sometimes called autobiographical memory) lets you remember events that you personally experience. It includes memories such as the meal you ate last night, the name of an old classmate, or the date of some personally important event. "Episodic" refers to the remembrance of specific episodes organized together as a sequential narrative. Importantly, these memories are revised by subsequent *similar* experiences. The most distinctive feature of episodic memory is that you see yourself as an actor in the events you remember. You therefore memorize not only the events but also the entire context or narrative surrounding them. The emotions you experience at the time of the event condition the quality and detail of your memory of the episode.

According to Robert Burton and many others, our episodic memory isn't nearly as good as we think it is. "None of us have an instinctual belief that our memories are this fragile. Despite the proliferation of psychological studies questioning the accuracy of episodic memory recall, we cling to the belief that our pasts approximately correspond to our memories. Sometimes we sense that the details are a bit faded, but we rarely doubt the essence of a memory. We rely upon the notion that, at the very least, the memories of our past reflect fundamental truths."[18] Throughout the episodic memory retrieval (more like recon- struction) process, negativity biases arise as we retain the *impression* rather than the features or details of the episodic information. Since negative experiences and memories are more distinct in our minds, they are easily accessible and retrieved more rapidly.

---

18 Robert A. Burton, M.D., *On Being Certain: Believing You Are Right Even When You're Not* (New York: St. Martin's Press, 2008), page 83.

Semantic memory is the system that stores knowledge (facts and concepts) about the world, much of which can be accessed quickly and effortlessly. It includes the meanings of words, names of country capitals, social customs, functions of things, colors, odors, etc. Semantic memory also includes the rules and concepts that allow us to construct a mental representation of the world without any immediate sensory perceptions.

Thought Experiment:

How did you hear about the Challenger Space Shuttle Accident?

How certain are you about those memories?

Read the thought experiment. Ulric Neisser was studying the kind of memories people have for highly dramatic events. Within a day of the 1986 Challenger space shuttle explosion, he interviewed 106 Emory University undergraduates. He had them write down in a journal exactly how they heard about the disaster, where they were, what they were doing, and how they felt. About two and a half years later, Neisser interviewed them again. He found that 25% had second accounts that were significantly different from their original journal entries, more than 50% had some degree of error, and less than 10% specified the details the same as they had originally.[19]

Prior to reading their original journals, most of the subjects were certain that their current memories were absolutely correct. In fact, when confronted with what they had originally written down, many still had a high degree of confidence in their false recollections. They said their current memories felt correct even when faced with journals in their own handwriting. One student said, "That's my handwriting but that's not what happened." This is only one study of many documenting this phenomenon. Memories can and do change; we even create memories that never happened. The mechanism of episodic memory is not a retrieval process but a constructive process resulting in a reconstruction of the past. We need to be aware that our memories can be in error, and that these errors can significantly influence or taint our beliefs and decisions.

---

19 Neisser, U., & Harsch, N. "Phantom Flashbulbs: False Recollections of Hearing the News About Challenger," in *Affect and Accuracy in Recall: Studies of "Flashbulb" Memories,* Winograd, E., and Neisser, U., eds. (New York: Cambridge University Press, 1992), pages 9-31.

Key Point:

Our memories change over time, even when we are confident they have not. Negative experiences and memories are more distinct and are retrieved more rapidly and therefore are more accessible and more influential in decision making.

8. We "Know" Less Than We Think We Know

"Despite how certainty feels, it is neither a conscious choice nor even a thought process. Certainty and similar states of 'knowing what we know' arise out of the involuntary brain mechanisms that, like love or anger, function independently of reason."[20]
– Dr. Robert Burton, Neurologist and Author

JCPenney has been in the retail business for over 100 years. With well over 1,000 department stores in the U.S., it has been widely known as a discount retailer. JCPenney's core customers are drawn to shop by sales, coupons, and discounts. But by 2011, JCPenney was showing its age and needing a strategy to turnaround its shrinking sales and lackluster profits.

The company hired Ron Johnson, a former Apple executive known for launching Apple's successful retail stores, as CEO in November 2011. Johnson knew just what to do and set about re-branding JCPenney as a hip destination to shop with the Boutique (store-within-a-store) Concept. He modified the pricing strategy away from sales, coupons, and discounts toward everyday "fair and square" prices. The retailer's oldest and most loyal customers stopped showing up, and they were not replaced by the desired hip and youthful customer base. On April 8, 2013, Johnson was fired. During his 17-month tenure, JCPenney's revenue deteriorated sharply and its share price dropped by over 50%.

Thought Experiment:

♦ A newspaper is better than a magazine.
♦ A seashore is a better place than the street.
♦ At first it is better to run than to walk.
♦ You may have to try several times.
♦ Once successful, complications are minimal.
♦ Too many people doing the same thing can cause problems.

---

20 Robert A. Burton, M.D., *On Being Certain: Believing You Are Right Even When You're Not* (New York: St. Martin's Press, 2008) pg xi.

- ◆ One needs lots of room.
- ◆ A rock can serve as an anchor.

As a collection, are these statements collectively comprehensible or random and meaningless?

Read the thought experiment. As a collection of statements, are the eight statements in the thought experiment collectively comprehensible or random and meaningless? This is the question posed by Dr. Robert Burton.[21] Feel your mind search for potential explanations. Are these statements connected to something in some way or not?

Now pay attention to what happens and how you feel when I introduce just one word: *kite*. Reread the statements in the thought experiment. The prior discomfort of ambiguity is replaced by a pleasing sense of rightness or correctness. Every statement fits together and has meaning once we understand the statements are about "flying a kite." In an instant and without conscious deliberation, the collection of eight statements has been irreversibly imbued with what Burton calls "the feeling of knowing."

The question at the bottom of the thought experiment likely (due to cognitive dissonance) kick-started your System 2 and actively engaged your left hemisphere interpreter at both conscious and subconscious levels. This probably happened *even* if you consciously chose to not participate in the exercise. Once the word "kite" was introduced, you immediately and effortlessly switched to System 1 and glided through the confirmation-based thinking that followed. *A critical issue here is that "the feeling of knowing" makes contemplating alternatives difficult.* Can you go back to reading the eight statements as you did and felt before the word "kite" was introduced? You cannot. "The feeling of knowing" keeps you in System 1, nearly disallowing other theories or alternatives to compete as possibilities to connect the eight statements.

The implications to organizational decision making are profound. Once managers and executives believe they "know" the best alternative, they become firmly rooted in System 1 thinking with all its implications including confirmation-based thinking. This includes absorbing information, data, and analysis that support their firmly held belief and discounting or discarding anything that does not. We can all identify with "the feeling of knowing." You just experienced it if you read the thought experiment.

---

21 Ibid, page 5.

There can be a mismatch between what we consciously think we know and what we *actually* know. We can consciously choose a false belief simply because it feels correct. The more committed we are to a belief, the harder it is to relinquish, even in the face of overwhelming counter-evidence. Our physiology seems to be weighted in favor of feeling over logic implying conviction is not really a choice. Burton describes "the feeling of knowing" as a sensation, a subconscious "circuit breaker", that informs conscious thought that the brain has reached a conclusion.

Dr. Robert Burton concludes: "Without a circuit breaker, indecision and inaction would rule the day. What is needed is a mental switch that stops infinite ruminations and calms our fears of missing an unknown superior alternative. Such a switch can't be a thought or we would be back at the same problem. The simplest solution would be a sensation that feels like a thought but isn't subject to thought's perpetual self-questioning. The constellation of mental states that constitutes the feeling of knowing is a marvelous adaption that solves a very metaphysical dilemma of how to reach a conclusion."[22]

Burton characterizes "the feeling of knowing" and ties it to pattern recognition with the following excerpts: "The feeling of knowing is universal, most likely originates within a localized region of the brain, and can be spontaneously activated via direct stimulation or chemical manipulation, yet cannot be triggered by conscious effort. These arguments for its inclusion as a primary brain module are more compelling than those postulated for deceit, compassion, forgiveness, altruism, or Machiavellian cunning. One can stimulate the brain and create a feeling of knowing; one cannot stimulate the brain and create a politician[23] ... You mull over an idea; you contemplate, ruminate, meditate, and sleep on it. You gradually are convinced and say to yourself, 'Yes, that's right.' This apparent cause-and-effect temporal sequence—first the thought, then the assessment of the thought, and then the feeling of correctness—is what gives 'the feeling of knowing' its authority. Any other sequence wouldn't make sense and would strip 'the feeling of knowing' of any practical value[24] ... It would be foolish to suggest that the feeling of knowing is present in the unconscious—an unfelt feeling makes no

---

22 Ibid, page 125.

23 Ibid, page 61.

24 Ibid, page 66.

sense. The likely explanation is that unconscious pattern recognition contains a calculation of probability of correctness, which is consciously experienced as a feeling of knowing. The closer the fit between previously learned patterns and the new incoming pattern, the greater the degree of the feeling of correctness will be. A puzzling pattern that doesn't match with prior experience won't be recognized—the resulting low probability calculation might be felt as strange, unfamiliar, wrong, not right, or not felt at all."[25]

Burton postulates that the feelings of knowing, correctness, conviction, and certainty are not deliberate conscious conclusions or choices but rather mental sensations that happen to us. These sensations are preceded by associations that begin at the subconscious level. Once they are judged to be correct, they are passed on into consciousness and are experienced as an insight or an "aha" moment. Consequently, we can think we "know" something, when in fact we do not. We merely have the sensation of knowing.

Key Point:

> Think twice whenever decisions trigger strong emotions or snap "right" or "wrong" or "I know" judgments.

To improve our decision-making capabilities, we must learn the discipline of proactively addressing our propensities to make mistakes in thinking and to error in judgment. In this chapter, we focused on the mistakes in thinking that are most egregious to decision making. In the next chapter, we focus on the second source of cognitive concern, errors in judgment under uncertainty.

---

25 Ibid, pages 135-136.

"Good judgment comes from experience,
and experience comes from bad judgment."
– Mulla Nasrudin, 14th Century Sage

8
Judgment Under Uncertainty: Heuristics and Biases

Have you ever heard statements like these in your personal or professional experiences?

♦ "I want to base my decision only on the facts."
♦ "I looked at all the historical data and based my decision on that."
♦ "We couldn't measure that, so we didn't try to account for it in our decision."
♦ "We were not sure about that so we assumed ..."

These statements indicate that decisions are being made without accounting for some significant, often uncertain, future events or impacts. Decisions are being made using less than a complete accounting of critical information and insight. This is likely to lead to very disappointing results.

Of particular concern are the assumptions being used. We simplify our view of the future by making assumptions about what may happen. In situations where the truthfulness of the assumption can bear significant impact on the future of our organization or us, we must double check our assumptions. Assumptions often concern issues, situations, or events that are uncertain in nature. Treating uncertainties as assumptions is a common error in decision making. The untested or erroneous assumptions in *Operation Iraqi Freedom* (such as the Iraqi people welcoming the invasion force with open arms and the presence of weapons of mass destruction manufacturing capability) are examples of how entire nations' fates can be impacted by poor assumptions. Some assumptions undermine entire classes of decisions, especially casually stated assumptions such as:

+ "We're better than the competition so..."
+ "That won't work here because..."
+ "I've seen this situation before and so we need to..."
+ "Change is risky, so let's not..."

Material assumptions get slipped in with our casual System 1 thinking and language and these assumptions then slip past recipients as their System 2 thinking stays asleep without invocation. Peter Drucker had this to say about assumptions and uncertainty: "Errant assumptions are the root cause of all poor decisions[1] ... To take risks is the essence of economic activity. One of the most rigorous theorems of economics [Boehm-Bawerk's Law] proves that the existing means of production will yield greater economic performance only through greater uncertainty, that is, through greater risk."[2]

Rather than assume away uncertainty, it must be embraced and explicitly dealt with in a sound and rigorous way that engages how we think and form beliefs. Patrick Leach makes the point that uncertainty is a key source of value in business: "The only thing that allows businesses to provide rates of return greater than the risk-free rate to their shareholders – the only thing that allows them to provide greater value – is uncertainty. Granted, the uncertainty itself doesn't add the value; rather, it's how we manage it.[3] But if you don't understand it, you can't manage it." The 20th century Italian physicist, Enrico Fermi, provided some sound advice in this regard as shown in the Key Point below.

Key Point:

> When it comes to dealing with uncertainty and decision making, we need to stop making poor assumptions and follow Fermi's Rule: "Better to be approximately right than precisely wrong."

1   Peter F. Druckard, *The Effective Executive* (New York: HarperCollins Publishers, 1967, 1985, 1996 and 2002).

2   Peter F. Druckard, *Management: Tasks, Responsibilities, Practices* (London: William Heinemann Limited, 1974), page 125.

3   Patrick Leach, *Why Can't You Just Give Me The Number?* 2nd Edition (Gainesville: Probabilistic Publishing, 2016), page 12.

Our brains are designed to predict—to think about future issues, situations, and events. System 1 thinking does this casually and often superficially. System 2 thinking has its own limitations and biases, if and when it is invoked. The concern is the *quality* of our predictions and how best to improve these *predictive-in-nature* thoughts and beliefs. The English language has many words and expressions that connote the concept of uncertainty such as *probably*, *likely*, and *maybe*.

Thought Experiment:

Make a list of all the English words or expressions that you can think of that represent or connote "uncertainty." These include: "probably," "likely," "more likely," and "maybe", etc.

Consider the thought experiment above. When these words are used, there is very little precision in their use.

As an example, I ask you to meet me for lunch this Friday. You reply, "Well, I'm not sure I will be available for lunch this Friday, but I can probably make it." With that response, you would not be thinking of a precise probability associated with the word "probably" such as a 75% chance, or equivalently, a probability of 0.75. At most, you might have been thinking of a sense of a range of probabilities such as 0.20 to 0.60, but even this is stretching what likely constitutes your thinking. Your probability may be zero and there is no chance of a lunch, but you were just being polite in your response. In casual language, words that relate to the concept of uncertainty mostly give an attitude or sense about what may occur rather than a precisely thought-out probability.

The vagueness of our language about uncertainty leads to frequent misinterpretations that can result in significant consequences. Think of the poor man asking a woman for a date on Saturday night. She replies, "Yes, I *might* be able to make it. I'll *definitely* give you a call." Optimistically, he is [System 1] thinking the Saturday night date might have a 90% chance. If she is uninterested, the woman is thinking, "There is no way I'm going out with that person, let alone give him a call." Not only is there vagueness and ambiguity with our use of language connoting probability, but we can use that imprecision to create or manipulate perceptions. Similarly, corporate commitments and project planning suffer daily from these ambiguities in language and from our desire to create—often short-term—advantageous perceptions.

Key Point:

> Uncertainty arises in two different forms: (1) the uncertainty of the occurrence of a discrete event such as whether or not your company will win a specific contract; and, (2) the uncertainty in the outcome of a situation or process that results in a value from a continuous range [continuous distribution] of potential values such as the number of weeks to complete a project or the cost to complete a project.

In the case of a discrete event (see Key Point), we can ask the question, "What is your assessment of the probability that we will win the contract?" In the case of the continuous range of outcomes, we can ask the question, "What do you expect will be the number of weeks to complete the project, and how much variation could there potentially be in the number of weeks to project completion?"

As summarized by Daniel Kahneman and introduced in Chapter 6, System 1 creates biases in our judgment under uncertainty and decision making by:

♦ Generating impressions, feelings, and inclinations, and when endorsed by System 2, these become beliefs, attitudes, and intentions

♦ Linking a sense of "cognitive ease" to illusions of truth, pleasant feelings, and reduced vigilance (everything feels right)

♦ Neglecting ambiguity and suppressing doubt

♦ Desiring to believe and confirm (jumping to conclusions)

♦ Exaggerating emotional consistency (Halo Effect)

♦ Focusing on existing evidence and ignoring absent information (WYSIATI)

♦ Substituting easier questions for harder ones

♦ Overweighting low probability events

♦ Showing diminished sensitivity to quantity

♦ Responding more strongly to losses than to gains (loss aversion)

♦ Framing decision problems narrowly

♦ Influencing even the most careful decisions–it never sleeps

There are at least four major categories of biases in our judgment under uncertainty:

- ◆ Motivational Biases,
- ◆ Cognitive Biases,
- ◆ Errors in Logic, and
- ◆ Groupthink.

Organizational Motivational Biases

There are at least three organizational-related[4] motivational biases:

- ◆ Manager's Bias: "Tell the boss what he (or she) wants to hear." Managers prefer not to communicate bad news to supervisors and executives. Bad news can bring unwanted attention or guidance and is often perceived by the manager as tarnishing their reputation or, worse yet, inhibiting a future promotion. The manager's bias results in the under-reporting of problems and risks. Statements like "we have no significant risks" are typically an indication of manager's bias.

- ◆ Expert's Bias (or Authority Bias): "Experts should be certain rather than uncertain." We expect experts to be certain about their assessments because they *are* experts. even when the topic under judgment is inherently uncertain in nature. At times, experts can be uncomfortable in stating the full extent of the uncertainty for fear of being perceived as lacking expertise. Or, alternatively, the expert might truly believe in their understanding and intuition and underestimate the true underlying uncertainty in question.

- ◆ Analyst's Bias: "I don't want to be in disagreement with the corporate plan or existing forecasts." There are many types of analysts in business working in finance, R&D, engineering, operations, projects, and more. Analysts collect and model information in an attempt to assess the impact of an issue, situation, or event on some plan or policy that represents a status quo or other corporate expectation. As an example, corporate sales forecasts

---

4   When we use the word "organizational," the word "corporate" could also be used. However, these principles are not limited to business but apply to government and non-governmental organizations as well.

are grounded in both what the corporation is targeting as well as what is expected in the overall market environment. Once forecasts are established, individuals throughout the company are reluctant to discuss short falls, because it can label them as naysayers, pessimists, or under-performers. Likewise, analysts can be reluctant to communicate significant deviations from plans or forecasts and consequently sometimes under-report their information or knowledge.

We now move to the cognitive biases, which are more subtle and difficult to identify than the motivational biases.

Cognitive Biases that Impact Judgment Under Uncertainty

In Chapter 6, we introduced two pervasive cognitive biases, confirmation bias and negativity bias, as two major influences in the predict-perceive-confirm cycle of human cognition. Many other cognitive biases have been identified;[5] the following ten represent the most common and significant biases with respect to judgment under uncertainty.

- ◆ Optimistic Bias (or Optimism Bias, Illusion of Invulnerability): The mistaken belief that one's chances of experiencing a negative event are lower or a positive event are higher than others.
- ◆ Overconfidence Bias (or Overconfidence Effect): The tendency of individuals to have subjective confidence in the reliability of their judgments that is greater than can be justified by objective accuracy.
- ◆ Confirmation Bias (or Confirmatory Bias): A predilection to seek and find confirmatory evidence in support of already existing beliefs and ignore or reinterpret disconfirming evidence.
- ◆ Negativity Bias: The phenomenon by which individuals pay more attention to and give more credence to negative rather than positive experiences or other kinds of information.
- ◆ Present Bias (or Hyperbolic Discounting): Individuals

---

5   For a comprehensive list of cognitive biases see: http://en.wikipedia.org/wiki/List_of_cognitive_biases.

have a stronger preference for more immediate payoffs as compared to future or later payoffs. Individuals make choices today that their future selves would prefer not to have made.

♦ Believability Bias: Where individuals evaluate the strength of an argument based on the believability of its conclusion.

♦ Consistency Bias: The phenomenon by which individuals equate past issues, situations, events, and behaviors with current ones.

♦ Hindsight Bias (or Knew-It-All-Along Effect): The tendency for individuals to perceive events that have already occurred as being more predictable than they were before they took place. Hindsight bias may result in memory distortion, whereby the recollection and reconstruction of content can lead to false theoretical outcomes.

♦ Illusion of Control: The false belief by individuals that they can control or at least influence outcomes of issues, situations, or events that are outside of the control or influence of most people.

♦ Halo Effect: The phenomenon by which individuals judge a person's or entity's overall character by a single trait or impression (positive or negative).

Errors in Logic

Individuals routinely demonstrate a lack of ability to reason and to make appropriate inferences in the face of uncertainty. As discussed in Chapter 6, we think in terms of stories, scenarios, narratives, and causality, which are linear relationships. However, probability is a highly non-linear concept. And that non-linearity gives us trouble in making correct probability-related inferences.

Thought Experiment:

You are visiting your doctor and report a set of symptoms you are experiencing. Your doctor informs you that 20% of patients reporting these symptoms have the disease in question. The doctor also tells you some information regarding the accuracy of the test he suggests you take.

If you have the disease, the test accurately indicates you have the disease 90% of the time. If you don't have the disease, the test accurately indicates you don't have the disease 70% of the time. You take the test and test positive for the disease. What is the probability you have the disease?

Read the thought experiment. Answering the question it poses requires using a non-linear relationship called Bayes' Theorem or Bayes' Law named after Thomas Bayes, an 18th century English mathematician. The question can be restated as: "What is the probability that you have the disease, given that you show the stated symptoms and tested positive for the disease?" The answer is 43%.[6] If that strikes you as a surprising low probability that you have the disease after testing positive, it is because you under-weighted the base-line information that only 20% of individuals with the symptoms have the disease. The non-linear relationships of the underlying probabilities stated in the thought experiment are difficult to intuit short of performing the required calculations.

The gambler's fallacy is the mistaken notion that the odds for something with a fixed probability increase or decrease depending upon recent occurrences. For example, if you flipped a coin three times, got three heads in a row, and then concluded that the next flip was likely to be a tail, you would be committing the gambler's fallacy. This is an error in logic. Each coin flip, regardless of the outcome of the previous coin flip, has a 50/50 chance of resulting in a head or tail. Errors in logic are easy to make when thinking about probabilities. Probability theory is a subtle and often non-intuitive

---

6   To derive the probability of having the disease given you have the symptoms and test positive for the disease we need to apply Bayes' Theorem or Bayes' Law. The information provided to you in the thought experiment includes: (1) the probability of having the disease given you have the symptoms is P(Disease) = 0.20; (2) the probability you do not have the disease given you have the symptoms is P(Not Disease) = 0.80; (3) the probability you will test positive for the disease given you have the disease is P(Positive Test | Disease) = 0.90, which is a conditional probability; (4) the probability you will test negative for the disease given you do not have the disease is P(Negative Test | Not Disease) = 0.70, which is a conditional probability.

Bayes' Theorem states that the probability we are seeking, P(Disease | Positive Test)

= [P(Positive Test | Disease) x P(Disease)] / [P(Positive Test | Disease) x P(Disease) + P(Positive Test | Not Disease) x P(Not Disease)]

= [(0.90)(0.20)] / [(0.90)(0.20) + (0.30)(0.80)] = 0.18 / 0.42 = 0.428.

discipline that requires logically sound methods and models to ensure logically sound conclusions.

Groupthink

Groupthink is the term used to describe when a group makes a decision or comes to a conclusion and their process is characterized by uncritical acceptance or conformity to prevailing points of view. Groupthink occurs when members of a group try to minimize conflict and reach a consensus decision without critical evaluation of alternative ideas or viewpoints. This can happen when groups isolate themselves from outside influences or sources of information. Individuals in group settings tend to race to conclusions prematurely, not voice contrary perspectives, "Go with the flow" of the conversation and follow the consensus. System 1 plays a significant role in groupthink as it neglects ambiguity and suppresses doubt.

The *bandwagon effect* is a form of groupthink broadly documented in behavioral science. It has been shown that conduct or beliefs spread among people just as fads and trends do. The probability of an individual aligning with a position or adopting a belief increases with the proportion of individuals who have already done so. As more people come to believe in something, others likewise "hop on the bandwagon" regardless of the strength of the underlying evidence. The tendency to follow the actions or beliefs of others can occur where individuals prefer to conform or to incorporate information from others.

The *bandwagon effect* is a key driver of e-commerce. As an example, the business model of Groupon is premised on the *bandwagon effect* as it leverages the collective bargaining of a large number of buyers for local merchants' goods and services. If enough individuals sign up for a discount coupon, then the discount coupon becomes available to everyone in the group. If fewer individuals sign up than a predetermined minimum, the coupon is not available. The *bandwagon effect* drives fashion sales, music sales, social network adoption rates, and diet fads.

There are many examples of the downside bias caused by the *bandwagon effect*. Every significant stock market sell-off or market crash is the result of the *bandwagon effect*.

Heuristics Used in Judgment Under Uncertainty

In less regular or low-validity[7] environments, the heuristics[8] of judgment are invoked. Heuristics are mental shortcuts we all use when making judgments under uncertainty, and they can lead to cognitive biases. The following are five common heuristics we use in making judgments and probability assessments in the face of uncertainty:

♦ Availability
♦ Representativeness
♦ Adjustment & Anchoring
♦ Simulation
♦ Substitution (Effect)

These heuristics are used because they are economical and efficient. However, they can introduce systematic biases. Many of these potential biases can be mitigated, or at least minimized, via a well-defined probability assessment procedure.

Availability Heuristic

During the Great Recession of 2008, many individuals lost their jobs and sought new employment opportunities. Those who found new jobs tended to perceive the economy as recovering; those who did not perceived the economy as worsening or at best stalled. With respect to the state of economic recovery, the availability heuristic gave both groups a biased perspective. The availability heuristic is used whenever a probability (or range estimate) assessment is based on how easily instances of the event are recalled or visualized. This heuristic is summarized by the following statements:

♦ The easier it is to think of an occurrence of an event, the more likely it is judged to be.
♦ Recent events are easier to recall than past events.
♦ An infrequent disastrous event may be easier to visualize than an infrequent non-disastrous event.
♦ Individuals store and recall information better when it is ordered, redundant, dramatic, recent, imaginable, certified, or consistent.

---

7   Validity is the extent to which a concept, conclusion or measurement is well-founded and corresponds accurately to the real world.

8   Heuristics pertain to methods of learning using or obtained by exploration of possibilities rather than by following set rules.

- The cognitive ease with which instances come to mind is a System 1 heuristic, which is replaced by a focus on content when System 2 is engaged.
- Potential Bias: Available information is over-weighted.
- Example: A manager bases a time estimate of a given task on an actual occurrence of a recent, similar situation.

Representative Heuristic

A sample of a population is said to be representative of a population if the characteristics of the sample and the population are similar or the same. The representativeness heuristic is used whenever a probability (or range estimate) assessment is reduced to judgments of similarity. This heuristic is summarized by the following statements:

- This heuristic causes problems when too much emphasis is given to what is similar and not enough emphasis is given to what is different.
- Stereotyping is a form of the representativeness heuristic.
- Given specific information or evidence, people often discard (or under-weight) previous experience and general information.
- Potential Bias: Base case information is ignored or under-weighted.
- Example: A manager bases a time estimate of a given task on a perceived "similar" situation.

During the 2016 US presidential campaign, Hillary Clinton stated that "half" of Donald Trump's supporters were "deplorables," meaning people who are racist, sexist, homophobic, or xenophobic. The next evening, she apologized saying that she had been "grossly generalistic." Hillary Clinton generalized Trump supporters based on a small sample of individuals making media headlines and not on the fact that a large cross-section of Americans were his supporters.

Adjustment and Anchoring Heuristic

Consistently, across all business sectors, major capital projects are likely to cost more than their original budget. Contingency funds are set aside to cover unforeseen problems, however these funds are rarely sufficient. The adjustment and anchoring heuristic is used whenever a probability (or range estimate) assessment is constructed by perturbing some initial value or starting point.

- The anchor or starting point is often a mean or nominal value.

- Adjustments to the anchor are intended to account for possible problems or uncertainty.
- This heuristic is the basis for many engineering estimates.
- The adjustment is rarely adequate and the final estimate tends to be near the anchor regardless of how arbitrary the initial assessment was.
- System 2 works on data that is retrieved from memory in an automatic and involuntary operation of System 1.
- System 2 is susceptible to the biasing anchors that make some information easier to retrieve.
- Potential Bias: Range bounds on estimates are too narrow.
- Example: A manager bases a time estimate of a given task by first anchoring on the amount of time it "should" take. (Hidden assumption: "Everything will run as planned.") Then the manager makes insufficient adjustments to create range bounds to account for potential problems.

Simulation Heuristic

An executive has concerns over a competitor being first to market with a product that is similar to his company's product under development. The more detail the executive adds to the scenario he fears, the more concerned he becomes. He eventually believes that his firm must accelerate their product launch efforts in order to win the race to the marketplace. The simulation heuristic is used whenever a probability (or range estimate) assigned to an event is determined by mentally constructing a chain of hypothetical events (narratives or scenarios).

- Individuals tend to use this when they have little relevant experience.
- The more coherent and plausible the scenario, the more likely individuals judge the outcome.
- Potential Bias: There is a lack of accounting for scenario assumptions, and multiple different narratives or scenarios that can be created.
- Example: A manager bases a time estimate of a given task on imagining the work of each subtask and then adding the durations of each subtask to get an estimate of the duration of the overall task.

Substitution (Effect) Heuristic

A software game company has had several technical setbacks in pursuit of a new product release date. A new product development lead has been hired to get the overall project back on track. When the corporate executive of the company assesses the chances of a high-quality product being delivered on schedule, his assessment is influenced by how much he is impressed by and likes the new project leadership. The substitution (effect) heuristic is used whenever judgments or decisions are guided directly by feelings of liking or disliking with little deliberation or reasoning.

♦ Individuals tend to use this heuristic to replace a difficult question with an easier one.

♦ The stronger the like or dislike, the more confidence in the estimate.

♦ Potential Bias: Relevant, known information is ignored or at least under-weighted.

♦ Example: A manager bases a time estimate of a given task on how much he likes or dislikes the owner of the task.

We have significant, systematic shortcomings in thinking about risk and uncertainty and making judgments in the face of uncertainty. Our ability to predict future events is limited and can lead to spurious beliefs. Some conclude that our mental limitations and biases should preclude us from assessing probabilities altogether. They believe we are so inept at prediction and quantifying probabilities about future events that we should take a completely different tact to decision making under uncertainty. Nassim Taleb suggests building "a systematic and broad guide to *nonpredictive* decision making under uncertainty in business, politics, medicine, and life in general [because] risk is not measurable (outside of casinos or the minds of people who call themselves 'risk experts')."[9]

As discussed in Chapter 6, our brains are designed to predict. Because it is done at a subconscious level, you can't stop it from happening. You are "wired" to make decisions based on subconscious predictions. Furthermore, we have no internal mechanism for judging the quality of those predictions as they just happen. System 1 is constantly in the mode of predict-perceive-confirm offering immediate recommendations when it comes to decisions under uncertainty

---

9   Nassim Nicholas Taleb, *Antifragile: Things That Gain from Disorder* (New York: The Random House Publishing Group, 2012), page 4.

(regardless of the magnitude of the consequences of the decision or the degree of uncertainty).

It is incorrect to say that we can't predict or that we should avoid making predictions by doing something else. We should instead try to engage and inform System 2 to challenge System 1's rapid conclusions. This can be accomplished best by leveraging the way we think and form beliefs. When we attempt to avoid or ignore our predictive nature, we inadvertently leave these predictive thoughts unchecked and unchallenged, and then they subconsciously influence our decision making. The solution is not to avoid our natural predictive thought processes, but to engage them and work to improve the quality of their conclusions and ultimately the quality of our associated beliefs.

When it comes to decision making, it is difficult to overcome the predictive nature of our subconscious minds. It is easier to leverage and improve those skills while attempting to mitigate or at least minimize their biases. The issue isn't that we can't predict, but rather we can't predict well in many circumstances. But we always predict. There is no way around that fundamental property of the human brain when it comes to decision making.

Improving Your Thinking and Judgment Under Uncertainty

"Our mental limitations prevent us from accepting our mental limitations."
– Dr. Robert Burton, Neurologist and Author

Now that we understand eight basic mistakes in thinking and the biases we have in our judgment under uncertainty, the question becomes, "What can we *do* about this?" Let's start by reviewing the eight mistakes in thinking that were presented in Chapter 7:

1. We prefer stories to statistics.
2. We seek to confirm, not to question, our ideas.
3. We tend to over react to negative information.
4. We rarely appreciate the role of chance and coincidence in shaping events.
5. We sometimes misperceive the world around us.
6. We tend to oversimplify our thinking.
7. We have faulty memories.
8. We "know" less than we think we know.

Key Point:

> We should understand and be mindful of the strengths and limitations of our (and others') beliefs, knowledge, thinking, memory, and judgment.

An underlying culprit that feeds many of these thinking errors has been labeled "pseudoscientific thinking." It can also lead to poor quality decision making. *Pseudoscience* is a claim, belief, or practice which is presented as scientific, but it does not adhere to the scientific method and lacks supporting evidence or plausibility. In media, we are continually bombarded with pseudoscientific information. It can satisfy emotional needs like an unfounded cure for a terminal disease, or it can fascinate us as we watch a speculative show on the disappearance of planes in the Bermuda Triangle. We need to ensure pseudoscientific thinking does not creep into our decision making. Thomas Kida provides a summary of the characteristics of pseudoscientific thinking:[10]

1. Contains a preconceived notion of what to believe;

2. Searches for evidence to support a preconceived belief;

3. Ignores evidence that would falsify a claim or belief;

4. Disregards alternative explanations for a phenomenon;

5. Holds extraordinary beliefs;

6. Accepts flimsy evidence to support an extraordinary claim;

7. Relies heavily on anecdotal evidence; and

8. Employs very little skepticism.

The confirmation bias embedded in our System 1's predict-perceive-confirm thought process cycle results in many of the characteristics from Kida's list. Pseudoscientific thinking is a root cause of erroneous belief generation. Because of its impact on belief generation and decision making perspectives, we clearly need to eliminate or minimize our pseudoscientific thinking. "Trust but verify" (a skeptic's position) is a good starting point.

---

10 Thomas Kida, *Don't Believe Everything You Think: The 6 Basic Mistakes We Make in Thinking* (Amherst, New York: Prometheus Books, 2006), page 41.

Seven Ways to Improve Organizational Decision Making

Many of us share the common belief that reasonable discourse can establish the superiority of one perspective and line of thinking over another. The underlying presumption is that each of us, through rational thought, can see a problem, risk, or opportunity from an "optimal perspective" and rationally determine a best alternative or path forward. Robert Burton would argue that this is not the case. Burton argues, "The best that a rational argument can accomplish is to add one more input into this cognitive stew. If it resonates deeply enough, change of opinion might occur. But this is a low probability uphill battle; the best of arguments is only one input pitted against a lifetime of acquired experience and biological tendencies operating outside of our conscious control. To expect well-reasoned arguments to easily alter personal expressions of purpose is to misunderstand the biology of belief."[11]

The best we can do is to inform decision makers through a repeatable and efficient decision process that *builds into* decision making the eight elements of a high-quality decision as detailed in Chapter 2. Knowing the weaknesses and biases in our abilities to perceive, think, predict, and decide leaves us with no other choice when decisions are material with significant consequences. With the insights of this and the previous chapters in mind, listed below are seven ways to improve corporate decision making. There will be more specific detail in subsequent chapters.

1. Understand and be mindful of the strengths and limitations of your (and others') beliefs, knowledge, thinking, memory, and judgment.

2. Test your assumptions. (Are they truly assumptions, or are they wishes and desires about the future that are more appropriately represented as uncertainties?)

3. Think twice whenever decisions trigger strong emotions or snap "right" or "wrong" or "I know" judgments. (These are potentially subconscious, involuntary overrides in situations better suited for cost-benefit, System 2 thinking.) Corollary: Ask yourself, "How do I know what I know?"

4. Avoid pseudoscientific thinking.

5. Use decision processes, analytics, and supporting information systems to leverage the strengths of how we think

---

11 Robert Burton, Op. Cit., page 183.

and to minimize our innate and learned errors in thinking and judgment. (How to do this is the subject of subsequent chapters.

6. Adopt a long-term value perspective by considering "your future self as today's decision maker," a mental exercise to mitigate present bias in your decision making.[12]

7. Adopt and incorporate the Skeptic's Mantra, "Extraordinary claims require extraordinary evidence," into your and others' thinking.

Key Point:

Decision processes, analytics, and supporting information systems should leverage the strengths of how we think and attempt to minimize our innate and learned errors in thinking and judgment while leveraging the relevant, material information and knowledge residing across the enterprise in individuals and systems.

To paraphrase Carl Sagan, decision makers must strike that delicate balance of being open to new possibilities while remaining skeptical and requiring extraordinary evidence for extraordinary claims. The remaining chapters of this book focus on how to deploy these seven ways to improve corporate decision making. In our personal and professional lives, decisions fall into three categories: resolving problems, mitigating risks, and capturing opportunities. Of the three classes of decisions, *Problems* get the most attention at the expense of Risks and Opportunities.

---

12 Whenever you feel pressured to make a decision or feel the current decision-making situation is emotionally charged you run the risk of present bias, the tendency of individuals to give stronger weight to payoffs that are closer to the present time when considering tradeoffs between the present or near-term versus the long-term. In these circumstances I have found it valuable to use a mental exercise I call "Your Future Self as Today's Decision Maker".

In this exercise I imagine myself sometime in the future reflecting back on (1) the decision that I made and (2) what has happened as a result of the decision. Does my future self view the decision I made as a mistake? As short-sighted? Giving away a better future for something less? Or did I make the right choice from a long-term value perspective and consequently I or others lived through some short-term discomfort or hardship that is now only a memory? This exercise is helpful for both personal and professional decisions.

Key Point:

> With respect to the three classes of decisions, problems create the most cognitive dissonance, the clarion call from the subconscious mind for the need to change from the current situation, the status quo. Hence problems get the most attention and resources.

Decisions associated with *risk* are the least attended to and the worst managed. It is only when the risk *feels* real that we decide to meaningfully act. Without the stirring of our survival instincts, there is no action under an illusion of control and safety.

Key Point:

> From a decision-making perspective, we need to overcome our neurobiological "blind spot" to risks we have not personally experienced. Risks we can imagine but have not personally experienced have no emotionally-laden, long-term memory for our subconscious mind to dwell on and heighten our sense of urgency and need for response.

In Closing...

"Certainty is not biologically possible. We must learn to tolerate the unpleasantness of uncertainty. Science has given us the language and tools of probabilities. We have methods for analyzing and ranking opinion according to their likelihood of correctness. That is enough. We do not need and cannot afford the catastrophes born out of a belief in certainty." [13]
– Dr. Robert Burton, Neurologist and Author

"I can live with doubt and uncertainty and not knowing ... I have approximate answers and possible beliefs and different degrees of certainty about different things, but I'm not absolutely sure of anything ... It doesn't frighten me." [14]
– Richard Feynman, Nobel Laureate, Physics

"The third-rate mind is only happy when it is thinking with the majority. The second-rate mind is only happy when it is thinking with the minority. The first-rate mind is only happy when it is thinking." [15]
– Alan A. Milne, English Author and Playwright

---

13 Robert Burton, Op. cit., pages 223-224.

14 Richard Feynman, *The Pleasure of Finding Things Out: The Best Short Works of Richard P. Feynman*, edited by Jeffrey Robbins (New York: Perseus Publishing, 1999).

15 A. A. Milne, *War with Honour* (Macmillan and Company, 1940).

"It is far better to foresee even without certainty
than not to foresee at all."
– Henri Poincaré, French Mathematician and Philosopher of Science

9
Outcomes, Impacts, and Consequences

All through the day, you make estimates of future uncertain events, such as how long it will take to drive to work, what the temperature will be at noon, and how far you will drive the golf ball during a round of golf. In each of these cases, the uncertainty is a continuous value quantity, meaning the actual value comes from a continuous range of potential values. For most of the estimates we make, the accuracy of the prediction is not material because getting it wrong causes no real hardship. Additionally, both System 1 and System 2 engage in making predictions, and they suffer from biases. So how do we create high quality predictions about the future when getting it right is important and material?

From a corporate perspective, executives and managers need an estimation approach that leverages available relevant information, uses predictive analytics, and allows expert opinion and insights to address the unique aspects of situations not fully comprehended by information systems or data-driven analytics. In this chapter, we will focus on how to elicit expert opinion and insights of future uncertain outcomes, impacts, and consequences. We will assume that the experts have already had access to the insights gleaned from information systems and predictive analytics. A perspective on the role of future information systems and predictive analytics will be provided in Appendix 4.

As we discussed in the previous chapter, the correlation between the language we use and the numerical probabilities we ascribe to uncertain events is not strong—to say the least. To more precisely articulate our sense and degree of uncertainty, whether it is the likelihood of an event occurring (e.g., winning a contract) or the outcome of an uncertain continuous value quantity (e.g., the number of weeks to complete a project), we need to do this quantitatively. This chapter discusses how to estimate uncertain outcomes, impacts, or consequences for continuous uncertainties and how to do it with quality.

Estimating Surprising Outcomes, Impacts, and Consequences

Suppose I asked, "What is the distance, as measured in miles, of the Mississippi River from its headwaters in Northern Minnesota to the Mississippi River Delta at the Gulf of Mexico?" Your first inclination is probably to look the number up on the internet or "Google it." Don't do that for this exercise. Without further information, your first answer is likely that you don't know. If you think about it clearly for a moment, you will realize there is quite a bit of relevant information I have already given you in the question itself. The Mississippi River starts in Northern Minnesota and flows to the Gulf of Mexico. If you live in the United States, you probably have a general sense of the length and width of the contiguous 48 states—though Jay Leno on the "Tonight Show" found some serious comedic fun in asking pedestrians in Hollywood seemingly obvious geography questions and getting hilarious, erroneous responses.

Assuming you are uncertain about the length of the Mississippi River, there are ways for you to express your beliefs and the degree of your uncertainty as a continuous probability distribution. A common method for assessing uncertainty uses *fractiles*. (Readers interested in other methods for assessing subjective continuous probability distributions are referred to Hagen.)[1] Let's demonstrate how this works with the example of the length of the Mississippi River using the fractiles: 0.01, 0.25, 0.50, 0.75, 0.99.

To begin, I ask you for an estimate of the length of the Mississippi River so that there is a 50/50 chance that the actual length is either above or below your number. This is the estimate of *your* 0.50 fractile (also known as the 50th percentile or median). You might answer, "My 0.50 fractile is 3,000 miles." This means that in your opinion it is equally likely that the actual length of the Mississippi River is longer or shorter than 3,000 miles.

---

1   For an overview of assessing subjective continuous probability distributions see the Stanford University Dissertation published in 1991 by Brian W. Hagen entitled, "Constructing Discrete Marginal Distributions Via Redundant Probabilistic Assessment," Professor Ronald A. Howard, Principal Advisor.

I then follow with a second question regarding your 0.25 and 0.75 fractiles, "What is a range of values such that the actual length of the Mississippi River is equally likely to be within the range versus outside of this range?" The end points of this range represent the 0.25 and 0.75 fractiles, i.e., the middle half of the full range.

You might respond, "My lower bound or 0.25 fractile is 2,500 miles, and my upper bound or 0.75 fractile is 3,200 miles." This means that, in your opinion, there is a 50/50 chance that the length of the Mississippi River falls within the interval 2,500 to 3,200 miles. There is also a 50/50 chance for the length to fall outside this interval, either above or below.

To determine the outer extremes of your uncertainty (0.01 and 0.99 fractiles), I would ask two questions: "What is your value for the length of the Mississippi River such that there is only a 1% chance that the actual value is smaller than this number?" and "What is your value for the length of the Mississippi River such that there is only a 1% chance that the actual value is greater than this number?" Your responses might be, "There is only a 1% chance that the length of the Mississippi River is less than 2,200 miles or greater than 3,500 miles."

From this assessment, we would conclude that your beliefs and uncertainty about the length of the Mississippi River as measured in miles is captured in the five-fractile range assessment 2200, 2500, 3000, 3200, and 3500 as 0.01, 0.25, 0.50, 0.75, and 0.99 fractiles, respectively. According to Wikipedia, the length of the Mississippi River is 2,530 miles, which falls between your assessed 0.25 and 0.50 fractiles.

Thought Experiment:

Without using a reference and based solely on your current beliefs, perform a five-fractile range assessment (0.01; 0.25; 0.50; 0.75; 0.99) for the following three values and record your range assessments on a piece of paper or with your computer:

(1) How many miles is it across the Golden Gate Bridge in San Francisco?

(2) How tall is the Burj Khalifa building in Dubai, United Arab Emirates, the world's tallest building, as measured in feet?

(3) What year was Harvard University founded?

Read the thought experiment. The ability of individuals to quantify their beliefs about uncertain continuous values has been heavily researched since the 1960s. A summary of much of this research through the early 1980s is provided by Daniel Kahneman, Paul Slovic, and Amos Tversky.[2] The insights concerning mental heuristics and biases that were presented in the previous two chapters are based on this research. Of particular importance in assessing uncertainties is the research on the calibration of probabilities and the impact that the overconfidence bias has on that calibration.

Sarah Lichtenstein, Baruch Fischhoff, and Lawrence D. Phillips[3] defined two commonly reported calibration measures: *interquartile index* and *surprise index*. The *interquartile index* represents the percentage of items for which the actual value falls between the 0.25 and 0.75 fractiles (the interquartile range). If you were perfectly calibrated, you would have an interquartile index of 50. This means that over many uncertainty assessments, 50 percent of the actual values would fall within your interquartile ranges.

The second calibration measure, known as the *surprise index*, is more important for our discussion. The surprise index is the percentage of actual values that occur outside the most extreme fractiles assessed. In the five point fractile example, the most extreme fractiles assessed were 0.01 and 0.99. If the range provided was a perfect representation of the uncertainty, the actual value would fall below the 0.01 fractile only one percent of the time or above the 0.99 fractile one percent of the time. The range would capture the actual value 98 percent of the time. Therefore, a perfectly calibrated individual over many assessments would have a surprise index of 2 in this case. In one hundred trials, the perfectly calibrated individual would only have two actual values that fell outside the extremes of the assessed range. A large surprise index suggests that the individual consistently has too narrow a range in the fractile range assessment implying overconfidence in their assessments. This is a very common tendency resulting from the heuristics we use in making judgments. *Adjustment and Anchoring* is one such heuristic that consistently results in overconfidence bias.

2   Edited by Daniel Kahneman, Paul Slovic, and Amos Tversky, *Judgment under Uncertainty: Heuristics and Biases* (Cambridge: Cambridge University Press, 1982).

3   Sarah Lichtenstein, Baruch Fischhoff, and, Lawrence D. Phillips, "Calibration of Probabilities: The State of the Art" in H. Jungermann & G. deZeeuw, *Decision Making and Change in Human Affairs* (Amsterdam: D. Reidel, 1977). This is also a chapter in Judgment under *Uncertainty: Heuristics and Biases* edited by Daniel Kahneman, Paul Slovic, and Amos Tversky (listed above).

Now let's return to the previous thought experiment. You should have recorded three five-fractile range assessments. The length of the Golden Gate Bridge in San Francisco is 8,980 feet or 1.70 miles. The height of the Burj Khalifa building in Dubai, United Arab Emirates, is 2,717 feet with 163 floors. It is the world's tallest building. Harvard University was founded was 1636 and is the oldest institution of higher learning in the United States.

If you were well-calibrated in your assessments, we would expect not to be surprised by any of the three actual results. The actual values would have fallen within the three assessment fractile ranges of 0.01 to 0.99. Assuming you are like most people, you were probably surprised on at least one of these assessments; you may have been surprised on all three. At least that's what research has shown over the past five decades. In fact, even when the estimated values in the assessment are changed to represent more extreme outcomes (i.e., change the 0.01 and 0.99 fractiles to 0.001 and 0.999 fractiles), the surprise index remains significantly higher than targeted.

Lichtenstein, Fischhoff, and Phillips collected and analyzed many calibration studies performed until 1980, both fractile-based methods and other methods. They concluded: "The overwhelming evidence from research using fractiles to assess uncertain quantities is that people's probability distributions tend to be too tight. The assessment of extreme fractiles is particularly prone to bias. Training improves calibration somewhat."

The results of many of the fractile-based calibration studies done by Lichtenstein, Fischhoff, and Phillips are summarized in Table 9.1.[4] I added two columns to the table under the heading "Inferred Bounds," which I will discuss in a moment. The column labeled "n" represents the number of subjects in each of the studies. The two columns under the heading "Surprise Index" provide the ideal and the observed surprise indexes. Comparing the ideal to the observed surprise index, you can easily understand the conclusion regarding the underestimation of extreme outcomes.

The two columns under the heading "Inferred Bounds" give an indication of what the extreme fractiles would be if "inferred" from the observed surprise index. As expected, the inferred range is quite a bit narrower than the intended range of the assessment. This is not a scientifically grounded conclusion, but merely an observation of the relationship between what individuals assess as an extreme outcome and the associated outcome distribution.

---

4   Ibid.

Study	n	Surprise Index		Inferred Bounds	
		Ideal	Obs	Lower	Upper
Alpert & Raiffa (1969)					
Group 1-A (0.01, 0.99)	880	2	46	0.23	0.77
Group 1-B (0.001, 0.999)	500	0.2	40	0.20	0.80
Group 1-C ("min" & "max")	700	?	47	0.24	0.77
Group 1-D ("astonishingly" High/ Low)	700	?	38	0.19	0.81
Groups 2, 3, 4 Before Training	2,270	2	34	0.17	0.83
Groups 2, 3, 4 After Training	2,270	2	19	0.10	0.91
Hession & McCarthy (1974)	2035	2	47	0.24	0.77
Selvidge (1975)					
Five Fractiles	400	2	10	0.05	0.95
Seven Fractiles (incl. 0.10 and 0.90)	520	2	7	0.04	0.97
Moskowitz & Bullers (1978)					
Proportions: Three Fractiles	120	2	27	0.14	0.87
Proportions: Five Fractiles	145	2	42	0.21	0.79
Dow Jones: Three Fractiles	210	2	38	0.19	0.81
Dow Jones: Five Fractiles	210	2	64	0.32	0.68
Pickhardt & Wallace (1974)					
Group 1: First Round	?	2	32	0.16	0.84
Group 1: Fifth Round	?	2	20	0.10	0.90
Group 2: First Round	?	2	46	0.23	0.77
Group 2: Sixth Round	?	2	24	0.12	0.88
Lichtenstein & Fischhoff (1980b)					
Pretest	924	2	41	0.21	0.80
Post-test	924	2	40	0.20	0.80
Seaver, von Winterfeldt, Edwards (1978)					
Fractiles	160	2	34	0.17	0.83
Odds-Fractiles	160	2	24	0.12	0.88
Schaefer & Borcherding (1973)					
First Day, Fractiles	396	2	39	0.20	0.81
Fourth Day, Fractiles	396	2	12	0.06	0.94
Murphy & Winkler (1974)					
Extremes were 0.125 & 0.875	432	25	21	0.11	0.90

Table 9.1: Comparing Extreme Outcomes and Surprises to Fractiles of Distributions

In Table 9.1, there are 24 fractile-based calibration studies. The top seven best performance studies with the lowest number of observed surprises have been highlighted. Notice that these studies included either training or prior experience in making fractile-based range estimates of continuous uncertainties.

Also notice that the inferred extreme fractiles of these studies tended to be around the 0.10 and the 0.90 fractiles (10th and 90th percentiles) and not the 0.01 and 0.99 fractiles targeted. This suggests that when individuals provide estimates for the extremes of a continuous value quantity those estimates are more likely representative of the 10th and 90th percentiles as opposed to 1st and 99th percentiles. (See Table 9.2 at the end of this chapter for a list of the references cited in Table 9.1.)

Key Point:

When estimating extreme outcomes—such as "surprisingly good" or "surprisingly bad" outcomes—of continuous value events, individuals' subjective estimates more commonly are calibrated with 10th and 90th percentile values of an underlying continuous probability distribution as opposed to more extreme outcomes such as the 5th and 95th percentiles or the 1st and 99th percentiles.

Decision Quality Requires Reliable, Material Information

In Chapter 2, we introduced the concept of Decision Quality and the requirement of having reliable, material information as shown in Figure 9.1. Listed below are several key enablers and failure modes associated with capturing reliable, material information during decision-making processes.

Enablers include:

♦ Using material, historical data
♦ Techniques for capturing best "state of understanding" of subject matter experts
♦ Minimizing biases in beliefs and judgment
♦ Leveraging all the relevant insights provided by information systems and predictive analytics

Failure Modes include:

♦ Collecting only information that is easy to access as opposed to decision relevant

- ◆ Not knowing what information is most important to the decision
- ◆ Treating key uncertainties as assumptions
- ◆ Ignoring uncertainty
- ◆ Including insights from information systems or predictive analytics that are grounded in inappropriate or irrelevant data

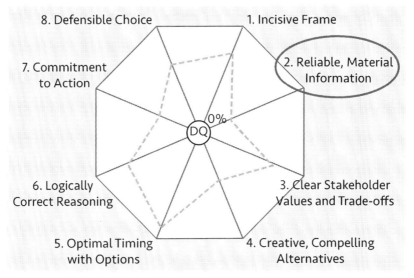

Figure 9.1: Reliable, Material Information is a Requirement of Decision Quality

Important decisions in government or corporations require input from subject matter experts. These experts can come from within the organization or from outside sources. Figure 9.2 shows the breadth of the information sources that should be leveraged by subject matter experts.

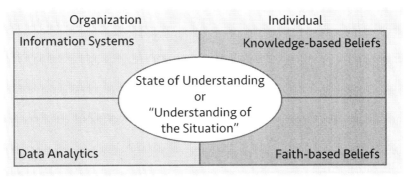

Figure 9.2: Targeted Components of a Subject Matter Expert's State of Understanding

Key Point:

> Critical to decision quality is ensuring that subject matter experts bring forth their best understanding of the situation during the decision-making process. Subject matter experts' state of understanding should consider all relevant and reliable information that exists within information systems and derived from predictive analytics, as well as the subject matter expert's own beliefs—both knowledge-based and inseparable faith-based.

The weakest link of the four components shown in Figure 9.2 is the subject matter expert's faith-based beliefs, which are intertwined with the subject matter expert's knowledge-based beliefs. In Chapter 6, we explored the limitations of human intuition, and the reasons why subject matter experts tend to have inferior predictive judgment compared to simple mathematical algorithms. These reasons included:

♦ Experts try to be clever, think outside the box, and consider complex combinations of features (low probability events and combinations) in making predictions.

♦ Simple combinations of features are more predictive.

♦ First order relationships are more informing than second order relationships with respect to prediction.

Also in Chapter 6, we introduced Daniel Kahneman's conclusions about what conditions need to be present to trust a subject matter expert's intuition and predictive accuracy. Expert's intuitions are likely to have predictive accuracy when the following two conditions are satisfied:

♦ The environment is sufficiently regular to be predictable.

♦ The expert has had the opportunity to learn these regularities through prolonged practice.

10–50–90 Range Assessments of Continuous Uncertainties

Organizations need a reliable and repeatable process for tapping into the four sources of information behind the expert's "state of understanding". The process should also try to minimize the biases associated with the judgment of subject matter experts. Additionally, a question that must be answered during the decision-making process is, "What would be the outcome, impact, or consequence of the problem / risk / opportunity should it occur?" From a financial perspective, the impacts are either in the form of revenue (sales) or costs, both of which are continuous value quantities where the value of the impact is typically uncertain.

Key Point:

> A 10–50–90 range assessment is a procedure for engaging subject matter experts to estimate uncertain impacts while comprehending their state of understanding and simultaneously attempting to minimize their biases.

The assessment targets the 10th, 50th, and 90th percentiles (0.10, 0.50, 0.90 fractiles also called the $p10$, $p50$, $p90$) of the underlying probability distribution associated with the subject matter expert's state of understanding as shown in Figure 9.3. Please note that some industries, most notably upstream oil and gas, numerically reverse the $p10$ and $p90$ percentiles. They use the $p10$ to refer to the larger number and the $p90$ to represent the smaller number. This can be considered just a change to the naming convention as all other math and definitions remain the same.

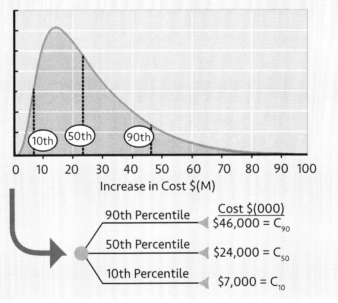

Figure 9.3: Example of a Subject Matter Expert's 10–50–90 Range Assessment for a Cost

The 10th percentile of a continuous cost distribution represents the specific cost (C_{10}) where there is only a 10% chance that the actual cost will be less than or equal to the value C_{10}. The 50th percentile, or median, represents the specific cost (C_{50}) where there is a 50% chance the actual cost will be less than or equal to the value C_{50}, which equates to a 50% chance that the actual cost will be greater than the value C_{50}. Likewise, there is a 90% chance that the actual cost will be less than or equal to the 90th percentile or C_{90}. Conversely, there is a 10% chance that the actual cost will be greater than the value C_{90} and a 90% chance that the actual cost will be greater than the C_{10}.

The Clarity (or "Clairvoyance") Test

"The single biggest problem in communication is the illusion that
it has taken place."
– George Bernard Shaw, Irish Nobel Laureate in Literature and
Co-founder of the London School of Economics

As conversations casually begin, System 1 is eager to confirm that the language being used is mutually understood by all parties involved until something feels wrong or disconnected. When that happens, System 2 is invoked and asks a question like, "Wait a minute, I think we're talking about two different things. What do *you* mean by the term _____?" If no one senses a disconnect in language, both parties will end the conversation believing that they have successfully delivered their messages. This is true in both our personal and professional lives. For conversations about decisions, especially material decisions, clarity in our language is of the utmost importance.

For example, the supply chain manager calls one of the company's suppliers and asks, "Are you going to make the delivery dates on this month's plan?" Is it clear to the supplier what the supply chain manager is asking? Is the supply chain manager referring to the current contracted plan or to the current plan plus the ad hoc requests made last week that have not yet been integrated into the plan? Is the supply chain manager referring to the fiscal month definition or the standard calendar month definition? Does this include all the products in the current plan or just the ones the supply chain manager is usually concerned with? There are many ways seemingly simple communications can be misunderstood by both parties. Sometimes the lack of clarity provides some perceived short-term advantage to one party over another so the lack of clarity is deemed as a benefit. However, this rarely results in a long-term benefit and usually results in a cost.

Ronald A. Howard, professor of Management Science and Engineering at Stanford University, coined the term *decision analysis* in the 1960s. As part of that discipline, he introduced the notion of the *clarity test*, also known as the *clairvoyance test*, to ensure clarity in our language during the decision making process.

The clarity test is a mental exercise that uses a hypothetical person known as the *clairvoyant*. Given clarity in language, the clairvoyant can accurately answer any question regarding past, present, or future events. If the clairvoyant cannot immediately tell us the outcome of an uncertainty and requires further information, clarity in language has not been reached. Let's try this out. An executive asks the clairvoyant, "What will be our sales next month?" Does that question pass the clarity test? The clairvoyant would say it does not and would ask:

♦ Which products and services are you referring to?

♦ Do you want the fiscal month or calendar month?

♦ Do you want to know gross sales or net sales?

♦ Do you want it measured in dollars or volumes?

♦ Do you want it for global sales or just North American sales?

♦ Do you want it for all Business Units or a specific Business Unit?

You get the idea. So, anytime we need to make an estimate of a continuous value quantity, we need to ensure the issue under discussion passes the clarity test.

A Five-Step 10–50–90 Continuous Quantity Range Assessment

The five-step method for estimating a continuous value quantity combines the probability distribution estimation concepts in Chapter 4, the heuristics and biases concepts from Chapter 8, and the concepts concerning the estimation of extreme values discussed in this chapter. This methodology uses a three-point range assessment as opposed to the five-point fractile range assessment discussed earlier in the chapter. As discussed in Chapter 4, a three-point range assessment sufficiently characterizes (with some modest assumptions about the shape of the probability distribution) the underlying uncertainty associated with the targeted continuous value quantity.

The range assessments will be discussed within the context of a problem, risk, or opportunity. The five steps are listed as follows; a detailed outline is included in Appendix 1:

1. Frame the assessment.

2. Leverage insights from information systems and predictive analytics.

3. Estimate the 90th and 10th percentiles (the tails).

4. Estimate the 50th percentile (the median).

5. Review and confirm the range assessment.

The eight elements of decision quality were defined in Chapter 2. Decision making processes in organizations should incorporate a quality review based upon these elements as well as a quality check of the range assessments. It is best if the assessment review is done by an individual or review team outside of the range assessment process. In order to establish the best state of understanding for problems, risks, and opportunities, we need to account for subject matter expert's best judgment beyond the often insufficient facts and data that reside in information systems. This requires range estimates of future uncertain outcomes, impacts, and consequences based upon a sufficient set of clearly stated scenarios.

These scenarios should be crafted using information systems and predictive analytics when available along with subject matter expert's System 2 intuition and judgment. The range assessment process must leverage the different types of heuristics experts use in making predictive judgments while attempting to minimize the biases that limit the quality of those judgments. Uncertainty and risk is not something to be avoided or assumed, but it should be understood, accounted for, and embraced in decision making. This chapter has provided the foundation for including subject matter expertise into the accounting of uncertainty and risk.

Alpert & Raiffa (1969)	Alpert, W., & Raiffa, H. *A progress report on the training of probability assessors.* Unpublished manuscript, 1969
Hession & McCarthy (1974)	Hession, E., & McCarthy, E. *Human performance in assessing subjective probability distributions.* Unpublished manuscript, September, 1974. (Available from Department of Business Administration, University College Dublin, Belfield, Dublin 4, Ireland.)
Selvidge (1975)	Selvidge, J. *Experimental comparison of different methods for assessing ther extremes of probability distributions by the fractile method.* (Management Science Report Series, Report 75-13). Boulder, Colo. Graduate School of Business Administration, University of Colorado, 1975.
Moskowitz & Bullers (1978)	Moskowitz, H., & Bullers, W. I. *Modified PERT versus fractile assessment of subjective probability distributions* (Paper No. 675). Purdue University, 1978.
Pickhardt & Wallace (1974)	Pickhardt, R. C., & Wallace, J. B. A study of the performance of subjective probabilty assessors. *Decision Sciences*, 1974, 5, 347-363.
Lichtenstein & Fischoff (1980b)	Lichtenstein, S., & Fischhoff, B. Training for calibration. *Organizational Behavior and Human Performance*, 1980, 26, 149-171.
Seaver, von Winterfeldt, & Edwards (1978)	Seaver, D. A., von Winterfeldt, D., & Edwards, W. Eliciting subjective probability distributions on continuous variables. *Organizational Behavior and Human Performance*, 1978, 21, 379-391.
Schaefer & Borcherding (1973)	Schaefer, R. E., & Borcherding, K. The assessment of subjective probability distribution: A training experiment. *Acta Psychologica*, 1973, 37, 117-129.
Murphy & Winkler (1974)	Murphy, A. H., & Winkler, R. L. Subjective probability forecasting experiments in meteorology: Some preliminary results. *Bulletin of the American Meteorlogical Society*, 1974, 55, 1206-1216.

Table 9.2: Studies Referenced in Table 9.1

"There is the risk you cannot afford to take, and there is the risk you cannot afford not to take."
– Peter Drucker

10

The Unnatural Act of Being Risk Neutral

In our personal and professional lives, we constantly face a portfolio of problems, risks, and opportunities. The recurring dilemma is which should be acted upon and which should remain side-lined without action. As we consider our resource limitations that determine the number and degree of actions we can take, we must ask the question, "For this problem, risk, or opportunity, do we act or not?"

Amos Tversky and Daniel Kahneman pioneered the research that resulted in a descriptive theory of decision making, i.e., a theory that describes how we act. Their findings revealed that *how* decisions are "framed" impacts the choices we make. They defined a *decision frame* as follows: "We use the term *decision frame* to refer to the decision maker's conception of the acts, outcomes, and contingencies associated with a particular choice. The frame that a decision maker adopts is controlled particularly by the formulation of the problem and partly by the norms, habits, and personal characteristics of the decision maker."[1]

Prospect Theory: Decision Framing and the Psychology of Choice

Read the thought experiment on the next page. Amos Tversky and Daniel Kahneman performed this thought experiment with 150

---

1   Amos Tversky and Daniel Kahneman, "The Framing of Decisions and the Psychology of Choice," *Science*, New Series, Vol. 211, No. 4481 (Jan. 30, 1981), page 453.

individuals to test their hypothesis that response to losses is more extreme than response to gains.[2]

Thought Experiment:

Imagine that you face the following pair of concurrent decisions. First examine both decisions, then select the options you prefer.

Decision 1-Choose between:

(A) A sure gain of $240.

(B) 25% chance to gain $1,000 and 75% chance to gain nothing.

Decision 2-Choose between:

(C) a sure loss of $750.

(D) 75% chance to lose $1,000 and 25% chance to lose nothing.

If you are like most individuals, you chose (A) in Decision 1 and (D) in Decision 2. In Tversky's and Kahneman's experiment, 84% of participants chose (A) in Decision 1 and 87% chose (D) in Decision 2. Their explanation is that the majority choice in Decision 1 is risk-averse. We prefer a risk-free prospect to a risky prospect of equal or greater expected value in the realm of gains. Conversely, the majority choice in Decision 2 is risk-taking (risk-seeking). In the realm of losses, we prefer a risky prospect to a risk-free one of equal expected value.

The insight that individuals are risk averse regarding gains and risk taking (risk seeking) when dealing with potential losses is a key principle of Kahneman's and Tversky's *Prospect Theory*. The importance of this insight is tied to how decisions are framed, i.e., whether stated from the perspective of gains or losses. We need to approach this with caution as the framing of the decision can induce individuals to make different choices. As an example, if an individual is given $100 and is told they must choose between a gamble where there is a 50/50 chance of keeping the money or losing it all or giving back $50 and keeping $50 for certain, they prefer to take the risk on the 50/50 chance. This problem is framed in terms of losses and Prospect Theory suggests people will tend to prefer the risk.

---

2   This thought experiment was proposed by Amos Tversky and Daniel Kahneman in "The Framing of Decisions and the Psychology of Choice," *Science*, New Series, Vol. 211, No. 4481, (Jan. 30, 1981), page 454.

We can take the same problem and characterize it in terms of gains. In this version, the individual is given no initial stake, and then they are asked whether they prefer a 50/50 chance of winning $100 or a certain $50. In this instance, they tend to play it safe (risk-averse) and choose the certain $50. From an expected value point of view, all of the outcomes have identical expected values of $50. The only difference is that the first problem is framed in terms of losses which prompts a risk-seeking behavior, and the second problem is framed in terms of gains where individuals tend to be risk-averse.

Since individuals tend to be risk averse with regard to gains, this implies they tend to value positive uncertain monetary outcomes as something less than the expected value (sometimes referred to as the expected monetary value or EMV). Conversely, in the realm of losses where individuals tend to be risk taking, they tend to value negative uncertain monetary outcomes as something more (less negative) than the expected value. To be *risk neutral* implies that the individual values uncertain outcomes as the expected value. Figure 10.1 illustrates a hypothetical value function that is risk taking for losses and risk averse for gains.

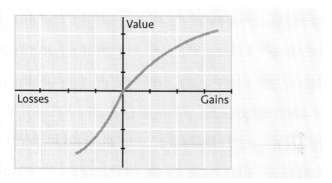

Figure 10.1: An Individual's Perception of Value for Gains Versus Losses

The value function shown in Figure 10.1 in the area of gains (positive values) is concave or negatively accelerating. This means the individual characterized by this curve would place a higher value on an incremental positive gain from $0 to $100,000 than they would on a gain from $1,000,000 to $1,100,000 even though the net gain is the same in each instance. Conversely, in the area of losses (negative values) on Figure 10.1, the value function is convex or positively accelerating. The incremental negative value associated with a loss from $0 to $100,000 is perceived as a greater loss than the incremental negative value associated with a loss from

$1,000,000 to $1,100,000. Viewing value through the lens of gain or loss represents a preference. This behavior is not desired when making corporate decisions where executives and managers should be risk-neutral.

The decision types shown in the bottom of Figure 1.1 of Chapter 1 constitute approximately 99% of corporate decisions and should be, for the most part, based on a risk-neutral risk preference. Only for high-stakes or "bet-the-company" type of decisions should risk-aversion come into play. Why? Because decisions are analogous to making bets. Large numbers of these bets are being made every day on behalf of the corporation. Maximizing the value created and protected for the corporation across these bets requires decision makers to be risk neutral. This corporate preference for risk-neutral based decisions is due to the law of large numbers. Let's walk through a few examples that illustrate why this is true.

Key Point:

> To maximize long-term enterprise value, corporate decision making should be based on an expected value (risk neutral) basis unless the decision is a high stakes or "bet-the-company" situation where accounting for corporate risk tolerance and risk aversion may be warranted.

Reconsider Decision 1 in the thought experiment, but this time use two players – Tom and Chris. Tom selected Choice (B) and was about to play the game with a 25% chance to gain $1,000 and a 75% chance to gain nothing. Before Tom can play, Chris intervenes and offers Tom $150 for the right to play the game. Even though the expected value of the game is $250, Tom accepts the lower amount. In this case, Tom's *risk premium* for this one-time lottery is $100 ($250 minus $150). A *risk premium* is defined as the expected value of the uncertain outcome minus the value the decision maker would accept for selling the uncertain outcome (the game).

Remember, Prospect Theory informs us that we tend to be risk averse in terms of gains. In the example, Tom is willing to forego $100 of the expected value gain to avoid the risk of gaining nothing. If this was a corporate decision, Tom just left $100 of value on the table due to his personal aversion to risk. As we mentioned earlier, the business world would prefer that Tom make decisions from a risk neutral perspective and take the 25% chance of gaining $1,000 as opposed to the certain option of gaining $150. In the realm of gains, the *risk premium* is a positive value for our assumed risk-averse decision maker.

Now reconsider Decision 2 in the thought experiment concerning losses. This time Tom had selected Choice (D) and was about to play a game with a 75% chance to lose $1,000 and a 25% chance to lose nothing. The expected value of this one-time game is a loss of $750. Again, Chris approaches Tom before the game and offers to take the game off Tom's hands if Tom pays him the expected value of $750. Tom decides to keep the game and take his chances. Chris makes a second offer and agrees to only charge $600 to take the game. Tom declines a second time. Tom thinks a little more, and offers Chris $500 to take the game. This time Chris declines, and Tom keeps the one-time game.

In this example, Tom's risk premium for this one-time lottery is −$250. The expected value of −$750 minus the −$500 certain amount of loss Tom was willing to accept to avoid the uncertain outcome. In the realm of losses, the *risk premium* is a negative value for our assumed *risk-taking* (or *risk-seeking*) decision maker. In other words, Tom was willing to keep $500 of the expected value loss and give up his chance of losing nothing.

At one point in this negotiation, Tom had the option of a certain loss of $600 versus the uncertain option of the one-time game with an expected value loss of $750. Tom chose the uncertain option which left $150 of corporate value on the table. The corporation would prefer that Tom choose the certain loss of $600 based on a risk-neutral risk preference. Once again, unless it is a high-stakes, "bet-the-company" type of decision, the corporation prefers risk-neutral decision making—neither risk-averse nor risk-taking.

Key Point:

> Both in our personal and professional lives, individuals naturally tend to be risk-seeking in their decision making in the realm of losses and risk-averse in their decision making in the realm of gains. Both of these tendencies are value destroying—for the vast majority of corporate decisions—from a long-term enterprise value perspective.

A second important feature of the value function in Figure 10.1 is the interpretation of the origin, the initial reference point. *Expected utility theory* is a normative decision-making theory (meaning it is based on how we *should* make decisions). Expected utility theory defines the origin to represent zero wealth. Utility (value) is then a function of total wealth, not incremental changes to total wealth. In prospect theory, Kahneman and Tversky argue that the normative theory assumption that we make judgements with regard to the total does not align with basic principles concerning how our perception actually works. Kahneman and Tversky elaborate on this point: "Our perceptual apparatus is attuned to the evaluation of changes or differences rather than to the evaluation of absolute magnitudes. When we respond to attributes such as brightness, loudness, or temperature, the past and present context of experience defines an adaptation level, or reference point, and stimuli are perceived in relation to this reference point. Thus, an object at a given temperature may be experienced as hot or cold to the touch depending on the temperature to which one has adapted. The same principle applies to non-sensory attributes such as health, prestige, and wealth. The same level of wealth, for example, may imply abject poverty for one person and great riches for another—depending on their current assets. The emphasis on changes as the carriers of value should not be taken to imply that the value of a particular change is independent of initial position. Strictly speaking, value should be treated as a function in two arguments: the asset position that serves as a reference point, and the magnitude of the change (positive or negative) from that reference point."[3]

A primary concern raised by prospect theory is that outcomes are perceived as positive or negative in relation to a reference point that is assumed to be neutral. However, variations of the reference point can determine whether a given outcome is perceived as a gain or loss and thereby invoking risk-averse or risk-taking preference in decision making. Once again, for the vast majority of decisions, corporations desire that their decision makers adopt a risk-neutral risk preference and avoid the value-destroying behavior prospect theory reveals. When framing and deciding on problems, risks, and opportunities, the reference point should be the corporation's or organization's deliberate strategy or plan as detailed in Table 3.1 in Chapter 3. Problems, risks, and opportunities should be framed as incremental changes (both positive and negative) with respect to a plan. This will leverage both the individual's innate incremental perspective as described in prospect theory, and the way individuals think and form beliefs when using side-by-side comparisons.

Expected utility theory can benefit from one further adjustment from prospect theory. Tversky and Kahneman assumed that

---

3   Daniel Kahneman and Amos Tversky, "Prospect Theory: An Analysis of Decision Under Risk," *Econometrica*, Vol. 47, No. 2 (March 1979), page 275.

individuals operate under a biased representation of probability in which they overestimate small probabilities near zero and underestimate large probabilities near one. While individuals are normally risk-averse for gains, they still play lotteries because they drastically overestimate the small probability of winning. Similarly, while individuals are normally risk-seeking for losses, they still buy insurance since they drastically overestimate the small probability of needing to file a claim on the insurance. In order to better calibrate their assessments of probability of occurrence, individuals should ground their assessments in available relevant information, learn best practice methods for making assessments, and make it a habit to compare their personal assessments to actual outcomes as a learning and calibration mechanism. Although this discussion has focused on monetary outcomes, Tversky and Kahneman found that the same risk preferences apply to decisions regarding human lives.

Neurobiological Explanation for Loss Aversion

An individual's tendency to strongly prefer avoiding losses to acquiring gains is called *loss aversion*. Animals, including humans, will fight harder to prevent losses than to achieve gains. For territorial animals such as lions, hippos, penguins, and even hummingbirds, this principle underlies the success of defenders. When a territory "owner" is challenged, the owner is by far the most likely winner. A lioness will give up relatively easily when chasing prey; however, once she has captured a zebra or gazelle, she will defend it fiercely and fight to avoid the loss. Clearly at that point the lioness has a new reference point with respect to her kill.

Daniel Kahneman said this about loss aversion and reference points: "Loss aversion is a powerful conservative force that favors minimal changes from the status quo in the lives of both institutions and individuals. This conservatism helps keep us stable in our neighborhood, our marriage, and our job; it is the gravitational force that holds our life together near the reference point."[4] As with the lioness, our fear and disdain of loss is much greater than our desire for gain.

When undisciplined gamblers experience a losing streak, they start to exhibit more risk-taking behavior as they attempt to claw their way back to the status quo and avoid a loss for the day. The same holds true for project managers who fall behind schedule or

---

4   Daniel Kahneman, *Thinking, Fast and Slow* (New York: Farrar, Straus and Giroux, 2011), page 305.

budget. They start making riskier decision choices that can drive projects into deeper trouble (in Chapter 14 of *Project Risk Quantification*, John Hollmann describes this phenomena in detail and cites observable characteristics of a project descending into chaos).[5]

Key Point:

An individual's innate loss aversion is a powerful conservative force that favors minimal change from the status quo and can bias corporate decision making towards inaction and/or late reactions.

Loss aversion causes the value function curve shown in Figure 10.1 to become convex in the area of losses. Consider the person who has lost $130 gambling at the race track and is now contemplating a final $10 bet on a 14:1 long shot in the day's last race. The likely reference point for the individual is in the realm of losses where risk-taking behavior is expected. They are drawn towards the high risk chance to get back to status quo and avoid a loss for the day. If they lose, the incremental increase in the day's loss by the additional $10 holds less value for them than the possibility of erasing their loss for the day.

What is the source of our aversion to losses? Is it a learned behavior or a biological consequence of being human? Functional magnetic resonance imaging or functional MRI (fMRI) is an MRI procedure that measures brain activity by detecting associated changes in blood flow. The procedure provides insight on neural activity by leveraging the fact that cerebral blood flow and neuronal activation are coupled. When an area of the brain is in use, blood flow to that region increases.

Benedetto De Martino, Colin Camerer, and Ralph Adolphs have determined that damage to the human brain's amygdala region eliminates monetary loss aversion. This implies that the amygdala plays a necessary role "in generating loss aversion by inhibiting actions with potentially deleterious outcomes."[6] It should come as no surprise that our brain's "emotion and fear center" plays a key role in our aversion to loss.

---

5   John K. Hollmann, *Project Risk Quantification* (Gainesville: Probabilistic Publishing, 2016).

6   Benedetto De Martino, Colin F. Camerer, and Ralph Adolphs, "Amygdala damage eliminates monetary loss aversion," *PNAS*, Vol.107, No. 8, (February 23, 2010), pages. 3788 - 3792. http://www.pnas.org/content/107/8/3788.full.

Other regions of our brains also play a role. Using fMRI responses, Sabrina Tom, Craig Fox, Christopher Trepel, and Russell Poldrack determined that loss aversion goes beyond the amygdala to include the ventral striatum (a reward center of the brain) and the prefrontal cortex (where thoughts and actions are coordinated with internal goals).[7]

Peter Sokol-Hessner, Colin F. Camerer, and Elizabeth A. Phelps provided evidence that regulating emotions with "reappraisal-focused strategies," meaning changing the decision frame and the way we think about the situation, can reduce loss aversion. Using the fMRI, they demonstrated that a reduction in loss aversion correlates with decreases in amygdala responses.[8] Benedetto De Martino has shown that while we all have an initial emotional response via the amygdala, some people can better control their initial emotional response via their frontal lobe, resulting in a more rationalized decision.[9] De Martino's conclusion is consistent with the Chapter 6 discussion of the evolution of the human brain. It illustrates the conflict that arises between the faster responding limbic system that includes the amygdala and the slower responding frontal lobes of the neocortex.

Key Point:

> While making decisions everyone has an initial emotional (amygdala-sourced) response. Some individuals can control these emotional responses better via their prefrontal neocortex.

There is irrefutable evidence that our loss aversion is innate in origin and not just a human trait. Prospect theory provides an understanding of our value-destroying decision-making behaviors when we become risk-seeking in the realm of losses (problems and risks) and risk-averse in the realm of gains (opportunities). Ongoing

---

7   Sabrina M. Tom, Craig R. Fox, Christopher Trepel, and Russell A. Poldrack, "The Neural Basis of Loss Aversion in Decision-Making Under Risk," *Science*, Vol. 315 (January 26, 2007), pages 515-518.

8   Peter Sokol-Hessner, Colin F. Camerer, and Elizabeth A. Phelps, "Emotion regulation reduces loss aversion and decreases amygdala responses to losses," *Social Cognitive and Affective Neuroscience*, Vol. 8, Issue 3 (March 11, 2013), pages. 341-350.

9   Benedetto De Martino, "How to Make Better Decisions", *BBC Documentary*, http://www.youtube.com/watch?v=cVqVJ0IXi_M, Minutes 16:26 - 18:26.

neurobiological research continues to investigate the source of these attitudes and behaviors in our brains.

In our continuing effort to improve the quality of both personal and corporate decision making, these learnings can help us create unbiased and appropriate decision frames and analyses. Understanding the way we naturally frame decisions and the influence that our human perspective has on our reference points should enable us to prescribe better methods of how to frame or structure decisions. We can use this information to leverage our innate skills while simultaneously mitigating the deleterious biases and outright decision-making mistakes associated with framing decisions.

"The man who insists on seeing with perfect clearness
before he decides, never decides."
– Henri-Frédéric Amiel, 19th Century Swiss Philosopher and Poet

11

Tipping Points and Decision Frames

To Act or Not to Act – That is the Question

Note: This chapter introduces a key concept of PRO Enterprise Management, the "tipping point of a material consequence." Executives and senior managers should read the introduction *but may skip or skim the detailed examples that are intended for analysts to demonstrate the breadth of approaches that can be used in practice. The concept of tipping points simplifies and structures the work of decision framing. Executives and senior managers may skim the discussions on decision framing without missing the core ideas of the book. And finally, for those individuals involved in enterprise risk management (ERM), the final sections of the chapter discuss the role of tipping points in ERM. Tipping points can simplify implementation of ERM and provide the sorely needed "narrative-based" bridge to ERM decision making.*

Sketching the Decision Frame: Act versus Not Act

Every executive or manager who oversees or provides input into a business plan owns a portfolio of problems, risks, and opportunities—PRO items—with respect to the plan. For each PRO item, the question is whether or not to act at this time? Do we intervene or leave the PRO item in status quo? This tense and often emotionally charged environment is typically caused by resource limitations. Additionally, various stakeholders inject their own risk behaviors into the decision-making process as they monitor the potential gains and losses resulting from any actions.

Figure 11.1 provides a standard decision structure (pattern) that can be used for sketching the decision frame of problems, risks, and opportunities. The decision is represented by the square on the left. The two choices—Investment and Action and No Investment and No Action—are shown as branches leading from the square. In both branches, the decision is followed by an uncertainty shown as a circle that represents the antecedent to the material consequences. This is an issue, situation, or event where the outcome is unknown. This uncertainty has a probability of either occurring or not. The probabilities for the uncertainties are shown as P and Q. These may be different for the same uncertainty if they are dependent on the decision. The final enterprise value is shown at the end of each branch.

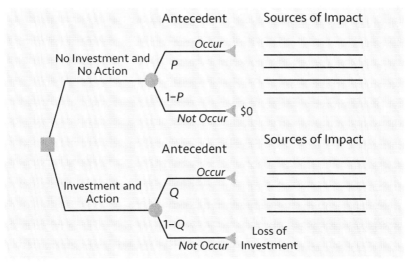

Figure 11.1: Sketching the Decision Frame: "What is the PRO Item Story?"

The consequences (impact) of the decision given the antecedent occurs are listed at the far right. In the case of deciding not to act (the upper half of the decision tree in Figure 11.1) and the antecedent *does not* occur, there is no impact to the plan and the end of that branch show $0 impact. No money has been invested in the PRO item, and no gains or losses resulted since the *problem, risk, or opportunity* did not occur. Conversely, in the case of deciding not to act and the antecedent *does* occur, there are consequences and the sources of economic impacts should be listed as well. You might not be able to quantify them at this point, but they can be identified.

In the case of deciding to act (the lower half of the decision tree in Figure 11.1) and the antecedent *does not* occur, there is an impact because there was an investment associated with the action taken. In the case of deciding to act and the antecedent *does* occur, there are still consequences. As above, the sources of economic consequences should be listed, and the value of the investment must be considered.

The decision structure in Figure 11.1 provides a clear representation of the narrative for the PRO item being framed. There are nuances and details that need to be understood, but for now, we will focus on this critical skill of sketching the decision frame.

Tipping Point of a Material Consequence

Using the decision structure in Figure 11.1 can help establish and clarify the tipping point of a material consequence associated with the PRO item before we get engrossed in the quantitative details. The probabilities P and Q in Figure 11.1 represent the likelihood of reaching the "tipping point of a material consequence." Many risk management methodologies neglect this and thereby reduce their usefulness.

Key Point:

> In every organization within an enterprise from the perspective of the CEO down to line managers, the concept of a "material consequence" should be well understood (if not documented). Material consequences are perceived with respect to a plan—the plan you are responsible for delivering. A material consequence to the CEO might be a loss of revenue within the year of $100 million dollars or more. For a line manager a material consequence might be a cost overrun within the year of $20,000 or more. The concept of material consequences can and should be applied to revenue, cost, and issues concerning environment, health, safety, and compliance.

Defining upfront what would be considered a material consequence with respect to a plan helps individuals sharpen their focus when identifying problems, risks, and opportunities. Risk identification processes that don't define material consequences result in long lists of risks that need to be filtered to get to risks that truly require attention and mitigation investment and action.

Six Sigma programs pursuing cost reduction opportunities often expend too much effort on less than material (significant) gains. Resolving every problem that emerges draws management's limited time and resources away from sorely needed risk and opportunity concerns and possibilities. Knowing what is a material consequence with respect to the plan you are managing is critical to effective management.

Key Point:

A *tipping point of a material consequence* is the point at which an issue, event, or situation crosses a threshold ensuring a material consequence will occur, though the *degree* of the material consequence may be, and is often, uncertain.

This concept is best explained through examples.

Tipping Point for Risks

The *Modified Mercalli Intensity Scale* is a seismic scale used to measure the *intensity* of an earthquake by assessing the effect as opposed to the Richter Scale that measures the magnitude or the energy released. Buildings and other structures can be designed to withstand an earthquake of a particular intensity. For example, the general structure of a building may have been built to withstand a Mercalli VIII intensity level (roughly equal to a magnitude 6.0 to 7.0 on the Richter Scale). However, if the plumbing in the ceiling is not properly strapped, even an earthquake of lesser intensity could result in a break in the plumbing inducing flooding—clearly a material consequence.

Suppose there is a manufacturing site in Southern California that was built along the lines described in the previous paragraph. Upon inspection, the general structure of the main building was assessed to withstand a Mercalli VIII earthquake. However, the strapping of ceiling plumbing and the methods used to mount some critical equipment to the floor were not up to that standard. In that case, a lesser earthquake could cause flooding from broken plumbing resulting in several material consequences including:

♦ Loss of raw materials and finished goods inventory,

♦ Ruined inventory,

♦ Comprehensive clean-up,

♦ Damaged equipment that needs to be repaired or replaced,

♦ Manufacturing shutdown until repairs are completed,

♦ Additional inspections,

♦ Lost sales due to inventory outage, and

♦ Replacement cost for lost inventory.

According to the U.S. Geological Survey (USGS), the probability of an earthquake of magnitude 6.0 or greater striking within 50 kilometers of this manufacturing site within the next five years is 0.20. The probability of an earthquake of magnitude 7.0 or greater striking within 50 kilometers of the manufacturing site within the next five years is 0.08.

In this case, the *tipping point of a material consequence* is an earthquake of magnitude 6.0 or greater. This magnitude of an earthquake could cause flooding of the plant with the associated consequences. You might question, "Why the five-year time window? Why not three years? Why not ten years?" These are all excellent questions and should be part of the framing discussion that includes the decision makers who ultimately would approve the decision frame and the risk-mitigation investment.

Tipping Point for Problems

We defined a *problem* as any issue, situation, or event that is certain to occur if no action is taken and will result in a material deviation from a planned goal and ultimately a loss. The problem (considered as the tipping point of a material consequence) may have already occurred, and the organization might already be experiencing losses. For a problem, the probability P in Figure 11.1 should be equal to 1.0, which indicates *certain occurrence of the tipping point,* that is, the tipping point has already happened. The probability Q in Figure 11.1 may or may not be equal to 1.0 depending on the timing of the problem and whether investment and action can reduce its likelihood of occurring.

As an example, a pharmaceutical company has a new breast cancer drug in their R&D pipeline that they are planning to launch in 24 months. They have submitted the results of a clinical trial to the U.S. Food and Drug Administration (FDA) and have been waiting on approval of their product based on the study results. Unfortunately, the FDA has just informed the pharmaceutical company that the study results were insufficient and that a subsequent toxicity study would be required before proceeding to FDA drug approval.

The risk of the first failed toxicity study *just* became a problem. Several material consequences ensue including:

♦ Potential change in the probability of FDA approval of the drug,

◆ Later product sales launch date,
◆ Potential for reduced sales over the lifetime of the product, especially if this is a first-to-market race with another emerging drug,
◆ Additional costs associated with the execution of an unplanned toxicity study, and
◆ Potential additional redo costs.

This is likely a situation that goes beyond the decision of whether or not to invest. The pharmaceutical company must decide what to do considering this new problem. Can the company minimize the time and cost of the additional toxicity study without risking another failed study or a failed FDA approval?

Tipping Point for Opportunities

An *opportunity* represents an issue, situation, or event that may result in an outcome that is better than planned and results in a net gain. In both your personal and professional lives, opportunities typically don't just fall into your hands unless you expend some effort and investment. Consequently, in many cases, the probability P in Figure 11.1 should be equal to 0.0.

As an example, an automotive parts supplier learned that one of their competitors just lost a major contract with an automaker. The competitor's terminated contract is now an opportunity that is currently not in the sales forecast of the automotive supplier. To capture a new potential contract, the automotive supplier will need to act and likely expend some resources currently not in the sales budget.

Given the automotive supplier decides to pursue this opportunity, probability Q in Figrue 11.1 will be some value greater than zero. Should the automotive supplier capture the new contract, several material consequences occur including:

◆ A new sales stream associated with the new contract and possibly other ancillary contracts,
◆ Additional unplanned tooling costs to fulfill the new contract,
◆ Potentially adding labor or an additional shift, and
◆ Other additional costs.

More Complex Tipping Points

So far, we have looked at PRO items with simple, single event antecedents. Let's consider a few examples and situations where the antecedent, the "tipping point of a material consequence," is a set of events that contribute to the probability of occurrence.

Example: A Defense Contractor Bidding on a Competitive Contract

Company A is a defense contractor currently in the bidding process for a U.S. Naval contract. With ongoing federal budget cuts, there is some uncertainty concerning whether the contract will be awarded or not. Moreover, the executives in Company A believe that the incumbent contractor Company B may have a slight competitive advantage. A first round of proposals resulted in the elimination of several potential bidders, narrowing the field down to three contractors. "Best-and-Final" proposals are due in four weeks. Company A considers the probability of their capturing the contract ("the tipping point of a material consequence") as 0.24 as shown in Figure 11.2.

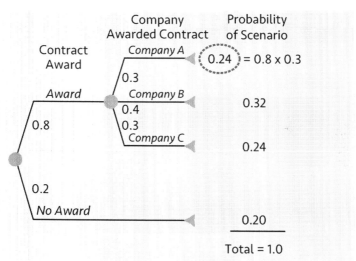

Figure 11.2: Calculating the Probability of Company A Capturing the Defense Contract

Whether this is an opportunity or a risk depends on how the contract is being accounted for in Company A's sales forecast and business plan, the reference point. If this contract is not in Company A's sales forecast and business plan, then this naval contract represents an *opportunity*. Moving forward, the dollars spent thus far are considered sunk costs, and the decision is whether or not to proceed and submit the "Best-and-Final" bid. If Company A decides to drop out of the competition (the "No Investment & No Action" branch shown in Figure 11.1), then the probability of capturing the contract is zero. If they decide to submit a "Best-and-Final" bid, then the probability of capturing the contract is 0.24.

An excellent strategic question at this point would be to consider what further actions could be taken, above and beyond the current "Best-and-Final" proposal plan. Additionally, what expenditures can be made and would those actions improve the probability of capturing the contract?

If this contract is represented in the current sales forecast as the total value of the contract (i.e., not risk-adjusted to account for probability of capture), then this situation is a *risk* to the current plan, the reference point. In that case, the probability of the risk occurring or not capturing the contract is equal to 0.76 (1.0 minus 0.24).

Example: A Pharmaceutical Company Considering a New Drug

Pharmaceutical companies follow a well-defined set of stages and gates leading to the product launch of a new drug (technically referred to as a New Molecular Entity, NME). Statistics exist on an industry-wide basis, a therapeutic area basis, and an individual company basis for the time and resources to complete each stage, as well as the probability of successfully completing each stage, allowing transition into the next. The first four stages of the process are considered the work of *drug discovery*. The second set of four stages are considered the work of *drug development*. Figure 11.3 provides the list of stages for drug discovery and development. The probabilities of successful transition from one stage to the next based upon industry benchmarks and data from Eli Lilly are also shown.[1]

If a pharmaceutical company is considering the opportunity of pursuing a new oncology drug, the tipping point of a material consequence could be considered as the launch of a new oncology product. This would require the successful completion of each of the eight stages of drug discovery and development. As indicated

---

1   Steven M. Paul, Daniel S. Mytelka, Christopher T. Dunwiddie, Charles C. Persinger, Bernard H. Munos, Stacy R. Lindborg and Aaron L. Schacht, "How to improve R&D productivity: the pharmaceutical industry's grand challenge," *Nature Reviews Drug Discovery*, Vol. 9 (March 2010), pages 203-214.

in Figure 11.3, the probability of occurrence for this is about a 4% chance (0.041). On the other hand, if the company has successfully completed their Phase II clinical studies, then the probability of reaching product launch is 0.637, which is calculated by multiplying the probability of a successful Phase III study or studies (0.70) by the probability of regulatory approval given Phase III success (0.91).

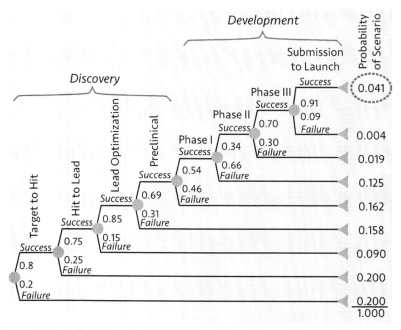

Figure 11.3: Calculating the Probability of Launching a Commercial Product for a Pharmaceutical Company

Once a potential NME reaches development (the final four stages), a stage-based project plan is established with a target product launch year and quarter. This plan and projected sales forecast becomes the reference point for all PRO items associated with the development project. Problems, risks, and opportunities will be handled with respect to potential changes in schedule, budget, stage transition probabilities, and projected sales forecast. Example strategic questions include:

♦ At what cost should we mitigate the risk of a two or three month delay in Phase III?

♦ Is it worth investing additional resources in improving the probability of a successful Phase III and what is the return on investment for those resources?

♦ What is the value of reducing the duration of Phase III by three months?

Example: A Pharmaceutical Company Pursuing the Launch of a First-to-Market Drug is in a Race with a Competitor's Potential New Drug

In the pharmaceutical industry, being first-to-market with a new class of drug can result in hundreds of millions of dollars more sales over the life of the product compared to entering second or later. Building off the information in the previous example, consider the situation where a pharmaceutical company is in Phase III with a probability of product launch of 0.637 and target launch in 24 months. A competitor is just beginning Phase III with a target product launch date in about 30 months. A possible tipping point of a material consequence could be the combination of regulatory approval and being first to product launch. Figure 11.4 suggests a means to quantify the probability of the tipping point of a material consequence for this situation. The conjunctive probability of being first-to-market and having a successful launch is 0.427. At this point, the pharmaceutical company should brainstorm ways to improve this probability, if possible.

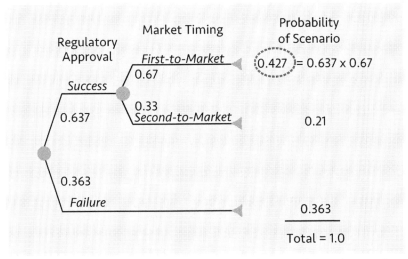

Figure 11.4: Calculating the Probability of Product Regulatory Approval and First-to-Market

Example: A Construction Company has a Cash Incentive Provided by a Customer for Delivering a Project within Budget and Schedule

A construction company is about midway through a 30-month construction project that includes a customer cash incentive of $25 million for completing the project within schedule and budget. The cash incentive is not included in the construction company's revenue forecast for the year, so the $25M cash incentive represents an opportunity. The project manager uses probabilistic analysis that includes a Monte Carlo simulation of the cost and schedule. The probabilities calculated in the analysis are shown in the probability tree in Figure 11.5.

As provided in Figure 11.5, the project analyst calculates the chances of the project being completed on time and within budget to be about 57%. The project manager should then ask additional questions such as:

♦ How can we increase the project's chances of capturing the cash incentive without adversely impacting the quality of the construction?

♦ What additional resources (labor and other costs) would be required to achieve this?

♦ What is the return on investment for these additional resources?

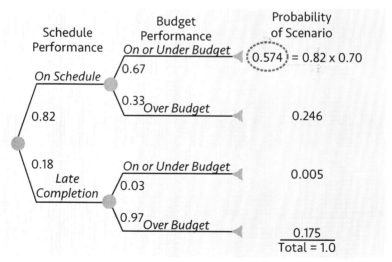

Figure 11.5: Monte Carlo Simulation Results, Project Schedule and Budget

Example: A Satellite Manufacturer is Creating a Proposal and Bid for a Contract and the Proposal Team is Concerned the Labor Hours are Insufficient

To improve the "competitiveness" of a proposal, executives have asked the proposal team to "sharpen their pencils" and determine how to reduce the amount of labor included in a bid. The proposal team gathered labor data from 25 previous contracts as shown in the Table 11.1.

The executives believe that in order to be competitive, the total labor hours need to be about 85,000. Based on an analysis of the historical data from similar programs, the proposal team concluded that 36% (9 of the 25) required more than 85,000 hours of labor. The team felt that the historical data would be a good representation of the future and concluded that there was a 36% chance that the program being bid would require more than 85,000 hours of labor (it can also be said to have a 64% chance of being below the 85,000).

Program	Total Hours	Program	Total Hours	Program	Total Hours
XRS 5	143,001	PRS 5	67,084	YUE 3	92,652
XRS 6	97,001	XQRAD-A	131,634	YUE 4	86,490
XRS 7	81,501	XQRAD-B	75,282	MORP	51,738
XRS 8	54,001	TELOQ	75,175	LEGES	51,221
PRS 1	69,838	OPRAND	75,175	TYPHON	57,185
PRS 2	52,859	OPRAND 2	78,234	XCALIB	96,456
PRS 3	58,001	YUE 1	106,217	DENTRO	83,765
PRS 4	49,551	YUE 2	92,652	SUPL-Q	87,000
				SUPL-R	61,345

Table 11.1: Example Project Labor Data

Example: A Food Services Company has Growing Concerns about the Possibility of a Warehouse Having HVAC Problems, Ultimately Destroying Inventory

The *annualized failure rate* (AFR) represents the probability of failure during any full year of service during the life of a device or component. The current HVAC system for the Food Services Company warehouse used for food inventory is eight years old. The service life is 15 years, and the system has an annualized failure rate of about 3%. A backup system is in place, but it is older than the primary HVAC system and is considered unreliable. The current capital plan calls for the HVAC system to be replaced in four years when it will be 12 years old.

The question is: What is the probability that the current primary HVAC system will have at least one failure in the next four years? Like many probability problems, it is much easier to calculate the converse–the probability of NO failures in the next four years and subtract from one. Consequently, the probability of at least one failure over the next four years can be calculated as:

Probability of at least one failure in four years $=$
$1 - (1 - 0.03)^4 =$
$1 - 0.885 = 0.115$

This represents a Risk to the Food Services Company. They will next need to determine the cost to the company if the HVAC system fails. If the probabilistically weighted cost is above the risk tolerance of the company executives, they should brainstorm ways to mitigate the risk.

Example: A Manufacturer is Performing a Failure Mode and Effects Analysis (FMEA) as Part of an Overall Risk Assessment of Raw Material Supply Risk

The executives of the manufacturing company asked the director of the quality organization to perform a risk assessment on the supply of raw materials. The quality team started by determining the set of key raw materials, and then they performed a *Failure Mode and Effects Analysis* (FMEA) study. A FMEA is a common single point of failure analysis used in many industries and governmental entities as part of reliability, safety, and quality engineering systems. It begins with a brain-storming session to determine a list of risk factors (failure modes) as shown in Table 11.2 for one of their key single-sourced raw materials. Next, they added a consideration of "tipping points of material consequence." They defined these as scenarios that would deplete both their six-month safety stocks of the raw material and final product, thus creating an out-of-stock scenario leading to lost sales.

Table 11.2 presents the quality team's identified risk factors for the key raw material under consideration. The quality team then debated which of the FMEA risk factors could plausibly result in the defined tipping point for the specific raw material. Those results are

Key Risk Factors	Tipping Pt?		AFR (Tipping Pt)	Summaries
	Yes	No		
Contamination:				
Quality (e.g. extraneous matter)	X		0.010	
Supply Chain control (e.g. adulteration)	X		0.010	
Exposure to heat in transport		X	0.000	
Total AFR for at least one Contamination Tipping Point failure				0.020
Market / Demand Changes:				
Significant change in Company's product forecast		X	0.000	
Potential ban of chemical or ingredient	X		0.005	
New product launch		X	0.000	
Change in supplied ingredient		X	0.000	
Emerging new competitor requiring raw material		X	0.000	
Adverse public event		X	0.000	
Changing trends in tax incentives		X	0.000	
Changing trends in offshore manufacturing		X	0.000	
Total AFR for at least one Market / Demand Changes Tipping Point failure				0.005
Supplier Compliance:				
Potential for supplier warning letter		X	0.000	
Potential for supplier consent decree	X		0.020	
Potential for stability failures		X	0.000	
Potential for supplier falsified documents		X	0.000	
Excessive or changes in number of deviations		X	0.000	
Total AFR for at least one Market / Demand Changes Tipping Point failure				0.020
Supplier Ability or Willingness to Provide:				
Change in supplier's control		X	0.000	
Change in supplier's ownership or financing		X	0.000	
Supplier loses a major client / contract		X	0.000	
Supplier gains a new major client / contract	X		0.020	
Change in supplier's union relations	X		0.010	
Potential supplier business disruption	X		0.050	
Change in supplier's revenue or earnings outlook		X	0.000	
Total AFR for at least one Supplier Ability or Willingness Tipping Point failure				0.080

Table 11.2: FMEA Study of Raw Material Risk Factors and "Tipping Point" Probability

indicated by "Yes" or "No". The probabilities of reaching the defined tipping point and thereby resulting in a material consequence for each of the critical risk factors (those with the Yes designations) were assessed. Those are shown in Table 11.2 in the form of *annualized failure rates* (AFR).

The final step is to calculate the total AFR across all the key risk factors. As an example, to calculate the AFR for the category "Contamination," which has two key risk factors, we calculate the probability of at least one tipping point failure occurring.

Again, it is easier to calculate the converse (no failures) and subtracting from one to give us the probability of at least one failure. Assuming the risk factors are independent events, the AFR for the category "Contamination" is calculated as:

$$P = 1 - [(1 - 0.01) \times (1 - 0.01)] = 0.020.$$

Similarly, to calculate the total AFR across all categories, we calculate the probability of at least one tipping point failure across all critical risk factors. Assuming the risk factors are independent events, the total AFR across all categories is calculated as:

$$P = 1 - [(1 - 0.01) \times (1 - 0.01) \times (1 - 0.005) \times (1 - 0.02) \times (1 - 0.02) \times (1 - 0.01) \times (1 - 0.05)] = 0.119.$$

These seven examples show that there are many approaches and tools that can be used to assess the probability of occurrence for the "tipping point of a material consequence." These include direct subjective assessments of the probability made by subject matter experts, statistical data analysis including predictive analytics, modified FMEA studies, and Monte Carlo simulation models.

Narrow versus Broad Decision Frames

Once material consequences are well understood within a decision-making domain (e.g., product sales or supply chain) and the tipping points of potential problems, risks, or opportunities are defined, the work of decision framing is simplified to the structure in Figure 11.1. However, this simplification has its limitations and potential biases. To understand and surmount these concerns we need to explore decision framing from a couple of different perspectives.

The term *narrow framing* can be used to describe two natural decision-making tendencies that we should try to avoid. First, it can refer to the tendency to consider, evaluate, and decide a risky prospect in isolation rather than as part of a larger portfolio of prospects. Kahneman observed that narrowly framed decisions depart more from risk neutrality than decisions made in the context of a decision portfolio.[2] By focusing decisions on a single prospect at a time, individuals forego the benefits of "portfolio effects" such as diversification in choosing a portfolio of stocks. The portfolio effects can only be identified and understood with joint evaluation.

Kahneman considered *accessibility*, or the ease with which mental contents come to mind, as the key cause of narrow framing. This is consistent with how individuals think in terms of side-by-side comparisons and specifically the side-by-side comparison of "status quo" vs. "change to status quo" as detailed in Chapter 6.

Narrow framing can also be used to describe the tendency to consider decisions as binary and having only two possible options. Chip Heath and Dan Heath use the analogy of "making decisions like teenagers" based on work by Baruch Fischhoff.[3] Teenagers exhibit the tendency to consider decisions from a "whether or not" or "A or B" type of perspective. There is a lack of consideration of multiple options that might be available. Heath and Heath argue that organizations tend to make decisions a lot like teenagers.

On the other hand, *broad framing* refers to the consideration and evaluation of a set of decisions that leverage inter-relationships of the choices, consequences of the actions, and other impacts. Broad framing is more complex and almost always requires analytics. It can easily overcome the capabilities of human thought unless the inter-relationships are few, simple, and linear in nature. Broad framing enables higher quality decisions, but the evaluations are resource intensive which can paralyze decision processes. In practice, it is currently only used for the most critical or strategic decisions in organizations, if it is used at all. A goal of PRO Enterprise Management is to enable narrowly framed decisions, meaning framed individually, to compete on a consistent basis of best value for the enterprise while identifying decisions that need to be considered and addressed within a *broad frame*.

Personal Frame versus Project Frame versus Enterprise Frame

2   Daniel Kahneman, "Maps of Bounded Rationality: Psychology for Behavioral Economics," *American Economic Review*, Vol. 93, No. 5, (December, 2003), pages 1449-1475.

3   Chip Heath and Dan Heath, Decisive: *How To Make Better Choices In Life And Work* (New York: Crown Business, 2013), page 34.

Companies typically have multiple types of projects underway simultaneously, including capital projects, product-related projects (R&D), six sigma projects, cost reduction projects, continuous improvement projects, efficiency projects, and software application projects.

There are at least three different and often conflicting frames that can be adopted during a project. Unfortunately, they can all be present and typically arise as dictated by the situation. These three frames include:

- ♦ Personal frame,
- ♦ Project frame, and
- ♦ Enterprise frame.

Project managers are prone to a form of cognitive dissonance especially when the stakes associated with a project are high, resulting in senior management oversight and increased scrutiny. As previously discussed, project managers will naturally be risk-averse in the realm of gains and risk-seeking in the realm of losses. If the project is running on schedule and within budget delivering a quality product, the project manager will tend to be satisfied with that performance and not try for improvements (the exception being when there is some type of incentive such as a cash bonus). But even with the incentive (a gain), project managers respond to their aversion to loss and risk and won't push hard given the project is tracking to plan, the *reference point.*

If the project is tracking behind schedule or over budget, the project manager perceives the project from the realm of losses. In this case, the project manager becomes risk-seeking. This can cause a bad project to get even worse. So we have a project manager potentially toggling between risk-averse and risk-seeking decision making behaviors depending on the status of the project.

But it's even more complicated. The dominant frame of the project manager is his or her *personal* frame due to our ever-present "loss aversion." If this is the manager's first project, they likely perceive the situation as a career-making or career-breaking assignment. To them personally, the project represents a "high-stakes" or "bet-the-career" situation. As we have discussed, neither the risk averse nor risk-seeking behavior is what the enterprise desires from the project manager (unless it is a "high-stakes" situation for the *enterprise* where risk-averse decision making may be warranted). The cognitive dissonance suffered by the project manager is the tension created by simultaneously holding a personal frame, a project

Potential Impact	Project-only Frame (Level-of-effort Contract)	Enterprise Frame
Labor * Internal Staff * External Staff	* Actual Cost * Actual Cost	* Little or No Impact * Actual Cost
Material	Actual Cost	Actual Cost
Schedule	Labor, Material, and Contract Impacts	Labor, Material, Contract, and Future Programs Impacts
Efficiency	Labor, Material, and Schedule Impacts	Labor, Material, Schedule, and Future Programs Impacts
Project Contract * Milestone Payments * Incentives * Penalties * Liquidated Damages	* Revenue * Revenue * Actual Cost * Actual Cost	* Revenue * Revenue * Actual Cost * Actual Cost
Sales by Product * Direct Follow-on * Related Programs	No Impact	Future Sales * Probability of Award / Capture * Contract Award Timing/Value

Table 11.3: Defense Fixed-price Contract Program Frame versus Enterprise Frame

frame, and possibly, an enterprise frame. But what is the difference between a project frame and an enterprise frame?

Let's consider a fixed price defense program being managed by a prime (chief or responsible) contractor. Table 11.3 identifies the potential financial/economic impacts that the program can incur and how they differ in translation to the limited frame of "Project-Only" vs. "Enterprise" frame.

As shown in Table 11.3, the potential impacts of project-related problems, risks, and opportunities can significantly differ depending on whether decisions are framed from a "Project-Only" perspective vs. an "Enterprise" perspective.

Consider the following scenario for a defense contractor and the tension created by having multiple frames held by the CEO, a Business Unit (BU) President, a Program Manager, and the Shareholders. A two-billion-dollar defense contract is in its third year of a four-year contract. It is the beginning of the fourth quarter of the company's fiscal year. A $500 million milestone payment is scheduled to be received by the corporation prior to the end of the quarter, given the contractor meets all the requirements of the milestone payment.

The $500 million milestone payment is included as part of the BU's and corporation's financial plan; it becomes the reference point. Anticipated annual performance-based bonuses (representing a second and more personal reference point) for the CEO, the BU President, and the Program Manager will be impacted by whether or not the milestone payment is captured. The situation is interpreted by all parties in the realm of potential losses. How does the "long arm" of loss aversion play out?

Let's start with the CEO. The CEO is balancing at least five frame perspectives:

♦ The shareholders,
♦ Wall Street commitments,
♦ Employees,
♦ The community, and
♦ Personal.

The CEO adopts an "Enterprise Frame" (see Table 11.3) and is fully focused to ensure this program meets the requirements and satisfies the customer leading to future sales. At the same time, the CEO has made a commitment to Wall Street on this year's financial performance that requires the milestone payment to be made before year's end. Employee bonuses and his personal bonus will also be impacted by the milestone payment. The CEO recognizes that the long-term value of the enterprise (the shareholders' and community perspectives) is driven by a satisfied customer maximizing the chances to win future contracts with the customer. However, the CEO naturally perceives the milestone payment from the realm of losses and ensures the gravity of the situation is clearly understood by the BU President. In other words, the CEO wants to make sure that milestone payment is captured before year's end.

Let's consider the situation from the BU President's point of view next. The contract represents the largest customer in the business unit. The BU President has weekly meetings with the Program Manager to ensure the program is on track. To reinforce the urgency of securing the payment, the BU President relays the CEO's message to the Program Manager, "Make sure the milestone payment is captured before year's end." The tension in these meetings is mounting as the fourth quarter approaches, and it becomes clear that the contract requirements for the milestone payment are not achievable. In an attempt to keep the BU President from providing unwanted outside-program support, the Program Manager (under a "Project-Only" frame, see Table 11.3) has not fully divulged some of the recent problems and risks in the program. The Program Manager assumed a risk-seeking position and bet that the obstacles could be resolved without BU or corporate involvement. However, the bets have not come through, making a delayed milestone payment nearly certain.

The Program Manager begins to explore ways to shift work from the current phase in the program to future phases in an attempt to be at least "low-side" compliant on the requirements for the milestone payment. The reshuffled work plan is risky as it pushes some critical testing later into the schedule and may result in costly rework. Yes, the program may capture the year end milestone payment which will be celebrated throughout the corporation—but at what future cost to the enterprise and its shareholders?

The above scenario is an example of how loss aversion with respect to reference points can lead to risk-seeking decision making that undermines the long-term value of the corporation. "Project-Only" decision-making frames represent the natural frame taken by almost all employees including senior, executive, and project management. Corporations and project teams need to review and measure decision outcomes from an enterprise frame along with the other frames. These types of decisions can impact long-term enterprise value, so management should understand the implications of project-related decisions. Management should endeavor to openly communicate and discuss the potential trade-offs between the differing frames prior to making these decisions.

Key Point:

> Corporate decisions are not always made based on long-term enterprise value creation or protection. However, it is the fiduciary responsibility of all decision makers (managers, executives, and board members) to at least *understand* the long-term enterprise value impact and the associated expenditure's return on investment prior to decision making.

A second example of impacts for *project-only frames* versus *enterprise frames* is shown in Table 11.4. This Table illustrates the differing frames of a clinical operations function in a pharmaceutical company. They are managing a clinical trial and outsourcing that trial to a Contract Research Organization (CRO) under a level-of-effort contract (as opposed to a fixed cost contract).

Potential Impact	Project-only Frame (Level-of-effort Contract)	Enterprise Frame
Labor * Internal Staff * External Staff	* Actual Cost * Actual Cost	* Little or No Impact * Actual Cost
Material	Actual Cost	Actual Cost
Schedule	Labor, Material, and Contract Impacts	Labor, Material, Contract, and Sales Impacts
Efficiency	Labor, Material, and Schedule Impacts	Labor, Material, Schedule, and Sales Impacts
Project Contract * Milestone Payments to CRO * Incentives to CRO * Penalties against CRO * Liquidated Damages	* Cost Timing * Actual Cost * Revenue * Revenue	* Cost Timing * Cost Timing and Value * Revenue * Revenue
Sales by Product * Current R&D Product * Existing Related Products * Future Related Products	No Impact	Sales by Product

Table 11.4: Pharmaceutical Company Clinical Trial Project Frame versus Enterprise Frame

The Relationship of Project Plans and Risk Behavior

Project plans heavily influence risk behavior throughout the course of a planned project. An overly aggressive project plan in schedule and budget leads to:

♦ More *problem* and *risk* value than *opportunity* value—which leads to

♦ Project distress with respect to schedule, budget, and quality—which leads to

♦ Managers perceiving the project from the realm of losses—which leads to

♦ Risk-seeking-based behavior and decision making—which leads to

♦ Value destruction via commission (acting) as risky choices are made in attempts to "claw back to plan" further degrading the long-term prospects and consequences of the project by taking an overall bad situation and most likely making it worse.

A too unambitious project plan in schedule and budget leads to:

♦ More opportunity-value than problem and risk-value—which leads to

♦ Project apathy with respect to schedule, budget, or quality improvement—which leads to

♦ Managers perceiving the project from the realm of gains—which leads to

♦ Risk-averse-based behavior and decision making—which leads to

♦ Value destruction via omission (not acting) of pursuit of opportunities to outperform the baseline project plan with respect to schedule, budget, or quality.

As all experienced executives and managers know, projects require a "Goldilocks Plan," meaning one that is not too aggressive while still being ambitious and deliverable. Executives and managers tend not to understand the risk behavior caused by the project plans. Regardless of the aggressiveness of the project plan, we need project managers making decisions on a risk-neutral basis unless the project is a "bet-the-company" initiative in which case risk aversion is important and should be addressed.

Risk Triggers and Key Risk Indicators

Risk triggers and *key risk indicators* (KRIs) are used by organizations in their general risk management processes and overall enterprise risk management. Risk triggers and key risk indicators are not risks, but they are metrics used to support the identification and management of risk. As an example, the left-hand column in Table 11.2 can be interpreted as a list of potential risk triggers that could result in the risk of depleted safety stock leading to lost product sales.

Key risk indicators (KRIs) are a more recent enterprise risk management development. The Committee of Sponsoring Organizations of the Treadway Commission (COSO), an established authority on Enterprise Risk Management, summarizes key risk indicators as follows: "KRIs are metrics used to provide an early signal of increasing risk exposure in various areas of the organization. In some instances, they may be little more than key ratios that the board and senior management track as indicators of evolving problems, which signal that corrective or mitigating actions need to be taken. Other times, they may be more elaborate, involving the aggregation of several individual risk indicators into a multi-dimensional risk score about emerging potential risk exposures. KRIs are typically derived from specific events or root causes, identified internally or externally, that can prevent achievement of strategic objectives. Examples can include items such as the introduction of a new product by a competitor, a strike at a supplier's plant, proposed changes in the regulatory environment, or input-price changes."[4]

Risk triggers and key risk indicators alone are insufficient for decision making as neither can answer a critical question: "What do we get in return for the allocation of our scarce resources?" In other words, what is the return on investment (ROI) for expenditures on risk mitigation? Risk triggers and KRIs are best defined only after the tipping point of a material consequence of a risk or set of risks is understood and specified.

Risk Tolerance, Risk Appetite...
...and tipping point of a material consequence

Executives often encourage their staffs to: "take on more risk," "be more risk-taking," "increase your risk tolerance," or "increase your risk appetite." Unfortunately, most people do not know how to translate those statements into action. The spirit of these statements is understood, but most people are still discovering and learning how to inculcate that type of thinking into their decision making.

The terms "risk appetite" and "risk tolerance" are related but represent distinct concepts. The Committee of Sponsoring Organizations of the Treadway Commission (COSO) defines *risk appetite* as: "the amount of risk, on a broad level, an entity is willing to accept in pursuit of value. It reflects the entity's risk management philosophy, and in turn influences the entity's culture and operating style. ... Risk appetite [assists] in aligning the organization, people, and processes in [designing the] infrastructure necessary to effectively respond to and monitor risks."[5]

---

4   Mark S. Beasly, Bruce C. Branson, Bonnie V. Hancock, "Developing Key Risk Indicators to Strengthen Enterprise Risk Management: How Key Risk Indicators can Sharpen Focus on Emerging Risks," Commissioned by the Committee of Sponsoring Organizations of the Treadway Commission (COSO), December 2010.

5   Dr. Larry Rittenberg and Frank Martens, "Understanding and Communicating Risk Appetite", Commissioned by the Committee of Sponsoring Organizations of the Treadway Commission (COSO), January 2012. page 3.

COSO defines *risk tolerance* as: "related to risk appetite but differing in one fundamental way: risk tolerance represents the application of risk appetite to specific objectives. *Risk tolerance* is defined as: The acceptable level of variation relative to achievement of a specific objective, and often is best measured in the same units as those used to measure the related objective. In setting risk tolerance, management considers the relative importance of the related objective and aligns risk tolerances with risk appetite. Operating within *risk tolerances* helps ensure that the entity remains within its risk appetite and, in turn, that the entity will achieve its objectives. Risk tolerances guide operating units as they implement risk appetite within their sphere of operation. Risk tolerances communicate a degree of flexibility, while risk appetite sets a limit beyond which additional risk should not be taken."[6]

As an example, consider a pharmaceutical company planning to "tech transfer" the manufacture of a drug product from a contract site that is scheduled for closure to an internal manufacturing plant. At the beginning of the year, the executive management communicated their related *risk appetite* with the statement: "We are not comfortable accepting more than a 10% probability that we will incur any lost sales resulting from changes in operations." The tech transfer project team translated the corporation's risk appetite statement into the related *risk tolerance* project statement: "The project team will not accept any risks with a probability of 10% or greater resulting in product lost sales." For the tech transfer project team, the tipping point of a material consequence is the narrative that leads to the lost product sales. For this example, a tech transfer schedule delay of ten weeks or more would result in the depletion of product safety stock leading to a stock out situation resulting in lost sales.

With this definition of the "tipping point of a material consequence," the tech transfer project team performed an FMEA study (see Table 11.2) to determine the probability of the risk occurring, i.e. the probability of lost sales resulting from this tech transfer. The FMEA study concluded that that probability of the tipping point was significantly greater than 10%. Consequently, risk mitigation plans were created. These will be discussed in subsequent chapters of this book.

---

6   Ibid., page 11.

Key Point:

The concept and application of the tipping point of a material consequence provides the narrative-based bridge from Enterprise Risk Management (ERM) concepts such as risk appetite and risk tolerance to investment and action while enabling risk mitigation investments to compete on a level-playing-field with spending on problem resolution and opportunities for improvement.

What are the Choices for the Decision?

This chapter has focused on framing of decisions, but nothing has been provided on how to determine the choices that should compete in answering the question "to act or not to act" for any given problem, risk, or opportunity. The creative work of crafting choices in the face of a decision easily deserves a full book. A common failure mode is considering only one alternative as Heath and Heath referred to as "making a decision like a teenager." To avoid the peril of "decision paralysis" resulting from considering many options, Heath and Heath recommend considering at most two or three options beyond "not to act." They recommend starting with a front-runner option and then considering the question: "What if that option disappeared?" What would your options be then? In PRO Management, each option should be compared against the status quo - "not to act" - to determine the best option. The best option should then compete with other best options of other problems, risks, and opportunities for the limited resources available at this time.

In summary, corporate decision making for problems, risks, and opportunities should be primed on an enterprise-based expected value. They should be made on a risk neutral basis unless the decision is a "bet-the-company" situation, in which case risk-averse decision making is appropriate. Unfortunately, as shown by Prospect Theory, individuals by nature do not make expected value-based decisions. We tend to demonstrate risk-seeking preferences in the realm of losses and risk-averse preferences in the realm of gains. Both of those positions are corporate value-destroying behaviors. Consequently, decision analytics are required to support executives and managers and inform desired risk-neutral decision making. These methods should easily integrate into existing decision processes including the emerging Enterprise Risk Management (ERM) methods.

Key Point:

Organizational decision making should be primed with an enterprise-value perspective and should then consider other value perspectives on a secondary basis.

"Don't be afraid to take a big step when one is indicated.
You can't cross a chasm in two small steps."
– David Lloyd George, Prime Minister of the United Kingdom

12

Narrative-Based Analytics

The Paradox of Business Modeling

The computer simulation and modeling of business performance has become extremely sophisticated and complex. It far outstrips an individual's ability to analyze and comprehend multifaceted situations without these tools. Yet executives routinely dismiss insights generated by complex business models whenever the results are not consistent with their fundamental beliefs about the business. Models are often "tweaked" until their results come into alignment with the executives' thinking. Business modelers have learned that analyses must be transparent in order for executives to embrace the results and act accordingly. Getting to a transparent model often means modeling first-order effects and no more. Moreover, modeling beyond first-order effects and relationships often results in built-in assumptions—at best, educated guesses—that can significantly impact the results of the analysis in not so obvious ways.

What is the bottom-line? In most decision-making situations, modeling business performance at the level of first-order effects is sufficient to generate insights to support high quality decision making. Business performance modeling should be "as simple as possible, but not simpler." It is now time to translate our understanding of neuroscience, cognitive psychology, corporate finance, and mathematics into an easy-to-learn and apply, yet rigorous and robust, decision-making analytical methodology. We will do this by establishing a universal decision-making structure designed to account for all of the key points in this book. The structure also simplifies and minimizes the required number of input parameters for enterprise value-based analysis and enterprise-wide decision making.

A Universal Decision Making Structure
Translating Neuroscience, Cognitive Psychology, Corporate Finance, and Mathematics into a Universal Decision-Making Structure

PRO Enterprise Management makes it possible to obtain the same enterprise decision-making solution (information, algorithms, and process) through four different story-lines based on:

♦ Neuroscience,
♦ Cognitive Psychology,
♦ Corporate Finance, and
♦ Mathematics.

From a *neuroscience* perspective, we know that our innate, hard-wired aversion to loss originates in an older part of our mammalian brain, the amygdala, causing risk-averse decision making and bias towards status quo. Both of these inclinations undermine enterprise value. Consequently, we need a decision-analytic method and decision-making process based on risk neutral (expected value) metrics to counter this ubiquitous value-destroying behavior.

From a *cognitive psychology* perspective, we know the heuristics, biases, and limitations individuals apply in judgment under uncertainty. We have methods for leveraging the strengths of those heuristics and countering their biases and limitations. Consequently, these understandings must be built into our decision-analytic method and decision-making process.

Though decisions are not always made based on long-term enterprise value creation or protection, it is the fiduciary responsibility of all decision makers from a *corporate financial* perspective to at least understand the long-term enterprise value impact and the associated expenditure's return on investment. They need to use this information for priming decision making at the time of decision.

From a *mathematics* perspective, we must employ mathematically sound algorithms and logic based on probability theory and expected value that integrate our understandings from neuroscience, cognitive psychology, and corporate finance.

Revisiting Discounted Net Free Cash Flow

Present value of net free cash flow used as the priming measure for corporate PRO Enterprise Management offers data collection and calculation efficiencies. Although I will not provide the development and mathematical proofs here, it is easy to prove that the delta Net

Present Value (NPV) of annual net free cash flows over *n* years before and after a PRO event/resolution is equal to the NPV of the annual deviations over *n* years. This means that when we use NPV of discounted net free cash flow as our enterprise value measure for problems, risks, and opportunities, we need only account for the *deviations* in cash flow to calculate impact to enterprise value. This provides a powerful and efficient short-cut methodology in estimating value impacts.

To illustrate these concepts, let's start with an example. A pharmaceutical company sells a product that has a gross margin of 90% (defined as gross profit/net sales—not an atypical gross margin for a pharmaceutical company). The company has an effective corporate tax rate of 40%. Working capital at the company runs at about 5% of sales. Table 12.1 provides an example of how lost sales of $200M in 2017 incrementally impacts net free cash flow for that fiscal year.

The 90% gross margin results in an incremental loss in gross profit of $180M. Since there are no incremental changes to any of the expenses or other income, the negative $180M gross profit becomes a net income before tax loss of $180M. Based on the corporate tax rate of 40%, this results in a decrease in corporate taxes of $72M. Adjusting for working capital at about 5% of sales, the net incremental effect to net free cash flow for the loss of $200M in sales is a reduction of $98M in fiscal year 2017.

Unfortunately, the pharmaceutical company is also contemplating additional lost sales for the product of about $100M per year for the years beyond 2017. In terms of real dollars, or 2016 (current year) dollars (as opposed to nominal dollars accounting for inflation), the net free cash flow impact of the lost sales for each of the fiscal years 2018 through 2025 is negative $49M per year.

To calculate the net present value of the cash flow impacts from the lost sales in years 2017 through 2025, we will need to use an appropriate *real, risk-free discount rate* for the pharmaceutical company. In this case, we will use 6% as the real, risk-free discount rate.

Consequently, the enterprise value lost as represented by the net present value of the cash flow impacts for the projected lost sales in years 2017 through 2025 is approximately $380M. Now let's reconsider the pharmaceutical company's lost sales as uncertain and assume that a 10–50–90 Range Assessment was performed as detailed in Chapter 9.

Fiscal Year 2017	$(M)
Gross Sales	(200)
Less: Discounts, Allowances, and Returns	0
Net Sales	(200)
Cost of Goods Sold	(20)
Gross Profit	(180)
Operating Expenses	
Selling Expense	0
General and Administration	0
Total Operating Expenses	0
Operating Profit	(180)
Other Income and Expenses	
Other Income	0
Other Expense	0
Total Other Income and Expense	0
Net Income Before Taxes	(180)
Taxes	(72)
Net Income After Taxes	(108)
Cash Flow Adjustments	
Add Depreciation and Amortization	0
Subtract Capital Investments	0
Subtract Changes in Working Capital	(10)
Cash Flow from Operating Activities	0
Cash Flow from Investing and Financing Activities	0
Total Cash Flow Adjustments	10
Net Free Cash Flow	(98)

Table 12.1: Example of Incremental Impact to Net Free Cash Flow from $200M Loss in Sales in Fiscal Year 2017

The results of the range assessment of lost sales over the years 2017 through 2025 are as follows:

♦ "Surprisingly High" or "Surprisingly Bad" (90th Percentile) lost sales would be lost sales of $300M in 2017 and $150M in the years 2018 through 2025.

♦ "Best Guesstimate" or "50/50" or "Median" (50th Percentile) lost sales would be lost sales of $200M in 2017 and $100M in the years 2018 through 2025.

♦ "Surprisingly Low" or "Surprisingly Good" (10th Percentile) lost sales would be lost sales of $50M in 2017 and $25M in the years 2018 through 2025.

Translating these scenarios into net free cash flow impacts is provided in Tables 12.2 and 12.3 (*note*: only affected items are shown in Tables 12.2 and 12.3).

Fiscal Year 2017	Percentiles ($M)		
	10th	50th	90th
Gross Sales	(50)	(200)	(300)
Less: Discounts, Allowances, and Returns	0	0	0
Net Sales	(50)	(200)	(300)
Cost of Goods Sold	(5)	(20)	(30)
Gross Profit	(45)	(180)	(270)
Operating Expenses	*not affected*		
Operating Profit	(45)	(180)	(270)
Operating Expenses	*not affected*		
Net Income Before Taxes	(45)	(180)	(270)
Taxes	(18)	(72)	(108)
Net Income After Taxes	(27)	(108)	(162)
Cash Flow Adjustments			
Subtract Changes in Working Capital	(2.5)	(10)	(15)
Total Cash Flow Adjustments	(2.5)	(10)	(15)
Net Free Cash Flow	(24.5)	(98)	(147)

Table 12.2: Incremental Impact to Net Free Cash Flow by Range Assessment Scenario for Fiscal Year 2017

The NPV for each of the 10–50–90 scenarios are enterprise losses of $95M, $380M, and $569M respectively. The 10–50–90 scenarios enable us to estimate the continuous distribution of the NPV impacts from uncertain lost sales (or other impacts to COGS, selling expense, etc.) with three data points. (See the discussion on 10–50–90 range assessments in Chapter 4.)

We can now estimate the expected value of the NPV loss:

$$\text{Expected NPV Loss} = (0.25)(95) + (0.50)(380) + (0.25)(569)$$
$$= \$356M$$

Fiscal Year 2017	Percentiles ($M)		
	10th	50th	90th
Gross Sales	(25)	(100)	(150)
Less: Discounts, Allowances, and Returns	0	0	0
Net Sales	(25)	(100)	(150)
Cost of Goods Sold	(2.5)	(10)	(15)
Gross Profit	(22.5)	(90)	(135)
Operating Expenses	*not affected*		
Operating Profit	(22.5)	(90)	(135)
Operating Expenses	*not affected*		
Net Income Before Taxes	(22.5)	(90)	(135)
Taxes	(9)	(36)	(54)
Net Income After Taxes	(13.5)	(54)	(81)
Cash Flow Adjustments			
Subtract Changes in Working Capital	(1.25)	(5)	(7.5)
Total Cash Flow Adjustments	(1.25)	(5)	(7.5)
Net Free Cash Flow	(12.25)	(49)	(73.5)

Table 12.3: Incremental Impact to Net Free Cash Flow by Range Assessment Scenario for Fiscal Years 2018 through 2025

In this example, we examined how uncertain impacts over time to a line item in the corporation's income statement (sales) translated into an expected net present value loss for the enterprise. We used the concept of 10–50–90 scenarios to account for the uncertainty in sales. However, the 10–50–90 scenarios can also be used in more complex situations to account for any number of income statement line items.

By simply focusing on the three 10–50–90 scenarios and considering each income statement line item as a part of a coherent and comprehensive 10–50–90 scenario, we can estimate the expected net present value impact of any combination of income statement items. In effect, we are performing a direct assessment of the continuous probability distribution of the net present value of net free cash flow given a tipping point has occurred. In doing so, we have bypassed the typical and often naive numerical assumptions of statistical independence and dependence of potentially numerous modeling variables. Any insight regarding dependence of variables should be built into the *coherent* assessment.[1] When models are available, all that will be required as output are the 10–50–90 net present values as detailed above.

As humans, we think and form beliefs in terms of narratives (scenarios). This approach provides the underlying mathematics to enable *framing* discussions regarding resolving problems, mitigating risks, and capturing opportunities. We will base these discussions on narratives—a critically needed efficiency in corporations—because the vast majority of decisions cannot be automated. As important, the approach preserves the requirement of making decisions based on the expected value of enterprise value creation or protection.

---

1   Probability is a very subtle and often non-intuitive discipline that when applied must be based on often subtle assumptions of statistical independence or statistical dependence of events, situations, or outcomes. The subtlety of statistical dependence is that two or more variables or parameters can be statistically dependent but not have a causal relationship. As discussed in Chapter 6, the human brain is designed to predict—which is a critical survival skill. Understanding causality enables prediction. Unfortunately, causality is over-applied in our thinking, which leads to erroneous beliefs and faulty decision making. Conversely, we misrepresent statistically dependent relationships that are not causal as independent because we tend to equate causality with statistical dependence in our thinking.

When there are large, typically historical, relevant data sets to draw upon (think of decisions on home loans or internet-based purchases), these statistical relationships can be inferred through statistical analysis and built into predictive models to support decision making. Unfortunately, the vast majority of decisions made in organizations have no such large, relevant data base to draw upon, leaving business analysts no choice but to make assumptions—too often, at best, educated guesses—about the statistical nature of issues, situations, and events in terms of statistical concepts including statistical independence and statistical dependence. By directly assessing the output variable (the net present value of incremental changes in free cash flow) through coherent and comprehensive narratives we can directly include our insights and understandings of dependence without detailed statistical modeling.

Mathematically, the type of probability assessment we are using is called a "Joint Direct Assessment of a Target Variable by Parts". For a detailed description of the approach and the underlying mathematics of estimation errors please see the Decision Empowerment Institute website.

Narrative-Based PRO Management Framing and Assessment

We introduced and discussed the concept of "Sketching the Decision Frame" in Chapter 11 (see Figure 11.1). We also discussed and provided examples of the concept of the "tipping point of a material consequence." We will now extend that discussion to include the comprehensive narrative-based framing of a problem, risk, or opportunity prior to the work of quantification. Figure 12.1 extends the Chapter 11 graphic to include the comprehensive narrative-based framing of a problem, risk, or opportunity.

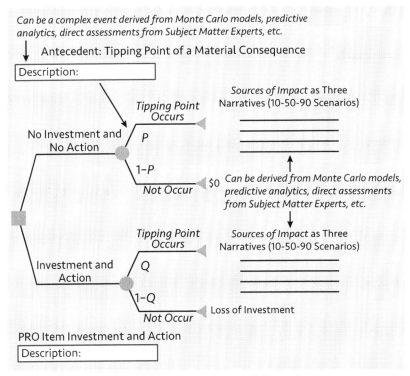

Figure 12.1: Sketching the Decision Frame as a Narrative Prior to Quantification

As indicated in Figure 12.1 and the Chapter 11 examples, the tipping point can be derived from a variety of methods, including Monte Carlo simulations, predictive analytics, FMEA type analyses, or simply through discussions with subject matter experts. It should be noted that we must first clearly define the tipping point and then assess or calculate the probability of its occurrence (P in the upper branch and Q in the lower branch of Figure 12.1). Though the simple graphic in Figure 12.1 has no indication of time, the probabilities used for calculations in PRO Enterprise Management will.

The narrative-based framing approach is designed to focus the initial framing discussion on narratives and scenarios and not get bogged down in simultaneously attempting to quantify the narratives. The separation of the narrative-based framing from quantification enables broader and more efficient participation of management and subject matter experts in the most critical element of PRO Management—PRO item framing—something that is sorely needed in practice throughout organizations.

Here is an example of a *risk* facing a pharmaceutical company.

Example: Stock-out Resulting from Delayed Tech Transfer

It is early 2016 and a pharmaceutical company is in the process of transferring the manufacturing of one of their products to an external manufacturer, a Contract Manufacturing Organization (CMO). This process is called a technology transfer (or tech transfer for short). A tech transfer has very specific requirements on how the transfer is performed and validated to ensure that the product manufactured at the new site is equivalent to the product manufactured at the originating site. Concern is rising over this CMO's ability to complete the tech transfer on schedule. An additional six-month inventory "safety stock" is already approved and built into the overall tech transfer plan and budget. Recent increases in the demand for the product coupled with a delayed tech transfer could result in a stock-out situation. Should the stock-out occur, customers would be lost as physicians change to a competitor's product.

The team starts the risk assessment by identifying the "tipping point of a material consequence." The primary concern is ensuring that the tech transfer is successful and that it is timely enough to ensure no lost sales (or at least minimal lost sales). The tech transfer team has a solid record of completing high quality tech transfers, but the projects also have a history of taking longer than their planned schedules. It is agreed that the tipping point is "a technically sound but delayed tech transfer that results in lost sales."

Given the tipping point occurs, the question now becomes, "What are the sources of impact?" To ensure comprehensive accounting of the sources of impact, we need to consider all of the line items in the income statement. This broad consideration of potential impacts will include the line items in *before* tax, *after* tax, and additional capital spending. Sources of impact (consequences) *before* tax include:

- ◆ Sales,
- ◆ Cost of Goods Sold (COGS),
- ◆ Selling expense,
- ◆ General and administration,
- ◆ Other income, and
- ◆ Other expense.

Sources of impact (consequences) *after* tax include:

- ◆ Cash flow from operating activities (tax impacts can be included here),
- ◆ Cash flow from investing activities, and
- ◆ Cash flow from financing activities.

Capital spending includes:

- ◆ Capital for buildings or land improvement (to be depreciated),
- ◆ Capital for machinery, equipment, or other.

There are three narratives (scenarios) that we will need to contemplate for their sources of impact given the tipping point occurs:

- ◆ The "Surprisingly Bad" or "Surprisingly High" (90th Percentile) Scenario,
- ◆ The "Best Guesstimate" or "Median" (50th Percentile) Scenario, and
- ◆ The "Surprisingly Good" or "Surprisingly Low" (10th Percentile) Scenario.

For reasons detailed in Chapter 9, you should start with either one of the extreme scenarios. I like to start with the most extreme impact scenario, 90th percentile, since the other two scenarios often only have a subset of the line items in the most extreme scenario, or they are a reductive form of the 90th percentile.

The tech transfer project and commercial operations managers review the tech transfer project plan, the inventory for the product including the approved additional safety stock, and the latest sales forecast to determine the potential timing of a product stock-out. They conclude that the potential stock-out would begin impacting sales in fiscal year 2017. They also conclude that, in the absence of any risk mitigation investment and action, there are no other sources of impact.

Considering Figure 12.1, the next step is to specify the investment and action to mitigate the risk of lost sales. The tech transfer team recommends hiring a well-respected outside contractor as a "man-in-the-plant" and building up another four months of safety stock. Providing some additional equipment to expedite test batches off the production line will reduce the overall schedule of the current tech transfer plan. The tech transfer team also recommends that executive management communicate their concerns with the management of the CMO.

The commitment to build up four additional months of safety stock amounts to pulling forward some manufacturing cost (COGS) and then burning off the additional safety stock the following year, thus reducing the manufacturing costs the following year. So the COGS impact has no significant cash flow impact (although this assumption should be challenged and analyzed). At this point, the risk of a *Stock-out Resulting from Delayed Tech Transfer* has been framed and now quantifying the frame is the next step.

The tech transfer project and commercial operations managers assess the probability of the tipping point occurring to be about 0.40. They also believe that the initial year of lost sales would be 2017, if the tipping point occurs. An investment and action plan to mitigate the risk of lost sales is developed. It includes two years of additional labor at $150K per year and purchase, installation, and validation of test equipment for $350K for a total cost of $650K. If this plan is implemented, the tech transfer project and commercial operations managers believe the probability of lost sales, i.e., the tipping point occurring, is reduced from the original assessment of 0.40 to about 0.10 (see Q in Figure 12.1).

The manager from commercial operations performed a 10–50–90 range assessment of the lost sales given the tipping point occurs. Those ranges are shown in Table 12.4 with the initial year being 2017. As an example, the 50th percentile scenario indicates lost sales of $200M in 2017, $100M in 2018, and $100M for years 2019 through the end of the ten-year time horizon. Given the investment and action plan is implemented, the probability of the tipping point occurring is reduced but the impacts given the tipping point occurs remains as depicted in Table 12.4.

Sales ($M)	10th	50th	90th
Initial Year	(50)	(200)	(300)
Second Year	(25)	(100)	(150)
Out Years	(25)	(100)	(150)

Table 12.4: 10–50–90 Incremental Impact Assessment of Sales for the Pharmaceutical Company

A summary of the PRO Management output measures for a single PRO item is presented in Table 12.5 for the Stock-out Resulting from Delayed Tech Transfer risk. This set of measures will be sufficient to answer the five questions of PRO Enterprise Management. The calculations for the numbers in Table 12.5 are detailed in Figures 12.2 and 12.3.

Before Investment and Action	$(M)
Current Year Cash Flow	0
Expected NPV	(142)
90th Percentile NPV	0
10th Percentile NPV	(569)
After Investment and Action	$(M)
Current Year Cash FLow	(0.3)
Expected NPV	(36)
90th Percentile NPV	(0.4)
10th Percentile NPV	(95.3)
Expected Gain (NPV After – NPV Before)	106
Current Year Investment	400
Total Long-term Investment	650
Current Year Investment Productivity	(0.81)
Investment Productivity	167.2

Table 12.5: Example Summary of PRO Management Output Measures for a Single PRO Item

Let's take a closer look at this important set of output measures.

Before Investment and Action

Expected Net Present Value Before Investment and Action represents the expected value of the risk in current year dollars as calculated in the probability tree in Figure 12.2.

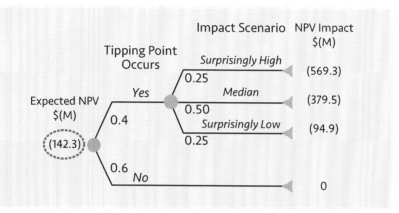

Figure 12.2: Example Expected Net Present Value Calculation Before Investment and Action

From the four discrete NPV Impacts in Figure 12.2, we can estimate the *10th* and *90th Percentile NPV* of the NPV Impact distribution as $(569)M and $0.0M, respectively.[2] Estimating the *10th* and *90th Percentile NPV* would have been more complex if there were multiple years representing the initial year of impact.

After Investment and Action

Expected Net Present Value After Investment and Action represents the expected value of the impact in current year dollars as shown in Figure 12.3. In the case of *After Investment and Action*, we must account for the impacts resulting from the capital expenditures.

The present value of the investment and action plan expenditures is about $0.64M. Since in the After Investment & Action case the risk mitigation spending occurs regardless of whether the risk

---

2   We use the 90th percentile scenario to represent the most extreme departure from the status quo when describing impacts. For losses (problems and risks), this implies the 90th percentile will be the most negative of the three 10-50-90 scenarios. For gains (opportunities), this implies the 90th percentile will be the most positive of the three 10-50-90 scenarios.

However, for the output distribution, the net present value of impacts to changes in net free cash flow, we use the standard convention that the 90th percentile will represent the right-hand tail of the distribution for net losses or net gains in net present value.

occurs or not, we must account for this investment in the cash flows (including depreciation and tax impacts) in all scenarios resulting in the values in Figure 12.3.

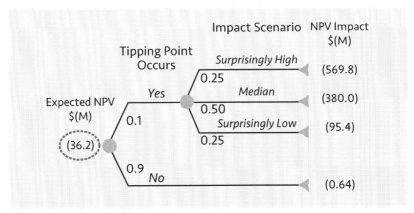

Figure 12.3: Example Expected Net Present Value Calculation After Investment and Action

Using the probability tree in Figure 12.3, we calculate the *Expected Net Present Value of the Risk After Investment and Action* to be about $(36)M. This is a significant reduction compared to the *Before Investment and Action NPV* risk liability of about $(142)M. From the four discrete NPV Impacts in Figure 12.3, we can estimate the *10th* and *90th Percentile NPV* of the NPV Impact distribution as $(95.4)M and $(0.636)M, respectively.

The *Expected Gain* listed in Table 12.5 represents the amount of enterprise value gained (lost) in current dollars resulting from the investment and action. It is calculated as the difference between the *Expected Net Present Value of the Risk* After *Investment and Action* minus *Expected Net Present Value of the Risk* Before *Investment and Action*. In our example, this equates to $(36)M – $(142) = $106M.

Investment Productivity is a return on investment (ROI) or "Bang-for-Buck" measure. It is the ratio of the *Expected Gain* divided by the present value of the investment. In our example, the present value of the $650K investment discounted at 6% is equal to $636K. So the *Investment Productivity* of the investment is about 167. In our example, a simple interpretation of the investment productivity is that every dollar expended on mitigating the risk protects about $167 of enterprise value. This is obviously a very high return on investment!

It is a good practice to check the sensitivity of the results to the probability of the risk occurring. How do the results change if the probability of the risk occurring is as high as 0.70? Or as low as 0.10? Figures 12.4 and 12.5 provide insights into how robust our conclusions are regarding the value of investing to mitigate the risk of Stock-out Resulting from Delayed Tech Transfer.

In Figure 12.4, we see that the NPV of the impact of the risk of Stock-out Resulting from Delayed Tech Transfer is more than $100M if the probability of occurring is greater than 0.30. The NPV impact is above $250M should the probability be greater than 0.70.

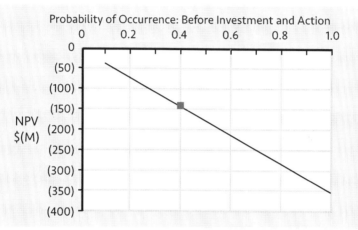

Figure 12.4: Example Sensitivity of Expected NPV to the Probability of Risk Occurring

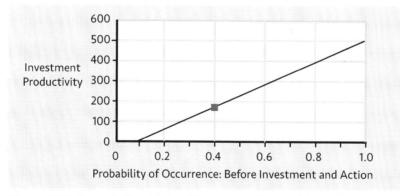

Figure 12.5: Example Sensitivity of Investment Productivity to the Probability of Risk Occurring

In Figure 12.5, we see that the investment productivity is positive if the probability of occurring is greater than 0.1. All of this suggests and gives us confidence that the risk mitigation investment and action is a good bet and should be pursued. Now let's consider a more complex example of narrative-based framing.

Example: System Security Breach of Customer Data Risk

Recent system penetration testing in an IT organization revealed two security vulnerabilities where customer data could potentially be compromised. The vulnerabilities were:

♦ Error message information that can reveal system back doors for hackers, and

♦ Old test application programming interfaces (APIs) that could allow hackers a direct path into the main enterprise resource planning (ERP) system.

The question for management is whether to mitigate the risk these vulnerabilities represent now or wait three years for the planned security system upgrade.

Beyond the potential for lost sales, a breach of customer data would cause several unplanned costs such as:

♦ Forensic examination,

♦ Notification of customers and third parties,

♦ Increased call center costs,

♦ Public relations costs,

♦ Legal defense and potential settlements, and

♦ Federal or state penalties.

If a breach of customer data did occur, the company would most likely immediately install the comprehensive security system upgrades it has planned as a future project.

The Director of Security believes there is a small chance, 5%, of a data breach over the next three years from the "error messages" back-door vulnerability. A breach of customer data from that event would impact consumers of their device products representing 20% of the company's $100M sales per year. The Director of Security believes the exposure of the main ERP system via the old test APIs represents a greater risk with a 10% chance of occurring over the next three years. That type of breach of customer data would potentially impact all customers.

The Director suggested a "patch" that would mitigate both risks and allow the company to proceed with a planned comprehensive security system upgrade in three years. The cost of the system "patch" is $135,000, including $35,000 in purchased software and $100,000 in IT labor.

The "tipping point of a material consequence" is the breach of customer data prior to the change to the security system upgrades. There are two risks in this case: the "error messages" risk and the "old test APIs" risk.

The Director of Security and the IT staff do some research prior to performing the 10–50–90 expense impact assessments summarized in Tables 12.6 and 12.7 for the "errors messages" risk and the "old test APIs" risk, respectively.

Impact	Description	Cost $(000)		
		p10	p50	p90
Forensic Examination	Not pursued.	0	0	0
Third Party Notification	State-by-state notification of only those affected by data breach.	10 ($0.50 each)	30 ($1.50 each)	100 ($5.00 each)
Call Centers	Call number included in notification letter is the company's internal call center, which covers related calls.	0	0	0
Public Relations	No external PR firm hired to address potential damage control.	0	0	0
Legal Defense and Settlements	Class action lawsuit from impacted consumers, including cost of defense and legal settlement.	600	1,500	7,500
Fines, Penalties, and Audits	No federal or state fines, penalties, or required audits are applicable.	0	0	0
Total Other Expenses		610	1,530	7,600

Table 12.6: Summary of the "Other Expense" Impact Assessment for the "Error Messages" Risk

These expenses are impacts that would occur in the year of the risk occurrence. The marketing and sales organization was asked to assess the impact of a data breach on sales. The "error messages" risk only involves device customers, which represents about 20,000 customers and roughly 20% of their total $100M in annual sales. The "old test APIs" risk is associated with all 50,000 customers and the total $100M annual sales. The marketing and sales organization believe that if either risk occurred, they would lose 3% to 5% of the impacted customer base.

Impact	Description	Cost $(000)		
		p10	p50	p90
Forensic Examination	Not pursued.	0	0	0
Third Party Notification	State-by-state notification of only those affected by data breach.	25 ($0.50 each)	75 ($1.50 each)	250 ($5.00 each)
Call Centers	Call number included in notification letter is a third party external call center. Costs are determined by call volume, number of weeks duration, and hours available per day.	30	60	90
Public Relations	PR firm hired to address potential damage control.	60	75	100
Legal Defense and Settlements	Class action lawsuit from impacted consumers, including cost of defense and legal settlement.	1,500	3,750	18,750
Fines, Penalties, and Audits	No federal or state fines, penalties, or required audits are applicable.	0	0	0
Total Other Expenses		1,615	3,960	19,200

Table 12.7: Summary of the "Other Expense" Impact Assessment for the "Old Test APIs" Risk

In this example, the investment to mitigate the risk is $135,000 in IT consulting and software. The impact of an "error messages" data breach is a loss of 3-5% of 20% of $100 million in sales. This represents a loss between $600k and $1,000k (median value = $800k). The probability of this occurring is 5% so the risk exposure (applying the 10-50-90 approach) is an expected value of -$40k.

The impact of an "old APIs" data breach is a loss of 3-5% of $100 million in sales. This represents a potential loss between $3,000k and $5,000k (median value = $4,000k). The probability of this occurring is 10% so the risk exposure is an expected value of -$400k.

Using a probability tree as shown earlier in this chapter with two uncertain events and combining the risks, the total risk exposure for the company is an expected value of $42 million. The investment of $135k mitigates a significant risk to the company and has a very high investment productivity.

Templates for Recurring Problems, Risks, and Opportunities

A critical component of PRO Enterprise Methods is using standardized, reusable templates for analyzing recurring problems, risks, and opportunities. Using templates enables efficiency, business process repeatability, and consistent comparisons based on enterprise value. As an example, risk segmentation (categorization) schemes used in Enterprise Risk Management (ERM) enable broad use of standardized, reusable templates to analyze specific categories of risk efficiently and to ensure consistent comparison of risks based on enterprise value.

Templates can be created for both framing and numerically assessing PRO items. Templates used for numerically assessing PRO items can be as simple or as complex as required. Assessment templates are designed to be either *parametric-based* or *time series-based*. If the impact narratives are individually defined by a coherent set of values for a small set of parameters that span the material consequence, a *parametric-based* template should be used. A *time series-based* template requires values for variables by year as the primary means of defining the impact narratives.

Let's consider a problem/risk framing template with a *parametric-based* assessment template used for clinical trials projects in a pharmaceutical company.

Example: Clinical Trial Enrollment Problem

A cardiovascular drug is scheduled for a phase III clinical trial. Unfortunately, one of the clinical trial sites has developed a troubling enrollment trend; it has a slow initiation and a high patient screening failure rate. Management at the site has been replaced, but the issues appear to be continuing. The company is concerned that the aggressive schedule for the trial is at risk. A back-up site was identified during the planning of the trial, and the question is whether to cancel the trial activities at the troubled site and pursue the back-up site. The risk of keeping the troubled site would be potential additional per patient cost and months of delay to trial completion. If that occurred, it could ultimately delay regulatory approval and initial sales.

For the clinical trial, the troubled site was to enroll 10,000 patients at a total cost of $45,000 per patient. Because of the site difficulties, the latest per-patient cost estimate was revised and increased by a range of $5,000 to $7,500. The scheduled completion was also revised to include a delay of an additional 14 months. The back-up site could enroll the same number of patients for $2,000 to $4,000 more per patient above the original $45,000 per patient cost, but changing over to the new site will cost an additional $13M in capital and expense. Closing the original site and lab would cost about $1.5M. Operating the original site beyond the planned schedule will cost about $200,000 per each additional month beyond the planned schedule. An executive contacted the Clinical Trial Project Manager to evaluate the option of "cutting-over" to the back-up site.

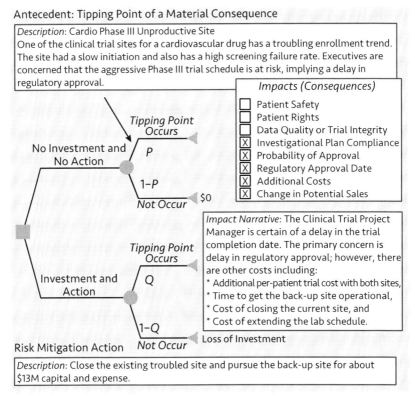

Antecedent: Tipping Point of a Material Consequence

Description: Cardio Phase III Unproductive Site
One of the clinical trial sites for a cardiovascular drug has a troubling enrollment trend. The site had a slow initiation and also has a high screening failure rate. Executives are concerned that the aggressive Phase III trial schedule is at risk, implying a delay in regulatory approval.

Impacts (Consequences)
- [ ] Patient Safety
- [ ] Patient Rights
- [ ] Data Quality or Trial Integrity
- [X] Investigational Plan Compliance
- [X] Probability of Approval
- [X] Regulatory Approval Date
- [X] Additional Costs
- [X] Change in Potential Sales

Impact Narrative: The Clinical Trial Project Manager is certain of a delay in the trial completion date. The primary concern is delay in regulatory approval; however, there are other costs including:
* Additional per-patient trial cost with both sites,
* Time to get the back-up site operational,
* Cost of closing the current site, and
* Cost of extending the lab schedule.

Risk Mitigation Action

Description: Close the existing troubled site and pursue the back-up site for about $13M capital and expense.

Figure 12.6: Example of a Clinical Trial Framing Template

The project manager understood that this was no longer a *risk* of regulatory approval delay; it was a *problem* as approval delay was inevitable if action wasn't taken immediately. But there is more than timing of regulatory approval at stake.

The template and checklist in Figure 12.6 make up the standard framing tool used by the company when assessing problems and risks for clinical trials and provide a summary of the initial framing of the problem. The company has a parametric-based template for defining the 10–50–90 impact narratives including the parameters:

♦ Modified probability of regulatory approval,

♦ Sales reduction as a percentage of current sales forecast,

♦ Months delay/acceleration to initial sales,

♦ Increase/decrease in cost per trial patient, and

♦ Other costs.

The actual template has a few other parameters, but they are not relevant for this example. Figure 12.7 provides the complete framing including the impact narratives defined by a coherent set of numerical values for each of the parameters.

The "Surprisingly Bad" and the "Surprisingly Good" scenarios are intended to represent the 90th and 10th percentile narratives, respectively. Both use net present value of free cash flow over the time horizon. The parametric-based impacts template requires the sales forecast for the drug and the projected gross margins given the planned regulatory approval dates and sales launches (U.S. and EU). The only other inputs to the template are the parameters listed above. Figure 12.7 shows a second method in which to summarize the 10–50–90 impact narratives as opposed to the method provided in Tables 12.6 and 12.7.

As shown in Figure 12.7, while the project team believes the impacts are inevitable, there is uncertainty around the magnitude of the impacts. Consequently, the probability of occurrence is 1.0 for both the *before investment and action* and *after investment and action* cases.

"Pay Now" versus "Maybe Pay More Later"

Many problems, risks, and opportunities have the pattern of "pay now" vs. "maybe pay more later." Aerospace and defense contractors regularly face this class of risk in their contract programs.

Example: Late Testing of System Component Risk

Let's consider an example for an aerospace/defense contractor. Built into the baseline cost and schedule of an on-going program is the

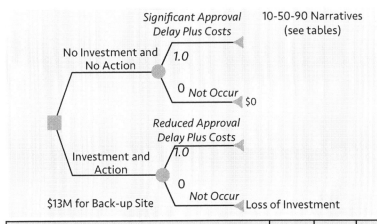

Before Investment and Action	10th	50th	90th
Probability of Approval - US	0.95	0.95	0.9
Probability of Approval - EU	0.95	0.95	0.9
Sales Reduction - US	0%	10%	15%
Sales Reduction - EU	0%	10%	15%
Months Delay to Initial Sales - US	6	8	14
Months Delay to Initial Sales - EU	6	6	12
Increased Cost per Trial Patient ($000)	5.5	6.0	7.5
Extend US Laboratory Operations ($000)	1,200	1,600	2,800
After Investment and Action	10th	50th	90th
Probability of Approval - US	0.95	0.95	0.95
Probability of Approval - EU	0.95	0.95	0.95
Sales Reduction - US	0%	10%	15%
Sales Reduction - EU	0%	10%	15%
Months Delay to Initial Sales - US	-1	1	2
Months Delay to Initial Sales - EU	-1	1	2
Increased Cost per Trial Patient ($000)	2.0	3.0	4.0
Extend US Laboratory Operations ($000)	1,500	1,500	1,500

Figure 12.7: Example of a Clinical Trial Framing Template with Impact Narratives Completed

assumption that an existing design for a component can be used in a new application by testing it in a different environment. This could be a risky assumption, and as Peter Drucker said, "Erroneous assumptions can be disastrous."[3]

The timing of the component test is scheduled to take place in about 24 months as it depends upon the completion of other tasks and milestones. There is a risk that the component will fail the test in the new environment, which would require the component to be redesigned and retested. Testing the component early, about 18 months ahead of schedule, increases the cost of the test, but it would allow for redesign and retest efforts should it fail. Conversely, if the test takes place as planned in 24 months and the component fails, the cost impact will be much higher. In this case the redesign and retest will be on the program critical path and will cost much more to avoid a project delay.

There is also an $800M follow-on contract scheduled to be awarded in 2019. Given that the aerospace/defense contractor performs well on quality, schedule, and budget for the current program, their chances of winning the follow-on contract are estimated at 80%, if the program is awarded. The follow-on contract is already included in the company's sales forecast. However, budget overruns and schedule delays will lower their chances of capturing the subsequent contract.

The aerospace/defense contractor has a *parametric-based* risk assessment template that enables both *program-only* impacts and an *enterprise* impacts frame. As per the company's program management processes, program staff must assess risks with both frames prior to the allocation of risk mitigation resources. The program risk assessment template has several *program-only* impact categories with the following four relevant to this risk:

- Program cost impact,
- Weeks added to critical path of program schedule,
- Level-of-Effort (LOE) labor costs per additional critical path week, and
- Other program costs.

The Program Risk Manager has worked with the relevant program stakeholders to assess the risk of the component failing testing. Table 12.8 provides the *program-only parametric-based* impacts assessment given the program continues with component testing in

---

3   Peter F. Drucker with Joseph A. Maciariello, *The Daily Drucker: 366 Days of Insight and Motivation for Getting the Right Things Done* (New York, New York: Routledge, 2011), page 2 (November).

about 24 months (*before investment and action*) and the component fails testing. Table 12.9 provides the impact assessment given the program pursues early testing of the component, and the component fails the early testing (*after investment and action*).

Impact	Description	Impact Value		
		p10	p50	p90
Cost of Redesign and Retest ($K)	Redesign and retest performed about 24 months from now.	$400 and 4 months	$500 and 5 months	$600 and 6 months
Weeks added to critical path Program schedule	Ability to overlap some component and system testing.	12 weeks; some overlap	16 weeks; minor overlap	24 weeks; no overlap
LOE labor costs per additional critical path week ($K)	Requires software test and quality assurance staff	$70	$80 (add system test)	$100 (add software)
Other Program costs ($K)	Corporate allocated lab costs	600	800	1,200

*Table 12.8: Program-Only Parametric-Based Impacts Assessment Given Component Fails Testing in 24 Months (*Before *Investment and Action)*

Impact	Description	Impact Value		
		p10	p50	p90
Cost of Redesign and Retest ($K)	Redesign and retest performed about 6 months from now.	$400 and 4 months	$500 and 5 months	$600 and 6 months
Weeks added to critical path Program schedule	Ability to overlap some component and system testing.	0	2 (minor impact)	4
LOE labor costs per additional critical path week ($K)	Requires software test and quality assurance staff	$70	$80 (add system test)	$100 (add software)
Other Program costs ($K)	Corporate allocated lab costs	0	100	200

*Table 12.9: Program-Only Parametric-Based Impacts Assessment Given Component Fails Early Testing (*After *Investment and Action)*

As per corporate policy, the program must also include an *enterprise impacts* assessment. *Enterprise impacts* include impacts to future program sales. In this case, the potentially impacted future program sale is the immediate $800M follow-on program. Corporate has a standard *parametric-based* impacts assessment template that consists of the following four types of impact:

♦ Change in future program award year,
♦ Change in future program probability of award,
♦ Change in future program probability of win given program award, and
♦ Change in future program award value.

The Program Risk Manager has worked with program management, marketing, and sales staff to assess the potential impacts to the follow-on program. Table 12.10 provides the *enterprise parametric-based* impacts assessment given the program continues with component testing in about 24 months (*before investment and action*) and the component fails testing. Table 12.11 provides the enterprise impact assessment given the program pursues early testing of the component and the component fails the early testing (*after investment and action*).

Impact	Description	Impact Value		
		p10	p50	p90
Future Program Award Year	Year	2019	2019	2020
Future Program Probability of Award	% (as currently forecast)	90%	90%	90%
Future Program Probability of Win Given Award	%	80%	70%	50%
Future Program Award Value	($M) (as currently forecast)	800	800	800

Table 12.10: Enterprise Parametric-Based Impacts Assessment Given Component Fails Testing in 24 Months (Before Investment and Action)

Impact	Description	Impact Value		
		p10	p50	p90
Future Program Award Year	Year	2019	2019	2020
Future Program Probability of Award	% (as currently forecast)	90%	90%	90%
Future Program Probability of Win Given Award	%	80%	80%	70%
Future Program Award Value	($M) (as currently forecast)	800	800	800

Table 12.11: Enterprise Parametric-Based Impacts Assessment Given Component Fails Early Testing (After Investment and Action)

Table 12.12 summarizes the risk evaluation from a program and an enterprise perspective. The evaluation includes both the COGS impacts and the sales impacts. The *investment productivity* of changing the test schedule is about 1.41—a productive use of the program's resources.

Before Investment and Action	$(K)
Current Year Cash Flow	0
Expected NPV	(432)
90th Percentile NPV	0
10th Percentile NPV	(1,870)
After Investment and Action	**$(K)**
Current Year Cash FLow	(150)
Expected NPV	(220)
90th Percentile NPV	(90)
10th Percentile NPV	(537)
Expected Gain (NPV After – NPV Before)	211
Current Year Investment	0
Total Long-term Investment	150
Current Year Investment Productivity	(1.0)
Investment Productivity	1.41

Table 12.12: Summary PRO Evaluation for Testing the Component Early

The Program Risk Manager also evaluated the risk and risk mitigation plan from a *program-only* perspective (only accounting for the COGS impacts). The investment productivity from a *program-only* perspective is also positive at 0.69. Of course, this expenditure should be compared with other current PRO items under consideration to truly determine whether this expenditure is as productive as other incremental program expenditures. An important question for the aerospace/defense contractor is, what is the corporate policy when a risk has a positive investment productivity for the enterprise but a negative investment productivity for the program?

Data Derived Impact Assessments

When relevant data is available for populating narrative-based analytics, it is straightforward to translate data into the standard PRO

Management structures. Recall that in Chapter 11 we introduced the notion of assessing the probability of a tipping point from a set of data for a satellite manufacturer.

Example: A Satellite Manufacturer's Labor Bid for a Competitive Contract

In the Chapter 11 example, the satellite manufacturer executives had asked a proposal team to determine the appropriate number of total labor hours to include in a bid to be competitive. Based on the historical data from 25 similar programs, the proposal team determined that 9 of the 25 programs required more than 85,000 hours of labor. This suggested that there was a 36% chance that the new program might require more than 85,000 hours (9 divided by 25). Table 12.13 presents the "total labor hours" data introduced in Chapter 11, only this time the data is ordered in ascending order from least to greatest number of hours required to complete a satellite program.

Program	Total Hours	Program	Total Hours
PRS 4	49,551	Conditional Probability Distribution Given that Tipping Point has Occurred	
LEGES	51,221	YUE 4	86,490
MORP	51,738	SUPL-Q	87,000
PRS 2	52,859	YUE 2	92,652
XRS 8	54,001	YUE 3	92,652
TYPHON	57,185	XCALIB	96,456
PRS 3	58,001	XRS 6	97,001
SUPL-R	61,345	YUE 1	106,217
PRS 5	67,084	XQRAD-A	131,634
PRS 1	69,838	XRS 5	143,001
TELOQ	75,175		
OPRAND	75,175		
XQRAD-B	75,282		
OPRAND 2	78,234		
XRS 7	81,501		
DENTRO	83,765		

Table 12.13: Historical Total Labor Hours to Complete a Satellite Program (in Ascending Order)

The nine programs highlighted in the right side of Table 12.13 provide the set of total labor hours given that the tipping point of requiring more than 85,000 hours of total labor has occurred. This set can be associated with a discrete approximation of the *conditional probability distribution* of beyond the tipping point occurrences.

A narrative-based impacts assessment given the tipping point has occurred would be based upon the conditional probability distribution of total labor hours greater than 85,000 hours. To translate the information in the discrete approximation of the distribution into a 10–50–90 set of narratives requires determining the 10th, 50th, and 90th percentiles of the data set. In MS Excel, this can be done with the "Percentile" statistical function.

In this case, we will use a PRO Enterprise Management template that calculates the probability of the tipping point and the 10th, 50th, and 90th percentiles of the underlying conditional probability distribution given the tipping point has occurred. The approximated 10th, 50th, and 90th percentiles of the total labor hours are 86,898; 96,456; and 133,907 hours, respectively. These numbers would populate another impacts template that would calculate the associated program cost as a Cost of Goods Sold (COGS) impact.

Monte Carlo Methods and Other Approaches for PRO Management Input

The outputs of a variety of analytical approaches are easily translated into the standard PRO Management input structures. Methods such as Monte Carlo models, predictive analytics, failure mode and effects analysis (FMEA), fault tree analysis, statistical analyses, and a variety of other methods can be used in concert with PRO Management analysis. Other analytical methods can help you find and quantify tipping points and assess narrative-based 10–50–90 impacts.

As an example, Monte Carlo models can calculate the probability of a tipping point based on a set of parameters that have a complex set of statistical relationships. The great benefit of using Monte Carlo models is their ability to estimate probability distributions for virtually any parameter as a function of input parameters. Moreover, given the estimated probability distribution of an output parameter, the Monte Carlo application can provide the 10th, 50th, and 90th percentiles of the distribution. This summary probability distribution information fits directly within the PRO Management input structure. The same is true for other predictive analytics methods and software applications. See Appendix 3 for a comparison of Monte Carlo methods and other methods to the direct assessment approach of PRO Enterprise Management.

A "Cost Savings" and "Cost Avoidance" Fallacy

A common mistake in continuous improvement initiatives and six sigma projects is measuring "cost savings" and "cost avoidance" for eliminating or reducing work performed by employees. If you eliminate or reduce the work associated with a specific task of a full-time employee, the value is likely not current year cost savings but rather the value-add of the work that fills in the available time. Or, if you avoided future hiring because of the work elimination, then that would be a true future cost savings equivalent to the fully burdened cost of a new hire. The fundamental test is whether the corporation's income statement for costs changes because of the work reduction. If the corporate income statement has not changed, then ultimately there has been neither effective cost savings nor cost avoidance.

Black Swans and the Antifragile

Some believe humans are incapable of assessing the probability of a tipping point and sizing the related consequences, and that to do so is folly. The more fundamental issue is that we make decisions based on our subconscious considerations of both likelihood and consequence. We can't help it. To ignore or attempt to bypass the operating system of the human brain is the true folly as long as humans have the final say in decision making. Let's reconsider Nassim Taleb's concept of Black Swans as an example.

Nassim Taleb has provided several important, iconoclastic insights into business thinking that are captured in his books *The Black Swan* and *Antifragile*. According to Taleb, "Black Swans (capitalized) are large-scale unpredictable and irregular events of massive consequence—unpredicted by a certain observer, and such unpredictor is generally called the 'turkey' when he is both surprised and harmed by these events."[4]

Further clarifying the concern with Black Swans, Taleb states: "An annoying aspect of the Black Swan problem—in fact the central, and largely missed, point—is that the odds of rare events are simply not computable. We know a lot less about hundred-year floods than five-year floods—model error swells when it comes to

4   Nassim Nicholas Taleb, *Antifragile: Things That Gain from Disorder* (New York: Random House, Inc., 2012), page 6.

small probabilities. *The rarer the event, the less tractable, and the less we know about how frequent its occurrence*—yet the rarer the event, the more confident these 'scientists' involved in predicting, modeling, and using POWERPOINT in conferences with equations in multicolor background have become."[5] Taleb raises concerns about the psychological and cognitive biases at play and the significant role of "hindsight bias" in rationalizing Black Swans once they have occurred (see Chapter 8 for the definition of "hindsight bias").

Taleb's antidote to Black Swans is the concept of *antifragility*. "Antifragility is beyond resilience or robustness. The resilient resists shocks and stays the same; the antifragile gets better ... It is far easier to figure out if something is fragile than to predict the occurrence of an event that may harm it. Fragility can be measured; risk is not measurable (outside of casinos or the minds of people who call themselves 'risk experts'). This provides a solution to what I've called the Black Swan problem—the impossibility of calculating the risks of consequential rare events and predicting their occurrence. Sensitivity to harm from volatility is tractable, more so than forecasting the event that would cause the harm. So we propose to stand our current approaches to prediction, prognostication, and risk management on their heads."[6]

The truth of the matter regarding the management of business risk is that you need both:

♦ The ability to assess and make decisions about mitigating risk based on the productivity options of the resources required to mitigate risk, and

♦ The ability to understand how antifragility applies to your business.

We need to build antifragility into the business as either a "must-have" expenditure or based on the careful assessment of the alternative uses of the resources required to attain some defined degree of antifragility.

When you dig into the details of compliance, there is always the fundamental issue of cost-of-compliance vs. degree-of-compliance. The concept of antifragility has the analogous issue. We must consider to what degree we build antifragility into the business and the cost based upon some measurable benefit. As with all business expenditures, enterprise investment productivity should be considered for issues regarding compliance as well as antifragility.

---

5   Ibid, page 7.

6   Ibid, pages 3-5.

Taleb argues that *the* odds (probability) of a rare event are "not computable." The fact is, in most cases of interest, it doesn't even exist. From a Bayesian perspective, probability merely represents the degree to which an individual or group believes a statement to be true based on their current beliefs (see Chapter 4). All probability does is provide clarity in expressing our beliefs—both knowledge-based and faith-based—numerically enabling comparison of expenditures based on best-value from the perspective of an individual, organization, community, or enterprise. Regarding small probability events (including Black Swans), you should never believe that you or experts know the probability of occurrence. But you can work to get an approximate assessment of the probability, based on all the historical data and other relevant insights available through analysis and subject matter expertise. Only then can you have a high quality discussion and make a high quality decision on expenditures to mitigate the negative consequences of a rare event.

While the concepts of Black Swans and antifragility are significant contributions to business management, they alone do not solve the fundamental enterprise-level PRO Dilemma: among competing and sometimes conflicting investments across problems, risks, and opportunities, how can you determine which investments should be funded to create or protect the most value?

The PRO Enterprise Management Advantage

To achieve a truly PRO Enterprise Management solution, a universal decision-making analytical structure is required to enable consistent comparison of problems, risks, and opportunities. For the first time, a single set of structures (patterns) applicable to problems, risks, and opportunities is provided. Traditional probability-based models (e.g., Monte Carlo Models) must directly address the subtle issues of statistical independence and dependence to ensure the models are mathematically sound. Unfortunately, this is difficult and variables often have conditional dependencies that are unknown and are consequently overlooked or ignored.

An alternative to these complex models is to think in the more natural terms of comprehensive scenarios or narratives and to perform direct assessments on the scenarios. This bypasses the complexities inherent in probability modeling. When more complex probability-based models exist or are desired, their results can be translated into the standard PRO Enterprise Management structures.

When relevant information and data exists, we want to leverage it. As suggested in Figure 12.1, we want to leverage all sources of information and data that resides in information systems, predictive analytics, and subject matter experts. We need to refine and structure this data with regard to specific problems, risks, and opportunities. An important advantage in the PRO Enterprise Management approach is the narrative-based framing as depicted in Figure 12.1. Be careful though: quantifying outcomes and impacts during the PRO framing process interferes with the critical mental activity of defining the 10–50–90 scenarios in terms of sources of impact that span the outcomes. The work of quantifying the sources of impact associated with the 10–50–90 scenarios should be separated from the work of describing the scenarios. This enables more efficient, more effective, and more natural framing discussions that all individuals, including executives, can participate in and understand. Quantifying the sources of impact in the 10–50–90 scenarios can be assigned and constructed apart from the framing activity. The lack of this separation in framing and quantifying is a common failure mode in the current practice of risk assessment and management across industries.

A foundational and pervasive axiom in PRO Enterprise Management method is that we think in terms of *patterns*. One set of *thought patterns* is how we think of and frame specific types of problems, risks, or opportunities. These thought and decision-framing patterns, often codified into business processes, inherently become beliefs; in turn, these beliefs dictate our decision making. A goal of PRO Enterprise Management is to identify existing, sometimes deeply embedded and often flawed decision-framing patterns that compromise or destroy enterprise value, and then to replace them with risk-neutral, enterprise-based, value maximizing decision-framing patterns that ultimately will employ narrative-based analytics for their evaluation.

According to Peter Senge, *learning organizations* are "organizations where people continually expand their capacity to create the results they truly desire, where new and expansive patterns of thinking are nurtured, where collective aspiration is set free, and where people are continually learning to see the whole together."[7] *Decision empowerment* (as defined in Chapter 2) coupled with PRO

---

7   Peter M. Senge, *The Fifth Discipline: The Art & Practice of the Learning Organization* (New York: Doubleday/Random House, Inc., 1990, 2006) page 1.

Enterprise Management methods are key enablers of Senge's vision for a learning organization. Improving patterns of thinking and ultimately decision making from the perspective of the *enterprise as the whole* is the essence of PRO Enterprise Management. For the first time, the approach leverages and integrates four different yet critical underpinnings of decision making:

- ◆ Neuroscience,
- ◆ Cognitive psychology,
- ◆ Corporate finance, and
- ◆ Mathematics.

In this chapter, we have introduced an efficient and effective standard practice for assessing and analyzing corporate decisions for problems, risks, and opportunities from a risk-neutral, enterprise-value based perspective.

"On an important decision one rarely has 100% of the information needed for a good decision no matter how much one spends or how long one waits. And, if one waits too long, he has a different problem and has to start all over. This is the terrible dilemma of the hesitant decision maker."
– Robert K. Greenleaf, Founder of the Center for Servant Leadership

13
Five Questions to Resolve the PRO Dilemma

Both in your personal life and your professional life, at any point in time, you own a portfolio of problems, risks, and opportunities—a *PRO Portfolio*. Consequently, at any point in time, you personally face (on at least two fronts) the challenge of the *PRO Dilemma*: among competing and sometimes conflicting commitments of time and money across problems, risks, and opportunities, how can you determine which commitments should be pursued at this point in time, based on creating or protecting the most value? Due to limited resources—time and money—you have to choose which PRO items to pursue. You can have *anything*, but you can't have *everything*. You have to choose.

It sounds daunting, yet isn't this in effect what you are doing on a regular basis anyway? Or at least what you *should* be doing? How well do you manage your *personal* PRO portfolio? How well do you manage your *professional* PRO portfolio? How well do you manage your *organization's* PRO portfolio? How well do you contribute to the management of your *corporation's* PRO enterprise portfolio? For most of us (if not all of us), there is significant room for improvement. And if you are what Greenleaf calls a "hesitant decision maker," it only intensifies the challenge of the *PRO Dilemma*.

Key Point: the *PRO Dilemma*

> Among competing and sometimes conflicting commitments of time and money across problems, risks, and opportunities, which commitments should be pursued at this point in time, based on creating or protecting the most value?

When left to our own devices, human behavior is fairly consistent. You can thank the development of the mammalian brain, and subsequently, the human brain for that (as we explored in Chapter 6). Primarily due to immediacy and potential for loss, we expend most attention and resources on problem resolution. Opportunity pursuits usually come in a distant second, and risk mitigation limps along in last place for attention and resource allocation. Like individuals, organizations have the same mindset for priority order when it comes to resource allocation across problems, risks, and opportunities. Humans evolved to the current state of PRO portfolio decision-making behaviors and capabilities (and so too did organizations).

When it comes to PRO management, the way corporations run today has everything to do with how corporations evolved, especially for older corporations. Early in the evolution of corporate management, Dupont provided an important PRO management breakthrough. In the early 1900s, companies were centrally controlled. During that period, Dupont transitioned from a single activity firm—making gunpowder—to becoming a chemical company with an increasingly wide range of products. Single-activity firms ignored how capital was used. As problems emerged they were recognized and resolved, often through standard procedures but with limited or no financial notion of cost-benefit. Beyond *problem* resolution, the focus was on gaining operational efficiency, which we call *opportunities*. But again, there was no rigorous notion of cost-benefit in making decisions on which operational efficiencies to pursue.

It became clear that a financially driven approach to managing investments and expenditures was required for the emerging, multi-activity corporations like Dupont. In these firms, management had to decide how to allocate capital against competing activities, some of which were more valuable than others given the firm's changing competitive situation. While the efficient and effective management of capital became a primary objective of the firm, there were no good solutions to achieving that objective. Ultimately, the question facing Dupont was, "How do we get the best value from limited resources?" It took nearly twenty years, but Dupont finally developed in 1919 the basic return on investment (ROI) formulation and calculation that is still in use today for capital investments. Not until this management breakthrough did these emerging corporations begin to move beyond problem management to problem *and* opportunity management (albeit not in an integrated way).

Though the practice of risk management in the form of insurance contracts dates back to at least the 14th century in Genoa with more sophisticated and specialized contracts emerging in 17th century London, its broader role in corporations did not emerge until well after World War II. Crockford,[1] and Harrington and Neihaus pinpoint the emergence of modern risk management to the decade of 1955-1964.[2] The primary emphasis in this period and for several decades thereafter was on the insurable type of risk, *pure risk*, with inroads slowly being made into *speculative risk*, both being managed separately from each other, and separately from problem and opportunity management.

Why the PRO Dilemma Remains Unresolved in Business and Beyond

In business and other formal organizations (including governmental entities and non-profit organizations), problems, risks, and opportunities (PRO items) are evaluated and managed separately. This is true at the enterprise, business unit, plant, function, and project levels. Universally, problems are managed best, with opportunity and risk management lagging sorely behind. This separation in management creates several critical, costly issues:

♦ It creates duplicative and conflicting efforts (businesses often have formal problem management processes or escalators and separate risk management functions with overlapping watch lists that are managed separately by different staff, resulting in confusion on who is responsible for what).

♦ It results in "stovepipe-based solutions" (each function of the business that employs risk management has its own unique risk management measurement system, language, and decision-making process).

---

1   G. Neil Crockford, The Bibliography and History of Risk Management: Some Preliminary Observations, The Geneva Papers on Risk and Insurance, 7 (1982), pages 169-179.

2   Scott Harrington and Gregory Niehaus, *Risk Management and Insurance* (New York, New York: Irwin/McGraw-Hill U.S.A., 2003).

- ◆ It results in an incomplete and misleading budgeting context as the thinking and understanding associated with problems, risks, and opportunities varies from none to inadequate.
- ◆ It results in unidentified alternatives.
- ◆ Ultimately, it results in the misallocation of resources due to under-informed decision makers with regard to an up-to-date and prospective understanding of problems, risks, and opportunities.

Separate measurement and management of problems, risks, and opportunities ensures that the PRO Dilemma remains unresolved.

Three Requirements to Resolve the PRO Dilemma

There are at least three enablers that must be in place to resolve the PRO Dilemma:

Create a Consistent Basis of Comparison

Problems, risks, and opportunities must be managed together and their management integrated into business and decision processes. Consistency in *measuring* their magnitudes, resource requirements, costs, and benefits enables direct comparisons of problems, risks, and opportunities across the enterprise. Consistency in *evaluating* the impacts of action and inaction is also required to enable direct comparisons.

Separate "Must-Haves" from "Like-to-Haves"

Clear articulation of "must-have" spends must exist, be well-documented and communicated, and be adhered to across the enterprise, including business unit, plant, function, and project levels. Must-haves include things such as resources required to:

- ◆ Implement past decisions,
- ◆ Ensure proper maintenance of facilities and operations,
- ◆ Operate safely,
- ◆ Sustain business operations, and
- ◆ Ensure quality and compliance requirements are met.

Must-haves also include things below a specified cost or schedule threshold that are considered discretionary to the responsible manager. Must-haves are expenditures that should not compete for the limited resources because they are expenditures the business must pursue to ensure the overall business is viable.

In short, "like-to-haves" include all expenditures not categorized as must-haves. Like-to-have PRO items must compete for resource allocation with all of the enterprise's other like-to-have expenditures, based on best value to the enterprise. Management must specify the triage guidelines that determine which PRO items should be treated as must-haves and which require evaluation as a like-to-have to compete for limited resources. Too many PRO items categorized as must-haves will erode the ultimate value of the enterprise. Too many PRO items categorized as "require evaluation" will paralyze the decision making in the business. Each organization must work to keep the list of must-haves as small as possible through policy and guidelines specific to the organization's domain. This entails minimizing "earmarking," "rubber stamping," and "shoehorning" things into organizational spending and budgets.

Measure "Best Value" Accounting for the Return on Committed Resources

The measurement of "best value" accounting for the return on committed resources used throughout this book is investment productivity as defined in Chapter 12. If another measure for best value is to be used it should be able to account for:

- All sources of and magnitudes of value and cost,
- Value trade-offs (some as straightforward as sales versus profit margins, with others more subtle such as cost of compliance versus degree of compliance, or cost of safety versus degree of safety),
- Time preference, that is, the value of having something today versus having it in the future,
- All sources of uncertainty associated with getting the value sought, and
- Both value creation and value protection.

Resolving the *PRO Dilemma* is a significant improvement in corporate management and corporate decision making.

PRO Management: an Essential Component of Budgeting Processes

PRO Management should be an ongoing activity in all organizations at all levels of the enterprise. However, PRO Management is an *es-*

sential component of all budgeting processes. Figure 13.1 illustrates the ongoing relationship of PRO items and planning, budgeting, and execution. PRO items should be considered at the outset of a planning and budgeting cycle, and emerging PRO items should directly influence the modification of budgets once budgets become sales and operating plans, or capital plans, or project plans.

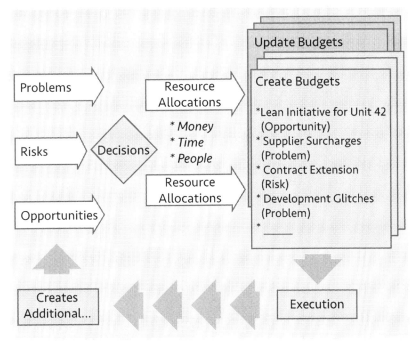

Figure 13.1: The Ongoing Relationship of PRO Items and Planning, Budgeting, and Execution

Every planning and budgeting process—including continuous budgeting processes and rolling budgets—should enable input on current and prospective problems, risks, and opportunities. This input should include both top-down and bottom-up perspectives. The bottom-up perspective should come from the front lines of the business and influence budget size and allocation, whereas the top-down perspective should provide the broader, "big picture" view including the clear articulation of must-haves. The final plan and budget should ensure that both perspectives are contemplated, resulting in a strong plan and budget as measured in potential enterprise value creation and protection. Consequently, the *deliberate strategy* of the enterprise (as defined in Chapter 3) must contemplate the problems *and* risks *and* opportunities facing the enterprise as a *whole*.

The capital budget is of particular importance when it comes to considering how to address problems, risks, and opportunities. Capital is often considered from three perspectives:

♦ Capital for operations and maintenance,
♦ Additional capital for improvement opportunities initiated in the current or previous year, and
♦ Capital for improvement opportunities to be initiated in the coming year.

Capital projects for improvement opportunities typically require a return on investment (ROI) evaluation to support determining which capital projects provide a sufficient return and create the most value for the organization. The ROI evaluation is part of the process in determining the capital project portfolio for the near term. Capital expenditures on operations and maintenance do not require an ROI evaluation since they are considered as must-haves. The capital budgeting process, as all budgeting processes, should enable consideration of all current and prospective problems, risks, and opportunities. In most organizations, the capital budgeting process does address operational problems and efficiency, and growth opportunities; however, few organizations directly attempt to address mitigating risks.

In all planning and budgeting processes, must-haves require clear articulation at the outset of the process. Based on policy statements from the Board of Directors, executives, and management, must-haves guidance is how management assert their influence based on strategy, values, beliefs, wisdom, risk tolerance, and overall perspective on the direction of the enterprise. Once must-haves are identified, they are dealt with as the top priority, with implementation based on cost-efficiency while ensuring must-haves are satisfactorily achieved. Must-have policy must provide enough emphasis and clarity that decision makers can distinguish between must-have PRO items and those that must compete for resource allocation based on value. Must-have policy applies to every organization and function.

PRO Management and Strategic Budget Cutting

"Doing more with less," "tightening our belts," and "sharpening our pencils" are all euphemisms for a seemingly constant message from today's executives to management—cut your budget or cut your spending. Unfortunately, budget cutting is rarely done well with respect to enterprise value. In the U.S. federal government, the *Budget Control Act of 2011* established evenly split cuts as measured in dollars to defense spending and non-defense spending (referred to as budget sequestration). Corporate executives often give directives such as "all departments must reduce their operating budgets by 5%." No one for a moment believes that these are smart ways to cut budgets—underscored by the hallway grumbling of managers—yet these simple evenly-spread approaches have an air of fairness and are the standard practice in corporate and governmental budget-cutting. Organizations have vastly different flexibility in absorbing budget cuts. Shouldn't that be a consideration as well?

Strategic budget cutting implies that budget cuts will be selective and different in degree or proportion based on the impact of the budget cuts on the enterprise's strategic position, or strategic goals and imperatives, or strategic initiatives, and ultimately, long-term enterprise value. But how should that work? Isn't this the reverse of creating a budget based on must-have spends and then spending on problems, risks, and opportunities?

- ♦ A budget-cutting *opportunity* is a budget cut that does not reduce enterprise value, or possibly increases enterprise value (such as an operational efficiency).
- ♦ A budget-cutting *risk* is a budget cut that results in a potential reduction to enterprise value.
- ♦ And a budget-cutting *problem* is a budget cut that will certainly reduce enterprise value.

From a loss-aversion perspective, the portfolio thought is, how can budgets be cut to minimize loss in enterprise value? *Investment productivity* is replaced with *divestment productivity*. So a budget-cutting PRO item that has divestment productivity of negative three implies that for every $1 of budget cut on the PRO item reduces enterprise value by $3. A budget-cutting *opportunity* with a positive *divestment productivity* would imply growth in enterprise value (such as the case for an operational efficiency).

Resolving the PRO Dilemma is the key to improved corporate decision making. This can be done in any organization by answering five questions.

The Five Questions of PRO Management

"The important and difficult job is never to find the right answers, it is to find the right question."
– Peter F. Drucker, Management Consultant, Author, and Educator

This quote from Peter Drucker's 1955 seminal book *The Practice of Management* provides the perfect starting point. Drucker's Chapter 28 is on "Making Decisions" and begins with the following passage, "Whatever a manager does he does through making decisions. Those decisions may be made as a matter of routine. Indeed, he may not even realize that he is making them. Or they may affect the future existence of the enterprise and require years of systematic analysis. But management is always a decision-making process. The importance of decision making in management is generally recognized. But a good deal of the discussion tends to center on problem-solving, that is, on giving answers. And that is the wrong focus. Indeed, the most common source of mistakes in management decisions is the emphasis on finding the right answer rather than the right question."[3]

Drucker's opening remarks on decision making, *from over sixty years ago*, couldn't be more true today—a testament either to the difficulty in improving organizational decision making, or the lack of efficient and effective organizational decision-making methods, or both. As Drucker understood and eloquently articulated, decision making is the primary job and work of management. And managers, just like each and every one of us, make decisions about only three things: problems, risks, and opportunities—*PRO items.*

Planning and status meetings need to focus on each executive or manager providing their updates to their answers for the same five questions at each of these meetings. This applies to:

♦ Business unit leaders,
♦ Executives and managers of business functions (such as sales, marketing, treasury, mergers & acquisitions, accounting, finance, research and development, manufacturing, supply chain, quality, compliance, and distribution),
♦ Plant managers,
♦ Program and project leaders, and
♦ Six-sigma and continuous improvement leaders.

---

3   Peter F. Drucker, *The Practice of Management* (London, England: William Heinemann Limited, Publishers, 1955, page 351.

In short, it applies *to anyone with a plan and a budget.* Having a full team of executives and managers present enables cross-organizational PRO item discussions and collaborative involvement.

The Five Questions

1. What are your PRO items?
2. Which erode the most value if not pursued?
3. Which, if pursued, create or protect the most value?
4. Which should/will you pursue at this point in time?
5. What are the implications to your plan and budget?

My guidance to the meeting presenters is to take a few minutes to communicate and discuss whatever else they deem relevant beyond these five questions. But the meeting should be about answering the five questions and determining what, if anything, you need, or that other organizational leaders can do to ensure that your five questions are answered and efficiently implemented in a manner that is—*foremost*—best for the enterprise.

To examine the five questions in detail, consider an executive at a pharmaceutical company. She holds a monthly, two-hour, cross-functional PRO Management Status Review that is the primary forum for deciding on significant expenditures that are funded by existing management reserve accounts, or are expenditure requests beyond current organizational budgets, or are emerging, cross-functional ("white-space") expenditure requests. Each director and manager in her organization manages their own PRO portfolio and each uses a common, standard, and consistent process by which they measure and manage their PRO portfolios. The executive's PRO Management Status Review (PMSR) is part of an ongoing process that tracks and decides on a Top 10 or so set of active PRO items across her organization.

The monthly PRO Management Status Review agenda has three topics:

◆ Quick Status on Implementation of PRO Items (committed to at previous PMSR meetings),
◆ Review and Make Decisions on the Current Top 10 PRO Item List, and
◆ Discussion on Proposed New PRO Items (to be analyzed prior to and discussed at the next PMSR meeting).

The following summaries represent the current Top 10 PRO items up for decisions on this month's agenda.

1. Clinical Trial Data Quality Concerns (Risk-CTDQ)

A colon cancer pivotal study is ongoing with enrollment complete. The last patient visit is scheduled for September, 2017, the final report is scheduled for December, 2017, and the Market Authorization submissions are scheduled for February, 2018, with regulatory approvals 12 months later targeting peak sales of $2B by 2022. The quality and interpretability of the patient data (compliance risk) has a chance of affecting the regulatory review timeline to approval and has a chance of even preventing approval. To prevent this quality risk, the Contract Research Organization (CRO) has indicated it needs an additional $5M in resource expenses, while we believe the CRO created the risk by not staffing as originally planned and funded.

2. Clinical Trial Enrollment Problem (Problem-CLTE)

A breast cancer pivotal study is scheduled to start enrollment in July 2017 and complete enrollment in June 2018 with 1,000 patients. Several individuals involved in managing the CRO relationship have raised concerns about the aggressiveness of the schedule and claim there is a 50% chance of enrollment being delayed by 6 months. The CRO predicts that it would cost an additional $13M on this $100M study to keep the timeline on track. Planned market authorization applications for the US and EU are scheduled for June 2019 with approvals 12 months later and targeted peak sales of $1B by 2025.

3. Single Source Stock Out Concern (Risk-SSSO)

A product that is becoming a higher-value product in the company's product portfolio is currently sole sourced. Should we invest in establishing a second manufacturing source to reduce the chance of product supply interruption? The cost of establishing a backup supplier is about $5.5M, including capital and expense, with additional annual costs of about $1M per year to maintain the manufacturing option.

4. Below Sales Forecast for Product Q (Problem-BSFP)

It is mid-year and one of the company's newer products is trending toward $5M below the annual forecast. The Marketing & Sales Organization wants to implement a multi-channel marketing campaign to create a sales lift before year's end. We will still miss this year's sales target but we believe we should reduce this year's sales gap so as not to send the wrong message to the marketplace. This requires a proactive investment of $750,000 in multi-channel marketing (including direct mail and an email program to an audience of physicians) that is executed over a five-month period.

5. Stockout Resulting from Delayed Tech Transfer (Risk-SOTT)

Concern is rising over a Contract Manufacturing Organization's (CMO's) ability to complete the tech transfer on schedule. A six-month safety stock is already built into the overall tech transfer plan and budget. Recent increases in the demand for the product coupled with a delayed tech transfer could result in a stockout. Some customers would be lost during the stockout as physicians change over to a competitor's product. To mitigate the risk of a stockout, the tech transfer team recommends hiring a well-respected outside contractor as a "man-in-the-plant" and building another four months of safety stock. Some additional test equipment will be installed at the CMO off of the production line to expedite testing of batches. The tech transfer team is also recommending that executive management step up their communications and concerns with the management of the CMO. The total cost of these risk mitigation efforts is $650,000 in capital and expense.

6. Clinical Hold of New Product C (Problem-CHNP)

The promising new product indicated for treating bacterial lung infections is currently initiating Phase 3 trials with an expected NDA submission date of 2018. The product has annual sales projections of $1 to $2 billion. The Phase II trial results have been positive. Unfortunately the company has been informed by the FDA that the potential drug has been placed on a clinical hold due to a safety issue based on its review of preliminary long-term rat inhalation carcinogenicity data. The FDA has requested that the company conduct a dog inhalational nine-month toxicity study to determine if the findings of the rat inhalation carcinogenicity study are also demonstrated in a non-rodent model. As a result we need to conduct another Phase 2 trial before re-starting Phase 3. This will extend the overall cost of the clinical program ($600K to $1M) and the NDA submission date will be delayed by about two years. The team is requesting $5.5M to implement an innovative trial design and recruitment process to minimize the time delay to regulatory approval.

7. Increase Capacity of the API Manufacturing Process (Oppor-tunity-ICMP)

The current manufacturing capacity of an active pharmaceutical ingredient (API) for Product M is sufficient; however, the capacity is likely insufficient for a recently reported uptick in the future sales forecast. Increasing API capacity by as much as 20% can be achieved fairly inexpensively if implemented within the next year and a half as it will require minor changes to the current manufacturing footprint. The requested expenditure is to buy and install new equipment for $2.15M in capital and expenses.

8. Customer Care Service Complaints (Risk-CCSC)

Customers are complaining about product customer service including Call Center and Web-Internet Response Time. Concern is rising over how this might negatively impact future sales. The likelihood of this event triggering lost sales is rising with time. Should the Customer Care Center (Call Center and Web-Site) be revamped this or next year or is it acceptable to wait, as planned, before we pursue this upgrade? The incremental cost of revamping the Customer Care Center earlier than planned is $1M over two years. The Customer Care Center operating cost should decrease by $100,000 per year after the new system is implemented. The potential lost sales resulting from frustrated customers is about $2.5M to at most $10M per year. We expect that 50% of the lost customers would not return even after the Customer Care Center is improved.

9. Unreported ADEs and Inconsistent NDA Safety Database (Risk-UADE)

For an ongoing clinical trial, medical coding responsibility was given to MDs and other clinical scientists. Unfortunately, no standardized coding guidelines were documented for terms. Concern is rising that the lack of standards could result in delayed regulatory approval due to inconsistencies in coding. The risk is of receiving a Not-Approvable Letter at the time of NDA filing. The recommendation is to immediately hire a CRO to redo the safety database at a cost of $10M. Also recommended is the creation of a centralized coding group by hiring a lead of medical coding and three coding specialists. The annual cost to the company is about $600K per year for the new staff.

10. Improve Clinical Trial Supply Forecasting (Opportunity-ICTF):

The Lean Six Sigma Initiative has identified the opportunity to improve clinical supplies planning, tracking, and reconciliation processes. The intent is to reduce the time and effort needed to develop, evaluate, and update clinical supply plans. Currently up to 50% of each CSO resource is expended managing, planning, and tracking spreadsheets and e-mail. As such, it is difficult to establish "one-version of the truth." We need to reduce the risk and cost of out-of-stock and clinical supply overages. The plan is to implement a clinical trial's supply forecasting and simulation application and interface it with each study's Interactive Voice Response System (IVRS). This will reduce clinical trial costs by about $5M per year by reducing supply overages, expired kits, and time needed to evaluate protocol and recruitment plan changes. The cost of implementing a Clinical Trials Supply Forecasting System with IVRS interface is $515,000 in capital and expense.

During the meeting session devoted to decision making, "Review and Make Decisions on the Current Top 10 PRO Item List," there are a standard set of analyses and graphs (depicted in the following sections) used to support the five central questions of the meeting. For this monthly meeting, thumbnail discussions of the TOP 10 PRO Items are distributed one week prior to the meeting along with supporting PRO portfolio analyses and graphs. The PRO portfolio analyses use the individual PRO item information as illustrated in Table 12.5 of Chapter 12, "Example Summary of PRO Management Output Measures for a Single PRO Item."

Question 1: *What are your PRO Items?*

At the outset of the meeting, updated/revised thumbnail PRO item descriptions—similar to those above—and updated/revised PRO portfolio analyses are distributed.

Question 2: *Which Erode the Most Value if Not Pursued?*

Due to all individual's strong aversion to loss, the second question jumps straight to the executive's primary concern: if we don't act, which PRO items can hurt us the most? This is the domain of *problems* and *risks*. Figure 13.2 provides a graphical representation of the answer to this question. This is a PRO portfolio analysis based on a before investment and action perspective.

In Figure 13.2, the PRO items are prioritized (ordered) by their expected net present value loss. In this case the problem "Clinical Hold of New Product C" has the greatest expected enterprise loss of $868M as measured in incremental net present value of discounted free cash flow. The bar surrounding the $868M expected loss represents the 10th to 90th percentile values of the underlying continuous distribution of the incremental net present value impact to discounted free cash flow associated with "Clinical Hold of New Product C" given no investment and no action.

The top four problems and risks with respect to expected loss range from $295M up to $868M, including

- *Clinical Trial Enrollment Problem,*
- *Clinical Trial Data Quality Concerns,*
- *Unreported ADEs and Inconsistent NDA Safety Database,* and
- *Clinical Hold of New Product C.*

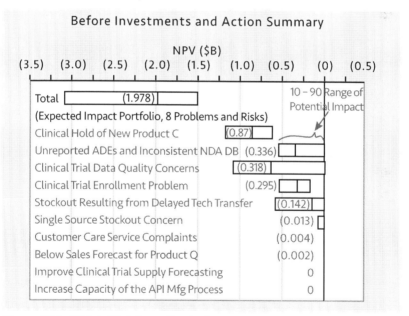

Figure 13.2: Which PRO Items Erode the Most Value If Not Pursued?

The bottom two PRO items in Figure 13.2 are *opportunities* and have no net impacts *before investment and action*. The top bar in Figure 13.2 represents the aggregate impacts of the ten PRO items (or eight non-zero impact PRO items). The expected loss of the portfolio of ten PRO items is nearly $2B (or calculated as $1.978B). The 10th

PRO Item	Investment Productivity	NPV Before ($M)	NPV After ($M)	Gain
Total	24.7	(1,978)	(644)	1,334
Clinical trial data quality concerns	62.3	(318)	(6)	312
Unreported ADEs and inconsistent NDA safety database	20.7	(336)	(33)	303
Cinical hold of new Product C	54.5	(868)	(578)	291
Stockout resulting from delayed tech transfer	167.2	(142)	(36)	106
Increase capacity of the API manufacturing process	47.2	0	101	101
Improve clinical trial supply forecasting	32.5	0	17	17
Customer care service complaints	67	(4)	3	7
Below sales forecast for Product Q	1	(2)	(1)	1
Single source stockout concern	(0)	13	13	(0)

Table 13.1: Top 10 PRO Items Prioritized By Net Gain

and the 90th percentiles of the distribution of the sum of ten PRO items can be approximated and in this case, the 10th percentile represents more than a $3B loss.

Question 3: *Which, if Pursued, Create or Protect the Most Value?*

The third question is all about which PRO items are impacted the most given resources are expended on them. A famous quote (incorrectly) attributed to Benjamin Franklin is: "A penny saved is a penny earned." My analog for corporations is, "A dollar of cash flow protected is equal to a dollar of cash flow created."

In Table 13.1, each PRO item has a value for "NPV Before" and a value for "NPV After." As defined in Chapter 12, the "NPV Before" value represents the expected enterprise value of the PRO item as measured in current year dollars prior to any investment and action in its pursuit. The "NPV After" value represents the expected enterprise value of the PRO item given pursuit of the PRO item with investment and action—including (or accounting for) the investments to pursue the PRO item—as measured in current year dollars. The expected net gain (labeled as *Gain* in Table 13.1) is simply the difference between these two values ("NPV After" minus "NPV Before").

Table 13.1 is a list of the PRO items ordered (prioritized) by the enterprise expected net gain achieved by pursuing each PRO item with their proposed investment and action plan. "Clinical Trial Data Quality Concerns" has the greatest net gain of about $312M. In fact, each of the top three net gain PRO items represents about $300M in enterprise value. Each of the top six net gain PRO items is over $100M in enterprise value. The remaining four PRO items have significantly less expected net gains. All of these insights are visually recognized in the graph provided in Figure 13.3.

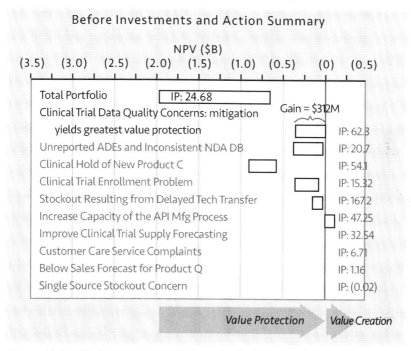

Figure 13.3: Which PRO Items, If Pursued, Create or Protect the Most Value?

The width of the bars in Figure 13.3 represent the magnitude of the net gain, whereas the placement of the end points of the bars represent the value of the "NPV Before" and "NPV After." As an example, the problem "Clinical Hold of New Product C" represents an expected loss of over $500M even after resources are allocated toward attempting to resolve this problem. The vast majority of the net gains are associated with *value protection* investments in *problems* and *risks* as opposed to the less significant net gains associated with *value creating opportunities*—again, all readily apparent in Figure 13.3.

PRO Item	Cumulative Investment ($M)	Cumula-tive NPV ($M)	Invest-ment Produc-tivity	Type
Stockout resulting from de-layed tech transfer	0.65	106	167	Risk
Clinical trial data quality concerns	5.65	418	62.3	Risk
Cinical hold of new Product C	11.15	708	54.4	Problem
Increase capacity of the API manufacturing process	13.3	810	47.2	Oppor-tunity
Improve clinical trial supply forecasting	13.8	827	32.5	Oppor-tunity
Unreported ADEs and incon-sistent NDA safety database	29.8	1,130	20.67	Risk
Clinical trial enrollment problem	42.8	1,327	15.32	Problem
Customer care service complaints	43.8	1,333	6.71	Risk
Below sales forecast for Product Q	44.6	1,334	1.16	Problem
Single source stockout concern	58.1	1,334	(0.02)	Problem

Table 13.2: Top 10 PRO Items Prioritized By Investment Productivity

The top bar in Figure 13.3 represents the expected net gain to the enterprise given all ten PRO items are pursued. Notice the *investment productivity* of pursuing all ten PRO items is over 24, a very high enterprise return on the portfolio. Unfortunately, even with this high investment return, the residual expected net loss is well over $500M, primarily driven by the net loss associated with the *problem* "Clinical Hold of New Product C."

Question 4: *Which Should/Will You Pursue at this Time?*

The initial *framing* and *priming* of this question is solely based on *enterprise investment productivity*. Table 13.2 prioritizes the PRO items based upon their *investment productivity*. Notice the broad range of investment productivity values from as high as 167 down to negative values, which is not an unusual spread for a pharma-ceutical company with high profit margin products. Executives and managers are typically unaware of the magnitude of this spread in productivity without this type of analysis and measurement.

The PRO item with the greatest investment productivity (about 167) is the *risk*, "Stockout Resulting from Delayed Tech Transfer." The total risk mitigation investment of this PRO item is $650,000 and the associated expected net gain from this investment is about $106M. Table 13.2 orders the PRO items by investment productivity and accumulates the investment and expected net gain as PRO items are added into a potential total portfolio spend (budget). As an example, if only the top two PRO items as measured in investment productivity were funded, the total cost of this would be about $5.65M for the enterprise value protection of about $418M. The diminishing return of PRO item expenditures is visually recognized in the investment productivity curve illustrated in Figure 13.4.

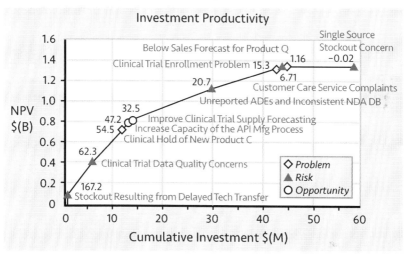

Figure 13.4: Initial Frame of Question 4, Which PRO Items Should We Pursue at this Time?

The starting point and initial frame of the discussion on which PRO items to invest in is represented by the investment productivity curve in Figure 13.4. The affordability of expenditures on PRO items must come into play during this discussion. For a variety of reasons—some good and some bad, but nonetheless reasons for organizational resource constraints—not all PRO items will be funded at this point in time. A line must be drawn on which PRO items to fund and which not to fund at this point in time—*the PRO Management portfolio decision.*

The executive starts the decision-making discussion by drawing a line that separates the PRO items based on investment productivity. The decision-making process has been primed and framed from

PRO Item	Cumulative Investment ($M)	Cumulative NPV ($M)	Investment Productivity	Type
Stockout resulting from delayed tech transfer	0.65	106	167	Risk
Clinical trial data quality concerns	5.65	418	62.3	Risk
Cinical hold of new Product C	11.15	708	54.4	Problem
Increase capacity of the API manufacturing process	13.3	810	47.2	Opportunity
Improve clinical trial supply forecasting	13.8	827	32.5	Opportunity
Unreported ADEs and inconsistent NDA safety database	29.8	1,130	20.67	Risk
Clinical trial enrollment problem	42.8	1,327	15.32	Problem
Customer care service complaints	43.8	1,333	6.71	Risk
Below sales forecast for Product Q	44.6	1,334	1.16	Problem
Single source stockout concern	58.1	1,334	(0.02)	Problem

Table 13.3: Initial Budget Solely Based on Investment Productivity

a long-term enterprise value perspective including the reality of budgetary constraints. The question the executive is asking at this point in the process and meeting is: "Why *isn't* this allocation the correct resource allocation for this PRO Portfolio?" Now is the time to debate all the ulterior reasons, motivations, and concerns that would result in a different PRO Portfolio resource allocation. This discussion sequence is important, that is, starting (priming the decision) with an enterprise perspective (which becomes the discussion anchor) versus not introducing an enterprise perspective until later in the discussion as a secondary thought and perspective.

As depicted in Table 13.3, all PRO items with investment productivity of greater than 15 are above the executive's line and all other PRO items are below. Spending about $43M creates or protects about $1.3B in enterprise value—an easily defendable use of investment resources for the enterprise.

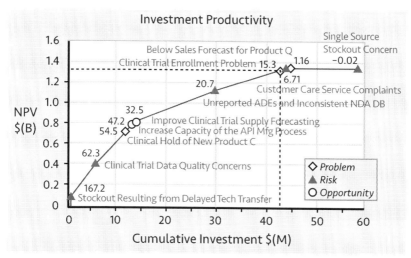

Figure 13.5: Initial Budget of Question 4, Which PRO Items Should We Pursure at this Time

Figure 13.5 graphically depicts this initial investment cut-off line for expenditures on PRO items.

But wait. It is almost *never* that simple. A debate ensues during the meeting on the valuation of the *risk* "Single Source Stockout Concern." A single manufacturing site produces the product associated with this risk. The corporation has struggled with establishing a policy on which products should be dual-sourced and which products are exempt from a dual-sourcing requirement. The risk of a product stockout resulting from potential issues at the manufacturing site was assessed and the cost of establishing and maintaining a second-source was estimated. The investment productivity of the second-source cost was determined to be negative, that is, an unproductive use of enterprise resources in the face of the potential product stockout risk.

A manufacturing director at the meeting made the point that another single-sourced product recently had a stock out due to a contamination issue at the manufacturing site. He had pledged to the Vice President of Operations that, "It wouldn't happen again!" The executive-in-charge at the PMSR meeting asked if the manufacturing director thought the risk assessment was flawed. The director stated he thought the assessed probability of risk occurrence was too small or "underestimated."

A sensitivity analysis of investment productivity to the probability of the risk occurring (similar to the example in Figure 12.5 of Chapter 12) was performed indicating that the investment productivity was negative or relatively low even when the probability of the risk occurring was doubled and tripled. Nonetheless, the manufacturing director maintained his position that a second-source manufacturing option should be established.

Is this just a case of availability bias, or manager's bias, or negativity bias, or groupthink clouding his judgment? (See Chapter 8.) Or has the manufacturing director uncovered issues that are beyond the supporting PRO management analysis?

PRO Item	Cumulative Investment ($M)	Cumulative NPV ($M)	Investment Productivity	Type
Must-haves: Below sales forecast for Product Q plus Update Oncologist Campaign	4.25	0.87	-	-
Stockout resulting from delayed tech transfer	4.9	107.2	167	Risk
Clinical trial data quality concerns	9.9	418.7	62.3	Risk
Cinical hold of new Product C	15.4	709.3	54.5	Problem
Increase capacity of the API manufacturing process	17.6	810.8	47.2	Opportunity
Improve clinical trial supply forecasting	18.1	827.5	32.5	Opportunity
Unreported ADEs and inconsistent NDA safety database	34.1	1,130.9	20.7	Risk
Clinical trial enrollment problem	47.1	1,327	15.32	Problem
Customer care service complaints	48.1	1,334	6.71	Risk
Single source stockout concern	61.6	1,333	(0.02)	Problem

Table 13.4: Final Budget Based on Must-Haves and Investment Productivity

The executive-in-charge remained unconvinced that this was a good use of corporate resources and she decided against funding the risk "Single Source Stockout Concern" at this point in time. A separate discussion was held regarding the problem "Below Sales Forecast for Product Q," which was ultimately categorized as a "Must-Have" spend. Additionally, a new PRO item introduced during the session regarding an urgent need to update an oncologist-focused advertising campaign was also categorized as a "Must-Have" spend.

Table 13.4 illustrates the PRO Management portfolio decision. $4.25M was allocated to the two "Must-Have" spends and a total of $34M was allocated to the PRO items above the dashed-line in Table 13.4, creating or protecting a total expected enterprise value of about $1.1B.

The Clinical Trials Director was asked to revisit his solution to the *problem* "Clinical Trial Enrollment Problem" as the discussion on this PRO item during the meeting revealed several potential improvements to his plan. He was directed to re-evaluate the PRO item accounting for these modifications "as soon as possible" and to schedule a follow-up meeting with the executive-in-charge to discuss funding on this urgent issue.

Figure 13.6 provides the investment productivity curve associated with the PRO Management portfolio decision made.

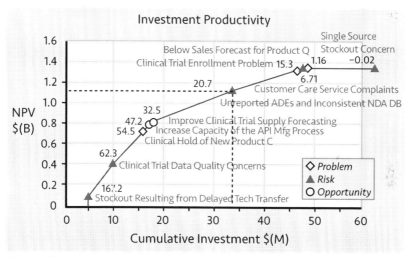

Figure 13.6: PRO Management Portfolio Decision and Budget of Question 4: Which PRO Items Should We Pursue at this Time?

Prior to finalizing the commitment to these expenditures, a final check is made by answering the fifth and final PRO Management question.

Question 5: *What are the Implications to Your Plan and Budget?*

Beyond the long-term enterprise value implications of PRO items, the associated plan and budget may have numerous other implications and impacts that must be addressed prior to finalizing the PRO Management portfolio decision on which PRO items to fund at this point in time. A strategic plan may have numerous measures and imperatives that must be considered and addressed prior to finalizing PRO item investments. Adjustments for such implications often find their way into must-have spending. Program and project PRO items can have quality or schedule implications that may have impacts that are difficult to assess and thus require further scrutiny that ultimately increases must-have spending. These are just two examples of potential broader implications that must be considered prior to committing resources to the PRO Management portfolio decision.

PRO items often require funding beyond what is available in existing budgets. Corporations have processes for addressing these funding requests so PRO Management decision making must be integrated into those processes. Consequently, the fifth question of PRO Management is not easily answered with a single graphic or standard discussion. However, there is a graphic that should be a part of answering the fifth PRO Management question and this graphic is illustrated in Figure 13.7.

Figure 13.7 provides the expected net present value loss for problems and risks, and expected net present value gain for opportunities as determined by their funding. PRO items that are targeted for funding are indicated by gray-scale bars implying their expected residual loss or expected gain given they are funded, that is, from the perspective of *after investment and action*. The remaining non-funded PRO items in Figure 13.7, as per the PRO Management portfolio decision, are graphed from the perspective of *before investment and action*, implying they are not being pursued at this point in time. By doing this we can determine the residual problem and risk liability given the proposed PRO Management portfolio decision and we can also determine the net comprehensive gain/loss to the enterprise given the proposed investments.

Given the expenditures proposed in Figure 13.6, the net result to the enterprise is an expected loss of $847M as indicated by the top bar in Figure 13.7. (Compare this to the enterprise expected loss of nearly $2B given no investments as indicated in Figure 13.2.) The 10-90 range on that expected loss is about $1.3B down to about $600M. The greatest source of loss remains with the *problem* "Clinical Hold of New Product C," even after allocating resources to resolve the problem. The second greatest source of expected loss is the unfunded *problem* "Clinical Trial Enrollment Problem," although this should improve once an updated problem resolution plan is resubmitted and approved.

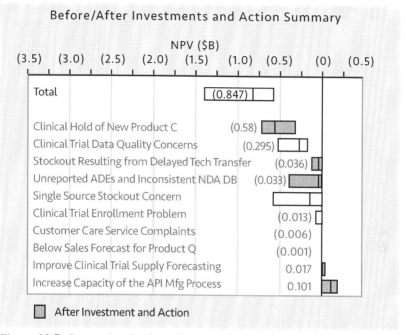

Figure 13.7: Supporting Analysis for Question 5, What are the Implications to Our Plan and Budget?

To calculate the residual problem and risk liability we simply need to add the expected losses of the *problems* and *risks* (linearity of expectation). Or conversely, subtract the expected gains from the two opportunities from the total ($-847 - 17 - 101 = -965$) resulting in a residual problem and risk expected liability of about $965M. Once again, the residual problem and risk liability is primarily due to the residual expected loss associated with the *problem* "Clinical Hold of New Product C."

The five questions of PRO Management are applicable to anyone, or any business activity, or any business entity that has a plan and a budget.

The Five Questions of Risk Management

Invariably, of the three types of corporate decision management—problem management, risk management, and opportunity management—risk management is the least understood, the most problematic, and the least effective in practice. So when executives and managers begin to implement PRO Management concepts, processes, and tools, they often start with risk management. And even though a tenet of PRO Enterprise Management is problems, risks, and opportunities should be managed together, not separately, since they all compete for the same limited resources, risk management is often the targeted initial focus for a corporate decision-making transformation.

The five questions of PRO Management can be easily modified to represent the five questions of risk management. The Five Questions of risk management are:

1. What are the risks?

2. Which risks potentially erode the most value if not mitigated?

3. Which risks if mitigated protect the most value?

4. Which risks should mitigation resources be allocated to at this point in time?

5. Given the expenditure of the risk mitigation resources, what is the residual risk liability and what is the impact to the associated plan and budget?

All of the analyses in the previous section and all of the Figures and Tables apply to risk management.

PRO Portfolio Analysis with Dependent PRO Items

The analyses and graphs in the previous sections have assumed that individual PRO items are *mutually independent*. There are degrees to which this assumption may not be true. In cases where two to several PRO items are dependent, they can often be modeled with methods beyond the scope of this book or the dependent PRO items can be combined into a single PRO item.

Sometimes there is a macro-level uncertainty that can impact the probability of occurrence, or the consequences and impacts, or both, across a set of PRO items. As an example, the macro-level uncertainty of the U.S. economy plunging into a recession creates at least two distinct narratives (scenarios) that can significantly impact the individual PRO item assessments. In this case, each PRO item should be assessed for each macro-level scenario. That is, assess each PRO item for the scenario of the U.S. economy advancing into a recession and then reassess each PRO item for the scenario of the U.S. economy continuing without plunging into recession. Perform two sets of PRO portfolio analyses just as we did in the previous section. Compare the conclusions of the PRO Management portfolio decision and determine how the portfolio decision changes with respect to the macro-level uncertainty scenario. Keep the decision making discussion grounded in the narratives and scenarios as the conclusions of any debate generated by this analysis will center around what the executives and managers believe regarding the likelihood of an ensuing U.S. economic recession.

In simple terms, improving corporate decision-making processes amounts to building the five questions of PRO Management into existing decision processes. And when there are no existing decision processes, use the five questions as requirements the decision process must satisfy. A central tenet of PRO Enterprise Management is that the *priming* and *framing* of corporate decision making should be based on a long-term enterprise value perspective. All other perspectives are subordinate to this.

Although material corporate decisions are not always made based on long-term enterprise value creation or protection, it is the fiduciary responsibility of all decision makers (managers, executives, and board members) to at least comprehend the long-term enterprise value impact and the associated expenditure's return on investment prior to decision making.

"The leader of the past knew how to tell.
The leader of the future will know how to ask."
– Peter F. Drucker, Management Consultant, Author, and Educator

14

Delegation, Escalation, and Collaboration

More and more executives and managers supervise *knowledge workers*—employees who know more about their work and associated problems, risks, and opportunities than their bosses do. It is ineffective for executives and managers to tell employees what to do and how to do it because usually the employees know and understand more than the executive or manager. Leadership involves collaborative involvement, decision making, and rare top-down directives.

In every organization, the questions are:

♦ "Where is the knowledge to make the best decision on behalf of the *enterprise*?"

♦ "Who, or what role(s), in the organization represents the appropriate point of decision?"

For each type or class of decision, we need decision makers to have the Harry Truman degree of conviction behind his famous quote, "The Buck Stops Here!" Where should the buck stop? The employee skills and supporting tools to enable individuals throughout the enterprise to consistently and quickly determine value *from the perspective of the enterprise* are missing in most if not all corporations today.

From a decision-making perspective, the central activity of PRO Enterprise Portfolio Management is making the *PRO Management Portfolio Decision* (at this point in time, which PRO items will be funded and pursued, and which PRO items will not be funded and either eliminated from further discussions, or placed on a "watch list," or re-analyzed/re-framed for subsequent decision making). As in all decision making, there exists a reference point from which decisions are framed and ultimately made. In corporations and government, the reference points are budgets and plans.

Back to the Inextricable Link Between Budgets and PRO Enterprise Management

Once a plan and budget exist, you have a PRO portfolio (whether you acknowledge it or not). This is true for all business entities (for-profit and non-profit), all organizations, and even for all individuals in their personal and professional lives. Moreover, for corporations, during the development of a plan or budget, there exists a PRO portfolio that should be accounted for in the planning and budgeting process (as discussed in Chapter 13). The feasibility of a plan depends on its associated PRO portfolio. An overly aggressive sales and operations plan (S&OP) will be heavily weighted with problems and risks and likely few opportunities for improvement. A sales and operations plan with neither stretch targets for sales nor operational improvements is likely to have many ignored opportunities coupled with minimal risk, ultimately undermining enterprise value creation potential. Embedded in the budgeting and planning approval processes should be the *quantitative* understanding and articulation of the enterprise's risk liability with respect to proposed budgets and plans.

Seasoned managers have a knack for crafting plans and budgets that have a personally acceptable perceived degree of risk in achieving corporate performance targets, which are then framed, packaged, and presented in a manner that maximizes their chance of approval. Personal beliefs, convictions, and perceived chances of success regarding the plan are largely based on intuition and experience (and typically not much else). Consequently, short of having a PRO portfolio analysis completed during the S&OP planning process, executives and managers are left to their own intuition regarding the degree of risk or degree of remaining opportunity in a plan and budget. The lack of PRO portfolio management built into planning and budgeting processes contributes to underperformance and budget overruns.

Jack Welch, former Chairman and CEO of GE, calls this "BS budgeting," where people spend most of their time following some mind-numbing ritual aimed at "delivering the budget."[1] Companies have to create a budget, of course, but it has devolved into something that he says is not only "disconnected from reality," but promotes "exactly what you'd never want ... It hides growth opportunities. It promotes bad behavior, especially when market conditions change midstream and people still try to 'make the number.' And it has an uncanny way of sucking the energy and fun out of an organization."

Budgets represent the corporate organizational blueprint for resolving problems, managing risks, and capturing opportunities over the course of the next year (or budget cycle) in order to support the ultimate goal of creating and protecting enterprise value. PRO Enterprise Management methods and tools employed during planning and budgeting processes will result in better plans and budgets. Employing these methods throughout the budget cycle will improve enterprise performance.

The Building Blocks of PRO Enterprise Portfolio Management

Chapter 6 introduced the basics of how we think and form beliefs and the important role of *patterns* in these mental processes. Our mental organizing skills often leverage the pattern of *hierarchies* in a "divide and conquer" mindset as we go about planning and executing our work. These hierarchies are ubiquitous in organizations for areas such as:

- ♦ Organizational structure (org charts),
- ♦ Sales geographies,
- ♦ Product groupings and product lines,
- ♦ Manufacturing sites and site capabilities,
- ♦ Business functions and sub-functions,
- ♦ Product supply chain and suppliers (raw materials through distribution),
- ♦ Work Breakdown Structures (WBS) for programs and projects (often with associated schedules),
- ♦ Budgets, and
- ♦ Enterprise Risk Management (ERM) classifications.

Embedded in each of these hierarchies is a basic unit or pattern of a

1   Jack Welch and Suzy Welch. "Stop the B.S. Budgets," *BusinessWeek*, 26 June 2006, page 114.

two-level hierarchy with a single, senior top node with subordinate distinctions beneath as illustrated in Figure 14.1.

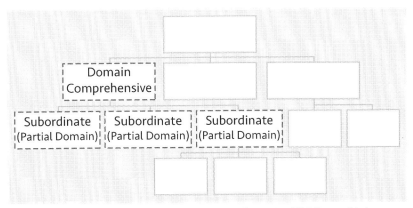

Figure 14.1: The Basic Two-level Hierarchial Unit in All Hierarchial Structures

This two-level management hierarchy also plays a significant organizing role in PRO *Enterprise* Management as indicated in Figure 14.2.

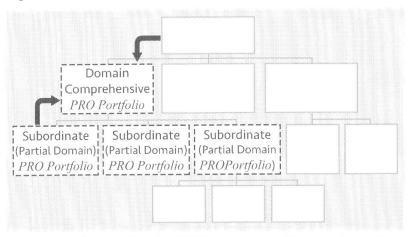

Figure 14.2: The Basic Two-level PRO Management Hierarchy Embedded in PRO Enterprise Management

PRO portfolios can be managed with a hierarchical structure consistent with the domain of the management hierarchies such as those listed above. The PRO portfolio of a product group can be managed via the hierarchy of the product group split across product lines. The PRO portfolio of a manufacturing network can be managed via the hierarchy of manufacturing sites within the network. The use of hierarchies is not perfect and certainly does not support all forms of relationships but it is a primary *pattern* of how we think and organize our thoughts. Hierarchies work well for PRO Enterprise Management given we add some management detail (summarized in Figure 14.3).

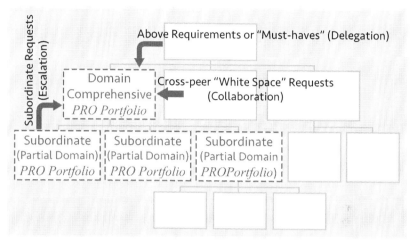

Figure 14.3: The Flow of PRO Portfolio Management Responsibility and Accountability

Everyone with a plan and budget has the "Basic Two-Level Hierarchical Pattern," where your position represents the Senior (Top) Node labeled as "Domain Comprehensive" in Figure 14.3. At the senior, Domain Comprehensive level, you must decide whether to manage PRO items by the comprehensive set across all subordinate levels versus have each subordinate PRO portfolio managed at the level of the subordinate with only white-space PRO items escalated to the "Senior" perspective. In short, this implies applying the five questions of PRO Management (detailed in Chapter 13) for the comprehensive set of PRO items at the node labeled Domain Comprehensive versus applying the five questions for each of the subordinate levels coupled with explicit policy on the nature of PRO items that must be escalated (including white-space PRO items) to the senior, Domain Comprehensive level.

A simple way to think about this is in terms of investment productivity curves. Do we *prime* the *PRO Management Portfolio Decision* with a single investment productivity curve at the senior, Domain Comprehensive level depicted in Figure 14.3? Or do we apply the *PRO Management Portfolio Decision* with an investment productivity curve at each of the three subordinate levels in Figure 14.3? If this was merely a mathematical optimization question, the answer would be to manage our limited resources with a single investment productivity curve at the Domain Comprehensive level, in fact just one investment productivity curve representing the enterprise's comprehensive set of PRO items. But this is not a mathematical optimization question. It is a question about the corporate culture senior executives must define and create, and more specifically, it is a question about senior executives' philosophy on decision empowerment throughout the enterprise.

It is the fiduciary responsibility of every executive and manager who creates and manages a budget to manage their associated PRO portfolio based on enterprise value. Where responsibility and accountability lie for decision making on a specific PRO item is the prerogative of the executive-in-charge. I use the term *responsibility* to mean the power to control, manage, and decide. I use the term *accountability* to mean the requirement to identify and record the reasoning behind all recommendations and decisions when preparing a budget and for all subsequent decisions on PRO items throughout the budget cycle. In general, the flow of PRO Enterprise Management responsibility and accountability is summarized as three source-flows with respect to the senior, Domain Comprehensive node in Figure 14.3:

♦ "Top-Down" across the individual subordinate PRO portfolios including *escalated* PRO items from subordinates;

♦ "Cross-Peer" white-space *collaboration* requests from within the hierarchy that you reside;

♦ "Above & Beyond" the boundaries of your hierarchy including *delegated* trickle-down must-haves and requirements, and roles in strategic initiatives, imperatives, and PRO item action plans.

ERM as a Decision-making Escalation Process

Enterprise Risk Management (ERM) must be both a top-down and bottom-up process. One without the other is insufficient. Escalation of existing problems, risks, and worrisome trends causes many enterprise risks. And often, new enterprise risks are the by-product of recent headline news on events or growing concerns. In Enterprise Risk Management there are recurring risks (e.g., contamination, batch failures, launch failures, process failures, etc.) where any single failure is not a material consequence; however, a large number or trend of such failures in a given time period (e.g. a year, or a quarter, or a month) is a material consequence.

A Common Hurdle: Cross-functional Collaboration

A common hurdle in the implementation of PRO Enterprise Management methods and tools is the degree of collaboration it requires across a variety of functions. As an example, individuals in business development or marketing and sales organizations may not routinely work with or share information with individuals in operational organizations. Collaboration and sharing of information doesn't happen for a long list of reasons. Senior management must ensure those barriers are removed and the necessary bridges created. Managing for the enterprise requires it.

The inextricable links between Enterprise Risk Management and PRO Management are becoming apparent. In the next chapter we will explore the natural extension of Enterprise Risk Management to PRO Enterprise Management.

"We cannot solve our problems with the same thinking we used when we created them."
– Albert Einstein

15
Beyond ERM to PRO-EM

Note: This chapter is written for individuals responsible for ERM, including CROs, CFOs, CEOs, heads of audit, and Board members. The chapter is also for ERM consulting service and software providers. Executives need an ERM story line that creates decision-making insights, which is the basis for integrating the ERM approach with the concepts that we have been discussing so far in this book. If your responsibilities do not include ERM, you should consider skimming the chapter and moving on to Chapter 16.

The roots of Enterprise Risk Management (ERM) can be traced back to the 1950s with the initial framing and development provided by insurance academia. The first risk management textbook was published in 1963 entitled *Risk Management in the Business Enterprise* by Robert Mehr and Bob Hedges.[1] The book broadened the objective of risk management to "maximize the productive efficiency of the enterprise." The breakthrough thought was that *all* business risks should be managed, not just those that could be "insured." This broadened objective is more closely aligned with the PRO Enterprise Management objective than what has transpired in the last fifty plus years of enterprise risk management evolution.

The term *risk* connotes potential for loss. Other than for companies whose core competence is risk management (such as insurance companies), the business enterprise has always poorly managed the potential for loss. However, the business enterprise solution is not found in a method and process that manages only risk; it is

---

1   Robert Mehr and Robert Hedges, *Risk Management in the Business Enterprise*, currently available from Literary Licensing, LLC (2012).

found in a method and process that manages uncertainty—both its upside and downside potentials. Clearly, Mehr and Hedges were grappling with this distinction but erroneously chose to frame the solution from the perspective of risk management. The evolution of ERM continues to attempt to merge the concepts of risk management and opportunity management; however it is still forced into an inappropriate, overly burdensome risk management framework for decision making.

ERM was ill-framed from its inception, promoting separating management processes of decisions on risks from other management decision processes on *problem* resolution and *opportunity* pursuits. ERM, in practice, has not recovered from this ill-framing of a management decision process regardless of the numerous tweaks and modifications made over the years. It will not recover until it is integrated into a coherent, repeatable, enterprise-wide method to manage the comprehensive portfolio of decisions across *problems*, *risks*, and *opportunities*.

ERM is primarily a decision-making process. Any ERM approach should be measured by its ability to answer the five questions of risk management detailed in Chapter 13 as well as be measured by the degree it satisfies any other requirements typically associated with ERM, including reporting and compliance. In this chapter we explore the relationship of existing ERM concepts to PRO Enterprise Management (PRO-EM) concepts to reframe ERM as part of a broader, comprehensive, enterprise-wide decision-making process solution across *problems*, *risks*, and *opportunities*.

The Current Standard for Enterprise Risk Management (ERM)

In 2004, the Committee of Sponsoring Organizations of the Treadway Commission (COSO) published the current standard for enterprise risk management (ERM) entitled, "Enterprise Risk Management—Integrated Framework." The "integrated framework" was intended to "help businesses and other entities assess and enhance their internal control systems." The introduction in the executive summary of the 2004 COSO publication provides a succinct vision of the role of enterprise risk management in a business entity:

"The underlying premise of enterprise risk management is that every entity exists to provide value for its stakeholders. All entities face uncertainty, and the challenge for management is to determine how much uncertainty to accept as it strives to grow stakeholder value. Uncertainty presents both risk and opportunity, with the potential to erode or enhance value. Enterprise risk management enables management to effectively deal with uncertainty and associated risk and opportunity, enhancing the capacity to build value.

"Value is maximized when management sets strategy and objectives to strike an optimal balance between growth and return goals and related risks, and efficiently and effectively deploys resources to pursue the entity's objectives. Enterprise risk management encompasses:

♦ Aligning risk appetite and strategy – Management considers the entity's risk appetite in evaluating strategic alternatives, setting related objectives, and developing mechanisms to manage related risks.

♦ Enhancing risk response decisions – Enterprise risk management provides the rigor to identify and select among alternative risk responses – risk avoidance, reduction, sharing, and acceptance.

♦ Reducing operational surprises and losses – Entities gain enhanced capability to identify potential events and establish responses, reducing surprises and associated costs or losses.

♦ Identifying and managing multiple and cross-enterprise risks – Every enterprise faces a myriad of risks affecting different parts of the organization, and enterprise risk management facilitates effective response to the interrelated impacts, and integrated responses to multiple risks.

♦ Seizing opportunities – By considering a full range of potential events, management is positioned to identify and proactively realize opportunities.

♦ Improving deployment of capital – Obtaining robust risk information allows management to effectively assess overall capital needs and enhance capital allocation.

"These capabilities inherent in enterprise risk management help management achieve the entity's performance and profitability targets and prevent loss of resources. Enterprise risk management helps ensure effective reporting and compliance with laws and regulations, and helps avoid damage to the entity's reputation and associated consequences. In sum, enterprise risk management helps an entity get to where it wants to go and avoid pitfalls and surprises along the way."[2]

Adding opportunities in the definition of enterprise risk management emerged later in ERM development as early attempts at ERM implementation revealed the inextricable relationship of risk and opportunity (which motivates what we characterize as the PRO Dilemma in Chapter 3). That said, the preponderance of ERM language and practice remains in the realm of avoiding losses, well short of a balanced effort between risk and opportunity management, while completely avoiding the third competing source of discretionary resource consumption, problem resolution.

The Comprehensive Perspective of Enterprise Risk Management (ERM)

Enterprise risk management (ERM) ideally uses an integrated or holistic approach to understand and manage the full spectrum and range of risks that an organization faces. ERM started in the late 1980s, when financial and insurance companies began to understand that they were taking dissimilar, independent, and sometimes competing approaches to managing a mounting number and types of risks they faced internally and externally. The uncoordinated, and sometimes conflicting, approaches to managing organizational risk led executives to ignore some risks while spending too much time and cost managing others. The result was that employees were not providing senior management a comprehensive picture of the risks they faced, thereby increasing the likelihood that the organization would be surprised by events that, in retrospect, were predictable.

During the past three decades ERM has grown from being a "good idea" into a more formal discipline to manage an organization's spectrum of risks. No universally accepted definition of ERM exists, so it's best to think of it as a common framework for managing five general types of risks, including: strategic, operational, financial, insurable, and governance. Charette and Hagen provide the following summaries of these five classes of risk:

♦ *Strategic risks* involve the organization's direction. Is the organization's deliberate strategy (see Chapter 3) and ability to adapt to market changes correct, or does it need to be changed to keep from stagnating or collapsing? Strategic risks are associated with the organization's

2   Enterprise Risk Management-Integrated Framework: Executive Summary", Committee of Sponsoring Organizations of the Treadway Commission, September 2004.

overall objectives, the assumptions that underlie those objectives, and the constraints the organization faces.

♦ *Operational risks* involve the people, processes, and technology that are needed to carry out the organization's strategic objectives. These risks include regulatory compliance in operations, how well information technology systems function, the effectiveness of information security to protect confidential data, and how well the organization uses communication media to inform the public on the status of its operations.

♦ *Financial risks* involve the strategic and tactical allocation of resources, including the organization's financial investments. For instance, are financial resources allocated so they create the best return for a public company's shareholders, or in the case of a government agency, do investments generate the best value?

♦ *Insurable risks* are amenable to being addressed by insurance (specifically, "pure" risks that involve only outcomes of a financial loss versus no loss).

♦ *Governance risks* involve compliance with legal and ethical standards, such as compliance with the Sarbanes-Oxley Act of 2002 (SOX).

According to Charette and Hagen, "Recently, a sixth class of risk, social risk (i.e., the risk of corporate decisions impacting negatively on society in which the organization operates), is being added to the list of enterprise risks that need to be considered, although some believe this to be an element of strategic risk."[3] For example, the potential for a Gulf of Mexico oil spill should have informed executives concerning decisions shortcutting safety that BP managers were making that ultimately led to the Deepwater Horizon fire and oil spill in 2010.

Of course, some risks include aspects of more than one of the five or six classes of risks. Some risks also evolve from one class to others. For instance, disclosure of personal information due to the loss of a laptop (an operational risk) may create both a reputational (a strategic risk) and monetary (a financial risk) consequence. Ideally, to simplify risk analysis and management of risks, we would like

---

3   Robert N. Charette and Brian Hagen, "Enterprise Risk Management: Time to Level the Playing Field, Part I," *Cutter Consortium Business Technology Strategies Executive Update*, Vol. 15, No. 19. (2012), page 3.

to create a hierarchical categorization scheme that is both mutually exclusive and collectively exhaustive with respect to the types or classes of risk facing an enterprise. However, from a practical standpoint, this is not possible due to interrelationships of risks and their interrelated consequences and impacts. Nonetheless, use of categories and hierarchies is helpful to ensure a comprehensive breath of risks is considered and accounted for in an ERM program. Once again, our inherent ability to organize our thoughts is limited to a few patterns and in this case a hierarchy seems to work best as an underlying structure as long as we explicitly include cross-hierarchical (white space) risks. Figure 15.1 illustrates the concept of a hierarchical categorization scheme for ERM in a pharmaceutical company.

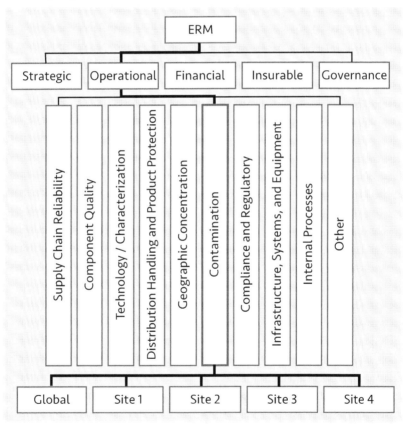

Figure 15.1: Example of a Partial Hierarchal Categorization Scheme for ERM in a Pharmaceutical Company

In practice, there is often the need to use multiple hierarchical categorization schemes to enable the various portfolio perspectives management desires to support decision making, more specifically, to make the *PRO Management Portfolio Decision*. In its best formulation, ERM identifies and manages the individual, collective, and cumulative effects of different types of risks an organization faces. The information created generates information previously ignored or glossed over that managers can use to understand and calibrate the level of risk the enterprise is actually assuming.

ERM: Good in Theory, Not So Much in Practice

As currently defined and practiced, enterprise risk management is too complicated and difficult to implement. ERM remains a "hard sell" in most corporations today, even though there is strong encouragement for its use by government regulators like the US Federal Reserve Board, the UK Financial Services Authority (FSA), and by credit rating organizations like Standard & Poor's (who began using it in 2009 to develop corporate credit scores) and Fitch Rating Service.

Paradoxically, even as ERM has proven itself not very useful in practice, board members and corporate executives truly want—in many cases demand—ERM. At the personal level, board members and corporate executives have seen over the past decade increased compliance and liability risk—not to mention the risk of personal embarrassment and risk to their reputations.

However, these same board members and corporate executives are also highly skeptical of *large-scale* ERM programs, not only because of their cost, but more importantly because the insights generated seem to add little value to the decisions board members and executives need to make. Lots of effort is expended in identifying and quantifying the five types of risks outlined above; however, little is done in regard to what you should do with that information. Moreover, if action is defined and taken, what is the value to the enterprise for taking such actions? How much enterprise value is created or protected? What is the enterprise's return on investment? ERM and decision making, regardless of the rhetoric to the contrary, are typically disconnected in practice.

What senior executives need is a way of understanding their organization's risks in a straightforward, non-confusing manner so they can make sensible decisions about what to do about them. This also means they need to be placed into a sensible decision context that includes *problems* and *opportunities*, as well as *risk*.

The (Confusing) Language of Enterprise Risk Management

Trying to define something as a *risk* or a *problem* can get confusing. When this question is extended to the enterprise, it can get even more confusing and frustrating. To keep from getting lost in the jargon, remember a key point from Chapter 3:

Key Point:

Knowledge about risk is only informative, meaningful, and useful if it supports decision making.

Currently there is no single, agreed-to set of definitions and distinctions for what the management of enterprise risk includes or doesn't include. Nonetheless, in this section I will attempt to introduce the broader language used in the literature to describe what ERM is supposed to do. Here are several terms you will see in use:

- ♦ *Risk Capacity*: This is the maximum risk that an enterprise (or other entity) can bear given its capital, liquid assets, borrowing capability, etc., in the pursuit of the *deliberate strategy* of the enterprise. At the enterprise level, you can think of risk capacity as defining the threshold or tipping point at which the power driving the enterprise is transferred from the board and senior executives to the debt holders—the banks, in this era, maybe the US Federal Government.

- ♦ *Risk Exposure*: This represents the amount of risk an enterprise (or other entity) retains, which includes the *residual risk* remaining from risks after risk mitigation actions have been taken into account and *accepted risk* consisting of those risks having no risk mitigation actions and that consequently are assumed by the enterprise.

The following terms were defined in Chapter 10 and repeated here, with the source being the Committee of Sponsoring Organizations of the Treadway Commission (COSO):

- ♦ *Risk Appetite*: "The amount of risk, on a broad level, an entity is willing to accept in pursuit of value. It reflects the entity's risk management philosophy, and in turn influences the entity's culture and operating style... Risk appetite [assists the organization] in aligning the organization, people, and processes in [designing the] infrastructure necessary to effectively respond to and monitor risks."[4]

Some argue that corporations need a formal *risk appetite* framework to help senior executives and managers make and defend decisions on how much and what kind of risk they should take. At the enterprise-level, *risk appetite* can be articulated as a statement. Rittenberg and Martens provide an example from a healthcare organization: "The Organization operates within a low overall risk range. The Organization's lowest risk appetite relates to safety and compliance objectives, including employee health and safety, with a marginally higher risk appetite towards its strategic, reporting, and operations objectives. This means that reducing to reasonably-practicable levels the risks originating from various medical systems, products, equipment, and our work environment, and meeting our legal obligations will take priority over other business objectives."[5] Risk appetite is then interpreted—both quantitatively and qualitatively—and cascaded down throughout the enterprise into organizational objectives and classes of risk.

- ◆ *Risk Tolerance*: "...relates to *risk appetite* but differs in one fundamental way: *risk tolerance* represents the application of risk appetite to specific objectives. *Risk tolerance* is defined as: The acceptable level of variation relative to achievement of a specific objective, and often is best measured in the same units as those used to measure the related objective. In setting *risk tolerance*, management considers the relative importance of the related objective and aligns risk tolerances with risk appetite. Operating within *risk tolerances* helps ensure that the entity remains within its risk appetite and, in turn, that the entity will achieve its objectives."[6] This is a term that is used in two distinctly *different* ways. In the second way, risk tolerance is used as a measure of a decision maker's risk attitude or preference.

---

4   Larry Rittenberg and Frank Martens, "Understanding and Communicating Risk Appetite," Commissioned by the Committee of Sponsoring Organizations of the Treadway Commission (COSO), January 2012. page 3.

5   Ibid, page 8.

6   Ibid, page 11.

In overly simplified terms from Prospect Theory (see Chapter 10), an individual who "weighs more heavily" the potential downside consequences of a decision is referred to as a *risk-averse* decision maker. An individual who "weighs more heavily" the potential up-side consequences of a decision is referred to as a *risk-seeking* decision maker. Individuals who equally weigh the potential up-side and downside consequences of a decision are referred to as *risk neutral*. Decision analysts will assess the risk tolerance of the decision makers of an enterprise and codify this in a utility function that is used during the evaluation of strategic alternatives in an attempt to account for the decision makers' risk preferences within the decision analysis process.

In the COSO view, *risk appetite* is defined in relation to the corporation's strategy creation process and is set by the corporate board and senior executive staff, whereas *risk tolerance* is defined (again by the board) in relation to corporate business objectives and their related activities that have been allocated resources for implementing that strategy (deliberate plan). There are a variety of risk measures in use to define risk tolerances including:

♦ *Value at Risk* (VaR),
♦ *Earnings at Risk* (EaR),
♦ *Cash at Risk* (CaR),
♦ *Cash Flow at Risk* (CfaR), and
♦ *Greeks* (a set of factor sensitivities used extensively by traders to quantify the exposures of portfolios that contain options).

Non-risk measures are also used in describing risk tolerances such as the dollar amount of credit outstanding or capital availability. Probabilistic thresholds are also used such as "the probability of violating a debt covenant."

♦ *Risk Targets*: These represent the bounds (as measured in the same units as risk tolerance) that an organization targets to operate within. Setting the *risk targets* requires the tricky balancing of the organization's resources, the organization's commitment to performance (goals, objectives, performance targets) and the acceptable degree of risk assumed in achieving those performance commitments.

Are you confused yet? Keep in mind the key point—*knowledge about risk is only informative, meaningful, and useful if it supports making a decision*. Making a decision is a commitment of resources—money or time—and resources are managed through budget setting and budget allocation. ERM needs to be integrated back into budget setting, budget allocation, and most importantly, management decision-making processes. PRO Enterprise Management can help accomplish this task.

PRO Enterprise Management Perspective on the Concept of Risk Exposure

PRO Enterprise Management requires *problems*, *risks*, and *opportunities* to compete for resources—money and time—based on enterprise value creation and protection, the ultimate measure for for-profit enterprises. ERM; however, is primarily focused on the protection of shareholder (enterprise) value. Protecting shareholder value requires the management of and investment in resolving problems and mitigating risk—managing the potential downside performance of the enterprise.

Consider a commonly used financial institution ERM measure, *Value at Risk* (VaR). *Value at Risk* is based on a statistical analysis used to quantify the level of financial risk within an enterprise or investment portfolio over a specific time frame such as a day or week or month or year. *Value at Risk* is used to measure and control the level of risk that the enterprise undertakes. The risk manager's job is to ensure that risks are not taken beyond the level at which the firm can absorb the losses of a "probable worst outcome," often using the 5th percentile of an outcome distribution as the "probable worst outcome."

Value at Risk is measured with three parameters: the amount of potential loss, the probability of that amount of loss, and the time frame. For example, an enterprise may calculate through a statistical model of profit and loss that this year it has a 5% annual *Value at Risk* of $300M. This means that there is a 5% chance that the enterprise could have a loss of $300M or more this year. Figure 15.2 provides a graphical representation of this example of *Value at Risk*.

In Figure 15.2, the 5th percentile of the estimated probability density function of this year's profit and loss is minus $300M. This implies that there is a 5% chance that the loss for this year could be $300M or more. The estimated probability density function spans the range of potential outcomes for the year. As an example, also illustrated in Figure 15.2, is that there is a 5% chance that this year's profit could be greater than $4.3B.

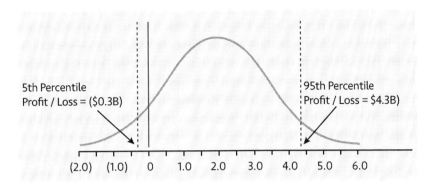

Figure 15.2: Example Output of a Statistical Evaluation to Determine an Enterprise's Annual Value at Risk

From an ERM perspective, the first question for senior executives (given the insights provided in Figure 15.2) is whether or not having a 5% chance of losing $300M or more is acceptable? Does this fall within the company's *risk target* bounds? Is this degree of *risk exposure* acceptable with respect to the senior executives' *risk tolerance*? If the answer to all of these questions is yes, then our analysis is complete. We could claim that ERM has done its job. We could claim that no decisions need be made at this point in time with respect to ERM.

On the other hand, Figure 15.2 typically results in the following types of questions:

♦ What scenarios or events are driving the "left-tail" of the distribution?

♦ What specific sources of risk or uncertainty are in the "left-tail" of the distribution?

♦ What can we do to reduce the $300M VaR?

♦ What scenarios or events are driving the "right-tail" of the distribution?

♦ What are the opportunities in the "right-tail" of the distribution?

♦ What can we do to push the "right-tail" of the distribution out further?

In other words, Figure 15.2 both *frames* and *primes* a discussion on:

♦ The specific scenarios or events culminating in company *problems* and *risks* that are driving the "left-tail" of the distribution, and,

♦ The specific scenarios or events culminating in company *opportunities* that are driving the "right-tail" of the distribution.

From a decision-making perspective, all of your work is still ahead of you. Much work and modeling have been done to create the distribution in Figure 15.2, but the "heavy lifting" of decision making remains. What decisions need to be made given the insights of the Value at Risk analysis?

To create the profit and loss distribution in Figure 15.2 it was necessary to create a comprehensive enterprise profit and loss model accounting for all of the "significant" sources of risk and uncertainty. However, notice that the focus of the conversation is about the "tails" of the distribution. What is driving the tails? From a decision-making perspective, the tails are the byproduct of the enterprise's *PRO portfolio* and the decisions made with respect to the enterprise's *PRO portfolio*. PRO Enterprise Management is a solution to engineering the shape of the profit and loss distribution in Figure 15.2. PRO Enterprise Management is a solution to ERM decision making.

We have already explored a risk exposure portfolio measure in Chapter 13 associated with the second question of PRO Management: "Which PRO items erode the most value if not pursued?" Each problem and risk has an associated PRO management measure of "Expected Net Present Value" *Before Investment and Action* as defined in Chapter 12. Consider the risk exposure due to network-wide (global) contamination as depicted in Figure 15.3. As per Figure 15.3 we can conclude that the *expected* risk exposure to the corporation due to network-wide (global) contamination risk is about $1.26B.

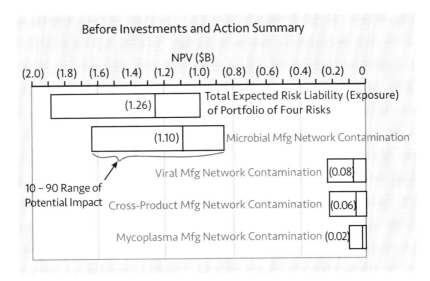

Figure 15.3: Expected Risk Exposure to the Corporation Due to Network-Wide (Global) Contamination Risk Before Investment and Action

Considering risk mitigation actions for each of these risks allows for the *priming* prioritization of expenditures by investment productivity as depicted in Figure 15.4.

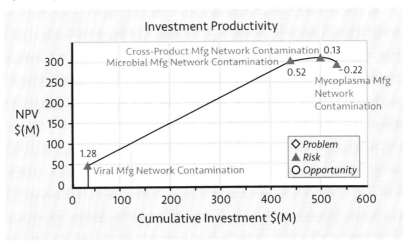

Figure 15.4: Network-Wide (Global) Contamination Risk Mitigation Investments Prioritized by Investment Productivity

Which enterprise risks should you pursue with investment and action? Let's consider all risks with positive investment productivity. In this example, that includes: (1) "Viral Manufacturing Network Contamination," (2) "Microbial Manufacturing Network

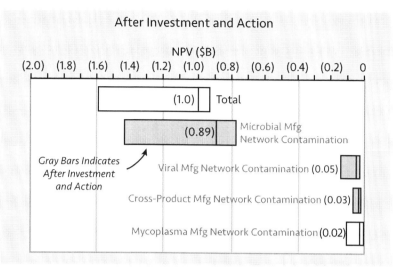

Figure 15.5: Expected Residual Risk Exposure to the Corporation Due to Network-Wide (Global) Contamination Risk After Investment and Action

Contamination," and (3) "Cross-Product Manufacturing Network Contamination." The residual risk given the risk mitigation actions are pursued is provided in Figure 15.5.

As per Figures 15.3 and 15.5, the expected risk exposure due to "Network-Wide (Global) Contamination" has been reduced from

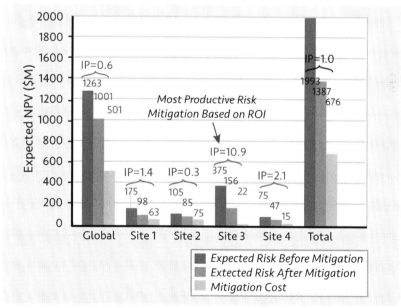

Figure 15.6: Expected Residual Risk Exposure Due to Contamination Risk with Investment Productivity (IP)

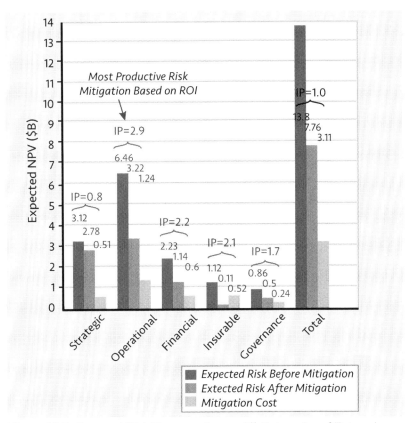

Figure 15.7: Expected Risk Exposure Across All Categories of Enterprise Risk with Investment Productivity

about $1.26B to about $1.0B. But how does this class of contamination risk compare to the other sources of contamination risk listed in Figure 15.1? Performing the same analytical approach to the other sources of contamination risk enables the comparisons and summary in Figure 15.6.

Figure 15.6 provides enterprise value-based insights to *prime* the decision discussion about which contamination risks to pursue with investment and action. The same process is used to compare classes of "operational" risks listed in Figure 15.1. And this can be further rolled up for a perspective across the entire enterprise risk management framework as shown in Figure 15.7.

These are the insights needed to appropriately *frame* and *prime* discussions on enterprise risk management decision making.

PRO Enterprise Management Perspective on the Concepts of Risk Capacity, Risk Appetite, and Risk Targets

As currently practiced, there is a broad range of qualitative and quantitative measures that are used for the concepts of risk capacity, risk appetite, risk tolerance, and risk targets. Net present value of discounted enterprise free cash flow is an example of an ERM measure that can be applied to each of these concepts. From a comprehensive ERM perspective it is not a sufficient measure, but it can be argued as a necessary ERM measure that easily bridges all of these concepts and a measure to be used to prime ERM decision making.

Analogous to the generalized notion of risk appetite, the Board and corporate executives can create a threshold point, measured

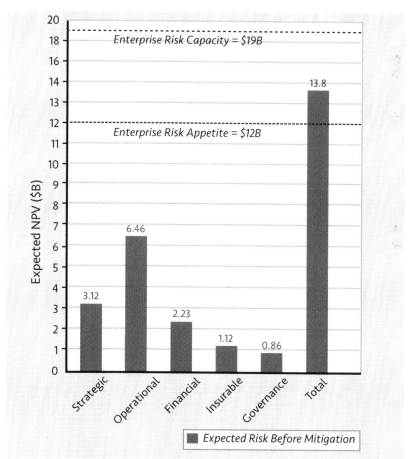

Figure 15.8: Setting Enterprise Risk Capacity and Enterprise Risk Appetite (Measured in Lost Expected Net Present Value of Discounted Free Cash Flow)

in lost shareholder value, which they want to ensure—or at least minimize the probability—the enterprise does not cross. From the PRO-EM perspective, this implies that risk appetite is the amount of risk (measured in shareholder value) that an enterprise is willing to bear while pursuing the deliberate plan of the enterprise. Figure 15.8 provides an example of setting the enterprise risk capacity and enterprise risk appetite as measured in expected lost net present value of enterprise discounted free cash flow—as discussed in Chapter 5, a good surrogate measure for lost shareholder value.

As illustrated in Figure 15.8, the current enterprise risk assessment is within the enterprise risk capacity threshold ($19B) but not within the enterprise risk appetite threshold ($12B) associated with the enterprise's deliberate plan.

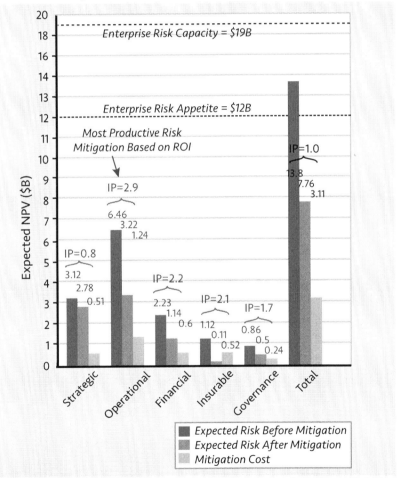

Figure 15.9: Potential Risk Exposures After Investment & Action in Relation to Enterprise Risk Capacity and Enterprise Risk Appetite

Figure 15.9 suggests that the enterprise can get well within the enterprise risk appetite threshold (given all potential risk mitigations are funded), reducing the enterprise risk exposure to about $7.8B. The risk appetite and the risk mitigation investment productivity measures now inform the decision making on which risk mitigation actions to fund. As in the PRO Management method, first the "must-have" risk mitigations are identified and funded, and then the remaining risks competing for funding are prioritized based on investment productivity using investment productivity curves thus ensuring Mehr's and Hedges' original objective of risk management: "maximize the productive efficiency of the enterprise."

As we cascade down into organizations and categories of risk, the concepts of risk capacity, risk appetite, risk tolerance, and risk targets can all apply. Figure 15.10 provides an example of using risk targets as bounds on the risk category of "contamination risk." The current expected value risk exposure of $1.26B in contamination risk is beyond an executive's risk target bounds of $0.6B to $1.1B; consequently, the executive will need to decide which specific contamination risks to fund for risk mitigation actions.

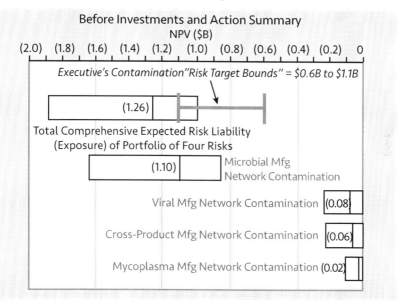

Figure 15.10: Example of Risk Target Bounds Applied to Contamination Risk

As detailed in Figure 15.11, funding risk mitigation actions for the risks with the top three greatest investment productivity values (and in this case also the largest top three risk exposures) the executive reduces the expected risk exposure for the category down to about $1.0B which is within the executive's risk target bounds.

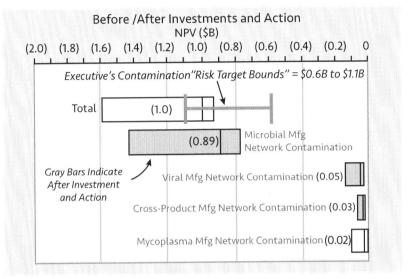

Figure 15.11: Risk Exposures After Investment and Action in Relation to Contamination Risk Target Bounds

Geopolitical Risk

Geopolitical risk (also known as *political risk*) is a risk of financial or market loss resulting from political decisions, changes, or disruptions. Political *decisions* by governmental leaders on taxation, currency valuation, trade tariffs, labor laws, or environmental regulations can have significant effects on business operations and profitability. Political *disruptions* such as terrorism, riots, coups, civil wars, international wars, and even political elections that may change the ruling government can dramatically affect businesses' ability to operate.

Example: Geopolitical Risk for Energy Industry Products and Services Provider

Executives at a multi-national energy services company were concerned of the potential for a geopolitical crisis in a country that generates significant revenue from their mature oil fields services. The energy services company had recently hired a consulting company to perform a geopolitical risk assessment project to help assess the situation in the region and provide some risk mitigation strategies to reduce the risk of losing sales in the region resulting

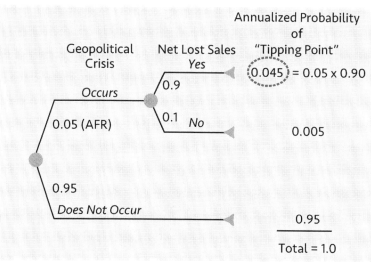

Figure 15.12: Annualized Probability of a Geopolitical Crisis Leading to Lost Net Sales Before Investment and Action

from a geopolitical crisis. The consulting company suggested five risk mitigation strategies to reduce the potential of lost sales due to a geopolitical crisis, including:

♦ Examine the political connections of the energy company's local partners. Close association with the current regime is advantageous now, but once key individuals are removed from power the energy company could lose most if not all of its business.

♦ Consider contributing to the country's economy and culture with a well-publicized public project.

♦ Cultivate connections with public officials outside the industry in which the company operates—they may become important allies in a crisis situation.

♦ Go beyond discussions with representatives of the national or local government—they may not be a good indicator of public opinion.

♦ Establish an informal dialogue with local journalists and human rights and environmentalist groups.

A Risk Assessment Team including internal subject matter experts and subject matter experts from the consulting company was assembled—by request of the region's VP of Operations—and they agreed to the tipping point of a material consequence being a geopolitical event that leads to any lost sales. Figure 15.12 and Figure

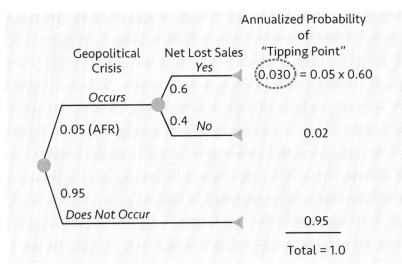

Figure 15.13: Annualized Probability of a Geopolitical Crisis Leading to Lost Net Sales After Investment and Action

15.13 provide the Risk Assessment Team's annualized probability or annualized failure rate (AFR) of a geopolitical crisis leading to lost net sales for the cases of before investment and action and after investment and action, respectively.

The Risk Assessment Team worked with individuals in the Business Development and Marketing & Sales Organization to assess the *before investment and action* impact to net sales given a geopolitical crisis leading to lost revenue. They agreed that a "surprisingly bad" scenario would be that all future sales would be lost. Further they believed that a "surprisingly good" scenario, given the tipping point occurred, would be a loss of 50% of future sales. Their 50th percentile net sales impact was assessed as an 80% loss of future sales. A similar logic was applied to the *after investment and action* net sales impacts. The consultant and the Marketing and Sales Organization staff argued that, from past experience, they believed the risk mitigation strategies would reduce the 10–50–90 net sales losses to 25%, 50%, and 100%, respectively, of total regional net sales. So there was still significant risk that a geopolitical crisis leading to lost net sales could eliminate all future net sales from the region—at least in the "surprisingly bad" 90th percentile scenario.

The Risk Assessment Team with the support of the consulting firm created a budget to implement the five risk mitigation strategies discussed above, including building two schools, one in each of two impoverished neighborhoods. The total cost of implementing these risk mitigation strategies was $4.8M. The geopolitical risk unmitigated has a total expected risk liability of \$195.7M. The expected risk liability can be reduced to \$142.3M by implementing the risk mitigation strategies. The expected net gain from this investment is calculated as the difference in these two numbers: \$53.4M. The expected investment productivity (IP) of risk mitigation strategies is 11.52.[7]

The geopolitical risk can only partially be reduced, largely the result of having no real way to mitigate the chances of a geopolitical crisis occurring in the region (see Figures 15.12 and 15.13). Having no real means to reduce the risk in the first two years during the time required to implement the risk mitigation strategy further reduces the company's ability to mitigate this risk. However, even with limited means to reduce the chances of a tipping point occurrence, the investment productivity is significantly positive: over 11! The region's VP of Operations felt this "minimal investment" to partially protect future net sales in the region was "obviously supported by the analysis" and he approved the budget request for pursuing the five risk mitigation strategies and he directed his staff to pursue implementation quickly.

Reputational Risk

Reputational risk (also known as *reputation risk*) is a risk of loss resulting from damages to a corporation's or an organization's reputation culminating in:

♦ Lost sales,
♦ Increased operating, regulatory, or capital costs, or
♦ Reduced market capitalization (stock price).

The tipping point of a material consequence can be any one or more of these three impacts triggered by an adverse or potentially criminal event—even when the company is not found liable or guilty. The underlying adverse events typically include one or more matters of ethics, safety, security, quality, innovation, and environmental sustainability. However, reputational risk can also result from poor or inadequate response to strategic or operational risks.

In extreme cases, reputational risk can lead to bankruptcy such as the case for Arthur Andersen—once a prestigious accounting firm—after its felony conviction for obstructing a federal inves-

---

7   The denominator in the investment productivity calculation is the present value of the investment and therefore it is discounted over time by the corporate discount rate.

tigation into Enron. Recent examples of companies suffering from damaged reputations include: Toyota, Oracle Corporation, Goldman Sachs, and BP. Damaged reputations are not always the company's fault as was the case in 1982 for Johnson & Johnson when seven people died from cyanide-laced Tylenol capsules, triggering a massive recall of the product and hundreds of millions of dollars in lost sales. In reputational risk there are concerns over market capitalization (stock price) and so some like to use market capitalization as a reputational risk measure. This is a measure of fear; but fear of what? Future lost sales? Increased operating costs? Downgraded credit rating? All of these show up in cash flow. Downgraded credit rating results in increased cost of debt, that is, increased interest expense. Net present value of discounted free cash flow is a good surrogate measure for enterprise value and enables financial measurement of all sources of risk—including *reputational risk.*

Meta-Risks

In 2000, Jack Gray introduced the concept of "meta-risks" for investors in capital markets, identifying the underlying source of "meta-risk" as people, organizations, and their interactions.[8] This includes issues such as:

◆ Rigidity in people holding material beliefs that are not sufficiently challenged and their selective acceptance of evidence and arguments confirming their beliefs,

◆ Data mining and predictive analytics that are too narrowly focused or grounded with flawed assumptions about the future,

◆ Complexity built into risk models coupled with insufficient insight on the implications of complexity to model results, and,

◆ Investment decisions made by an investor's agent based upon the agent's risk tolerance (as opposed to the investor's risk tolerance)—in our case a manager's decision based on the manager's risk tolerance rather than the enterprise's risk tolerance.

Although Gray's discussion was intended for investors in capital markets, the points he made are applicable at the enterprise level. A primary concern Gray raises is the lack of awareness of meta-

---

8   Jack Gray, "Meta-Risks," *Journal of Portfolio Management*, Spring 2000, Vol. 26, No. 3: pages 18-25.

risks because of high confidence in the assessment and control of the risks that are modeled.

The increasing complexity of risk resulting from the inter-relationships and combined impacts of global, market, financial, economic, environmental, and internal forces can defy rational explanations and simple narrative explanations. Models featuring excessive complexity will generate results that can be counter-intuitive to individuals, leaving executives suspicious of interpretations and recommendations. On the other hand, overly simplified models can fail to account for important interrelationships among risks, and their misrepresentations can misinform decision making.

Gray's view is a philosophical yin and yang perspective and recommendation. Every meta-risk has a complementary meta-risk:

- ◆ Insufficient challenge of thoughts and beliefs is complemented by excessive challenge and delayed decision making,

- ◆ Too narrowly defined data collection, decision frames, and analyses are complemented by overly consuming data collection and overly broad frames and analyses,

- ◆ Overly complex models are complemented by simple models, and

- ◆ Individual's short-term needs and tolerance for risk are complemented by the enterprise's long-term needs and tolerance for risk.

Gray concludes that organizations need a "balanced culture" explicitly focused on the dual nature of meta-risks and that debate, discussion, and challenge are key ingredients that need to be built into risk management processes. PRO Enterprise Management methods and analytics are explicitly designed to be part of the complementary nature of managing meta-risks. Both simple and complex decision frames and models are at times simultaneously needed, as eloquently articulated by Gray.

Eliminating or Modifying "Dead End" Risk Management Practices

Any risk management process or risk analysis method that does not directly and naturally enable the answering of the Five Questions of Risk Management is a "dead end" decision process. A good example of a dead end decision process is use of risk matrices (see

Appendix 5). To answer the Five Questions of Risk Management you will need to abandon the risk matrix at some point and transition to something else. The risk matrix is inefficient and results in rework and often requires reframing the risks. Any initial or preliminary risk assessment should support answering the five questions and also be easily and naturally expandable when more granularity or complexity is needed to ensure a high quality decision. *This* is a critical enabler of Enterprise Risk Management (ERM) and ultimately, PRO Enterprise Management.

Extending Enterprise Risk Management (ERM) to PRO Enterprise Management (PRO-EM)

By extending current ERM concepts and methods to include PRO Enterprise Management framework and methods, we can enable the broadened objective of risk management to "maximize the productive efficiency of the enterprise." Missing from ERM as practiced today is the ability to answer many important questions such as:

- ◆ What will it cost to reduce the enterprise's risk exposure to fit within the Board's and Corporate Executives' *Risk Appetite*?
- ◆ What is the ROI in terms of enterprise value for reducing the enterprise's (or other entity's) risk exposure?
- ◆ Which problem and risk pursuits have the greatest ROI in terms of enterprise value?
- ◆ What does it cost to support an organization's (or other entity's) reduced *Risk Tolerance* and what is the ROI in terms of enterprise value for the reduction?

An ERM trap executives fall into is the notion of pursuing more or bigger *opportunities* to balance or mitigate the potential downside associated with their existing *problems* and *risks*. As we have pointed out many times, PRO-EM brings these investments together to compete consistently for investment, making this balancing act of potential downside and up-side transparent. But all of these questions and thinking are best framed by the simple risk maxim:

Key Point:

Knowledge about risk is only informative, meaningful, and useful if it supports decision making.

It is becoming common wisdom that the understanding of enterprise risk needs to be an integral part of strategic planning and strategic decision making. For the vast majority of enterprises, the link between risk and strategic planning and decision making remains woefully insufficient. The PRO-EM perspective is that enterprise problems, risks, and opportunities all need to be an integral part of strategic planning and decision making—not just risk.

Why so much emphasis on risk management and ERM? Risk management remains the weakest link in corporate decision making across problems, risks, and opportunities. Leveraging and surgically refining current risk management and ERM infrastructures and business processes is an efficient path to enable broad implementation of PRO-EM methods and analysis. Risk Management is a speculative decision process; in the end, we are merely haggling about the quality and efficiency of these speculations and their subsequent decisions. The vision of Robert Mehr and Bob Hedges in 1963 was to broaden the objective of risk management to "maximize the productive efficiency of the enterprise."[9] PRO Enterprise Management enables that vision unlike current ERM in practice. PRO-EM bridges the abstraction of current ERM practices into and throughout organizational decision making.

---

9   Robert Mehr and Robert Hedges, *Risk Management in the Business Enterprise*, currently available from Literary Licensing, LLC (2012)

16

Implementing PRO Enterprise Management

Into today's globally-connected, competitive marketplace there are no *long-standing* successful corporations that were just lucky. The ability to make high quality decisions followed by sufficient execution is a must—just to stay in business. Fortunately, the laws of nature—survival of the fittest—influence corporate longevity. So having an advantage on the competition *might* be good enough to stay in business. Marcia Blenko, Michael Mankins, and Paul Rogers of Bain & Company believe *decision effectiveness*[1] in organizations is determined by four elements:

- ♦ Quality,
- ♦ Speed,
- ♦ Yield, and
- ♦ Effort.

In a survey of some 760 companies world-wide, they found, "The overall correlation between decision effectiveness and performance was extraordinarily strong, holding up at a 95 percent confidence level or higher for every country, industry, and company size we studied. Companies with the highest scores on decision effectiveness consistently generated higher levels of revenue growth and return on invested capital. Top-quintile companies on decisions produced an average total shareholder return about six percentage

---

1   Marcia W. Blenko, Michael C. Mankins, and Paul Rogers, *Decide & Deliver: 5 Steps to Breakthrough Performance in Your Organization* (Boston, MA: Harvard Business Review Press, 2010), pages 21-26.

points higher than that of other companies."[2] Important in Blenko's, Mankins', and Rogers' message is that *decision effectiveness* does not apply solely to big, strategic decisions; it applies to the day-to-day operational decisions too.

The vision of a *PRO* Enterprise is a corporation or governmental entity in which every individual who owns and manages a budget can efficiently answer the five questions of PRO Management with respect to their domain from an enterprise-value perspective, and successfully execute the resultant decisions both on a regular and repeatable basis. Is anything missing in this vision? If that vision were true in your corporation, would your corporation have reached the pinnacle of enterprise-value performance? Stop and think about what else must be true in an organization for it to reach the pinnacle of enterprise-value performance. What would you add or modify to articulate your vision of a *PRO* Enterprise?

Why Change Now?

There are at least four forces at play that pressure corporations and governmental entities toward a decision-making philosophy and practices (such as PRO Enterprise Management). All of these forces underscore the need for straightforward, consistent, "simple as possible but not simpler" methods and practices for enterprise-wide decision making based on enterprise value.

Economic Forces

- ◆ Business is becoming more complex and risky.
- ◆ Speed and complexity of decision making is increasing.
- ◆ Cost cutting continues to thin out staffing in organizations.
- ◆ There is not enough time for complex, detailed analyses.
- ◆ Organizations are required to do more with less.

Organizational Forces

- ◆ Regular reorganizations keep breaking processes that previously worked.
- ◆ Merger and acquisition activities result in distractions and loss of focus.
- ◆ New partners and supplier relationships are constantly being added.

---

2   Ibid, page 27.

Technological Forces

- Information technology suppliers are providing more complex and more specialized, costly solutions.
- Current IT firms have no long-term vision for integrated corporate decision making.
- There is no way to get to consistent, best enterprise-value decision making based on technology alone.

Regulatory Forces

- Regulatory agencies and organizations continue to evolve towards more requirements ensuring decision-making transparency.
- Requirements for broad considerations of risk, including the reporting of risks, are increasing.
- Stakeholders impacted by decisions must be considered.
- Organizations need to justify and document why one alternative was chosen and why other alternatives were not chosen.

Integrate the Five Questions into Decision Making

Broad-based change in corporations and governmental entities is difficult and is fraught with many risks. Change management is outside the scope of this book. If you are thinking about the broad implementation of PRO Enterprise Management in your organization, you will need expertise beyond the concepts in this book. A difficulty in changing existing business processes and decision processes is that when an outsider reviews the details of a process, the process can appear to be highly inefficient and possibly ineffective. But as you dig deeper into the existing process you find there are reasons—sometimes subtle and sometimes bad—for why the process runs in the manner that it does. Making wholesale changes to business processes often leads to failure or at least short-term failure until the changes are fixed to fit into the broader context and challenges within the organization.

I've found that the most effective means to implement PRO Enterprise Management methods and practices into existing business processes is to take a more careful approach. For business processes involving decision making, determine where and how the five questions of PRO Management are addressed. Typically you will find that these processes do not address the five questions; nonetheless, often there will be obvious ties or links to where placement of the work required to answer the five questions should be integrated into the process. In effect, you should try to create as little change to the business process as possible while ensuring sound PRO Enterprise Management methods are well integrated into the process.

The Critical Role of Corporate Culture

Anyone who has led or has attempted to lead a program of change in a corporation or governmental entity knows that culture matters. Corporate culture can be an enabler of change but most of the time it is an obstacle. Ignoring corporate culture in any transformational program guarantees failure.

Culture is commonly defined as the values, beliefs, attitudes, and assumptions shared within a company or organization. Much has been written about corporate culture and its influence on decision making, but, in general, I have not found the documented insights and recommendations very actionable (with a few exceptions).

In their 2013 book entitled, *Creating a Culture of Profitability*, Rob and Aviva Kleinbaum have provided a logical framework and powerful toolkit for analyzing and improving corporate culture. They simply define a "good" corporate culture as "a culture that leads to a profitable, sustainable, healthy business."[3] Peter Drucker claimed, "The first responsibility of business is to make enough profit to cover the costs for the future. If this social responsibility is not met, no other social responsibility can be met."[4] The Kleinbaums share this perspective by stating "without profit, your business will be neither sustainable nor healthy." Neither Drucker nor the Kleinbaums claim the objective of a business is to make a profit, but they claim it is necessary to be profitable if you want to be in business at all for the long haul to enable all other social-economic benefits. Both positions are completely consistent with the PRO Enterprise Management tenet of priming corporate decisions with a long-term enterprise value measure.

---

3   Rob and Aviva Kleinbaum, *Creating a Culture of Profitability* (Sugarland, TX: Probabilistic Publishing, 2013), page 4.

4   Peter F. Drucker, *The Frontiers of Management: Where Tomorrow's Decisions Are Being Shaped Today* (Oxford, United Kingdom: Butterworth-Heinemann Ltd., 1987).

Taking the First Step

"The secret to getting ahead is getting started."
– Mark Twain, American Author and Humorist

Over the years, much has been written about how to effect changes in organizations and, more specifically, about what steps should be taken to improve decision making. According to Peter Senge, author of a seminal change management book, *The Fifth Discipline: The Art & Practice of the Learning Organization*, there are four challenges to initiating changes:[5]

- There must be a compelling case for change.
- There must be time for change.
- There must be help during the change process.
- As the perceived barriers to change are removed, it is important that some new problem, not before considered important or perhaps not even recognized, doesn't become a critical barrier.

These four challenges are real and if not addressed will undermine (if not completely derail) an initiative's desired changes and constrict the value sought that is associated with the changes. Senge's first challenge is a compelling case for change, which was outlined in the section entitled, "Why Change Now?" With Senge's four challenges as a backbone, let us consider how to go about improving decision making in organizations by implementing PRO Enterprise Management.

Launching a PRO Enterprise Management Program

In this era of business management, many if not most companies and governmental entities have codified business processes for executing change projects or larger-scale change programs. Therefore, you should utilize your proven methods and processes for implementing PRO Enterprise Management in your organization or enterprise. If you are in an organization that does *not* have such change-based processes, you can find numerous practical change management references to use as a foundation for implementing PRO Enterprise Management. Whichever way you choose to implement PRO Enterprise Management, and, whether it is local or enterprise-wide, keep in mind and address Senge's four challenges to initiating changes.

---

5   Peter M. Senge, http://www.openfuture.co.nz/petersenge.htm.

Start with Pilot Projects

At the outset of every initial engagement I have with a new client I say, "I know what needs to be done and how to improve your organization's decision making and we have the tools to do it. What I don't know and what we must understand is what tailoring must be done to fit within your organization."

To understand this, we work through several pilot projects targeted on different areas that will provide the greatest benefits to your enterprise. The pilots will uncover several important characteristics about your organization, including:

◆ Leadership's preference for level-of-detail in analysis and data,

◆ Current leadership's decision-making style and process preferences,

◆ Current decision-making processes and capabilities,

◆ Barriers to information flow and cross-functional coordination,

◆ Capability of information systems to provide information, data, and insights supportive of PRO item assessments,

◆ Cultural barriers to enterprise value-based decision making, and

◆ Current capabilities to enable answering the five questions of PRO Management.

A primary insight to be gleaned from the pilot projects is the necessary granularity of data and analytics to ensure that decisions are implemented and that decision quality is achieved.

If the PRO Enterprise Management pilot projects are not sponsored through the finance organization, it is important to get finance involved at the outset. In corporations, the finance organization is typically the source of any ROI-based analysis (including PRO Management analytics). Finance will need to understand the general analytical approach to ensure they agree that it is sound and so that they can understand and interpret the analytical results and compare the results with their methods. Often times PRO Enterprise Management templates are owned and maintained through the finance organizations to ensure consistency with financial policies. A single pilot project in a targeted area requires several weeks to several months depending on the number of PRO items assessed and the number of individuals involved. Although pilot projects can be pursued in parallel, I recommend starting with a single pilot project to get an initial broad understanding of the seven organizational characteristics listed above.

A single pilot project includes the following tasks:

1. Train individuals on PRO Enterprise Management.

    ♦ The level of training depends on the goals and objectives of the pilot and can be anything from a brief introduction to PRO Enterprise Management to detailed training on PRO Enterprise Management analytics.

For each PRO item within the scope of the pilot project, perform steps 2, 3, and 4:

2. Frame the PRO item.

    ♦ Define the PRO item and metrics.
    ♦ Define the "Tipping Point of a Material Consequence."
    ♦ Define decision alternatives.
    ♦ Define 10–50–90 narratives (no numbers, just story-lines).
    ♦ Specify information sources (internal and external—people, information systems, and reports).

3. Analyze the PRO item.

    ♦ Specify investment and action by decision alternative.
    ♦ Assess "Tipping Point" probabilities.
    ♦ Perform 10–50–90 numerical assessments of narratives.
    ♦ Perform PRO analysis.
    ♦ Review PRO analysis results.
    ♦ Document insights and recommendations.

4. Commit to the PRO item decision.

    ♦ Vet insights and recommendations.
    ♦ Present to decision makers for commitment.
    ♦ Revise analysis and recommendations (as required).
    ♦ Present to decision makers (as required).
    ♦ Create a decision record.

5. Create and communicate the lessons learned from the pilot.

   ◆ Identify individuals to interview and consult for lessons learned.

   ◆ Create a simple template to capture lessons learned based on organizational characteristics listed above.

   ◆ Collect and document lessons learned.

   ◆ Review and revise (as required) any templates used in the pilot.

For most corporations, no more than three or so pilot projects in different areas should be sufficient to lead to an enterprise-wide PRO Enterprise Management transformation program. Risk management in one or more functional areas (e.g., supply chain, quality, or enterprise risk management) is often one of the pilot projects, as risk management tends to be perceived as necessary from a compliance perspective yet adding limited value as practiced. On the other hand, effective risk management has the potential for adding significant enterprise value; consequently, it is often at the top of the list of target areas for a pilot project.

Pursuing a PRO Enterprise Management Transformation Program

When transforming an enterprise to using PRO Enterprise Management methods and tools throughout—what I call a *PRO Enterprise*—start by understanding the breadth of the lessons learned from the pilot projects, and take a hard look at how your corporate culture could potentially derail such a transformation, and then review Senge's four challenges to initiating changes. All of these perspectives are critical for successful transformation. A PRO Enterprise Management enterprise-wide transformation strikes at the core of corporate culture—how decisions are made.

Improving decision making alone will not result in the enterprise benefits being sought. You will also need to ensure that the timely and effective implementation of decisions is a repeatable and dependable process. The critical component of decision implementation is transitioning from a decision being made to the successful launch of its implementation. Consequently, included in a PRO Enterprise Management transformation program is detailing the work associated with transitioning from decision making to implementation.

FACT is an acronym for Frame-Analyze-Commit-Transition. This decision-making process represents the standard from which enterprise decision-making processes are tailored. A PRO Enterprise Management transformation program incorporates this four-step process (FACT) into all decision-making processes. Ability to answer the five questions of PRO Management throughout the enterprise is also integrated into the process. The resultant set of concepts and tools cover the unique nature of a PRO Enterprise Management transformation.

RADIC Charts

The first tool is a RADIC chart that summarizes the roles and responsibilities of individuals in a PRO Management decision-making process. RADIC is an acronym for the following decision-making roles:

- *R*: Individual responsible for completing the task,
- *A*: Individual accountable for decision quality of the process,
- *D*: Individual who decides on the decision alternative to pursue or the action to take,
- *I*: Individual who is informed of the decision or result of a task, and
- *C*: Individual consulted for information or insight.

Role	Frame	Analyze	Commit	Transition
PRO Item Sponsor	C / I		I / D	D
PRO Assessment Lead	A	A	R / A	C
PRO Assessment Team	R	R	R	C
PRO Item Analyst	C	R	C	
Finance	C	C	I	
Marketing and Sales	C	C	I	
Manufacturing	C	C	I	
Change Management Team	C			R

Table 16.1: Simplified RADIC Chart: Tasks, Roles, and Responsibilities of a PRO Item Through Transition to Implementation

Table 16.1 provides a simplified example of a RADIC chart that spans the four-step process of decision making and transition to implementation. During a transformation program, a RADIC chart should be created for each class of decision within the scope of the transformation.

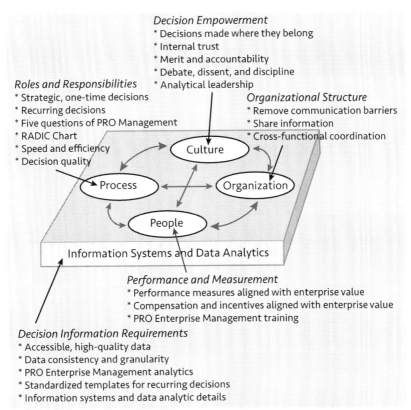

Figure 16.1: Overview of the Components of a PRO Enterprise Management Transformation Program

Figure 16.1 illustrates the breadth of components of a PRO Enterprise Management transformation program including:

♦ Processes,

♦ Culture,

♦ Organization,

♦ People, and

♦ Information Systems & Data Analytics.

The transformation's basic building block is building the five questions of PRO Management into the organization's or enterprise's business processes. For most functional areas of an enterprise (e.g., supply chain, quality, risk management, procurement, mergers & acquisitions, research & development, marketing & sales, plant management, project management) the breadth of decision making can be covered with (at most) three to five patterns or templates.

The role of the pilot projects is to identify these patterns and draft PRO Management templates that, through use, can be improved and refined over time.

A PRO Enterprise Management transformation program is ultimately about creating *PRO Managers* throughout the enterprise. A *PRO Manager* is an individual who can answer the five questions of PRO Management with respect to their domain and successfully implement the resultant decisions:

1. What are your PRO items?

2. Which erode the most value if not pursued?

3. Which, if pursued, create or protect the most value?

4. Which should/will you pursue at this point in time?

5. What are the implications to your plan and budget?

Advice on Meetings and Presentations

Presentations made and given by analysts are notoriously too long on numbers and too short on storytelling. The corollary of this is, if you want your audience to go to sleep, focus on the numbers. I'm going to look to a professional pitchman for advice on giving presentations, Oren Klaff, an investment banker. In his 2011 book, *Pitch Anything: An Innovative Method for Presenting, Persuading, and Winning the Deal,*[6] Klaff leverages Kahneman's notion of System 1 and System 2 thinking and provides valuable insights and tips for giving effective presentations. Although the book is crafted for closing deals, much of the contents is about giving effective presentations. He uses the notion of the "crocodile brain" and "neocortex" for roughly what Kahneman refers to as System 1 and System 2 respectively. [See Chapter 6 for discussion of Kahneman's System 1 and System 2.]

The following is my top 10 list of favorite quotes from Oren Klaff's book on the topic of giving effective presentations that connect with the minds of executives:

1. "All the important stuff must fit into the audience's limits of attention, which for most people is about 20 minutes."[7]

---

6   Oren Klaff, *Pitch Anything: An Innovative Method for Presenting, Persuading, and Winning the Deal* (New York, NY: McGraw-Hill, 2011).

7   Ibid, page 111.

2. "What's important here is not your mastery over the details but your mastery over attention and time."[8]

3. "It doesn't matter how much information you give, a lot or a little, but instead how good your theory of mind is. In other words, it's important how well you can tune your information to the other person's mind."[9]

4. "When frames come together, the first thing they do is collide. And this isn't a friendly competition—it's a death match. Frames don't merge. They don't blend. And they don't intermingle. They collide, and the stronger frame absorbs the weaker."[10]

5. "The brain of the person on the other side of the desk isn't reacting to any of those highly evolved, relatively complicated ideas. It is reacting exactly as it should. It is trying to determine whether the information coming in is a threat to the person's immediate survival and, if it isn't, whether it can be ignored without consequence"[11] (the lazy System 2 and the always responding System 1).

6. "Its [the brain's] reaction to your pitch basically goes like this: 'Since this is not an emergency, how can I ignore this or spend the least amount of time possible on it?' This filtering system of the crocodile brain has a very short-sighted view of the world. Anything that is not a crisis it tries to mark as 'spam'."[12]

7. The croc brain's filtering instructions:[13]

    ♦ If it's not dangerous, ignore it.
    ♦ If it's not new and exciting, ignore it.
    ♦ If it is new, summarize it as quickly as possible—and forget about the details. (Think simple narrative.)
    ♦ Do not send anything up to the neocortex for problem

---

8   Ibid, page 96.

9   Ibid, page 111.

10 Ibid, page 22.

11 Ibid, page 11.

12 Ibid, page 11.

13 Ibid, page 12.

solving unless you have a situation that is really unexpected and out of the ordinary (lazy System 2).

8. "The croc brain is picky and a cognitive miser whose primary interest is survival. It doesn't like to do a lot of work and is high maintenance when it is forced to perform. It requires concrete evidence—presented simply in black and white—to make a decision. Minor points of differentiation don't interest it."[14]

9. "Ironically, the mistake most people make when they see their audience becoming fatigued is to talk faster, to try to force their way through the rest of the pitch. Instead of imparting more valuable information faster; however, they only succeed in helping the audience retain less of their message."[15]

10. "Never get flustered, even when bad guys are closing in."[16]

You have to determine the best way to present PRO Enterprise Management analytical results and recommendations through short narratives backed up by sound information to explain analytical results that are uniquely crafted for your company, your organization, your audience, and ultimately, your decision makers. PRO Enterprise Management analytics are enjoyable to perform and generate many quantifiable insights. Analysts by nature like discovering the multitude of insights and want to share these in presentations. The problem is that the audience is thinking at a different level of detail. They are not interested in all of the great stuff you have discovered. Presentations should be targeted for 20 minutes but be prepared to give it in five minutes with one or two slides. The thrust of the presentation should be on the narratives. Numbers support the narratives and are necessary to understand the enterprise-value story.

Strive to become a *star* presenter and *PRO manager* in the eyes of senior management. Become someone senior management enjoys to hear from due to your ability to speak directly and succinctly about issues based on narratives supported by solid data and easy-to-understand analytics. Never be boring. Minimize small talk.

14 Ibid, page 15.

15 Ibid, page 50.

16 Ibid, page 167.

Inform, answer questions with directness and simplicity, be polite and respectful but never kowtow. If you don't know the answer to a question, say so and offer to quickly explore it. Have a sense of humor, but don't strive to be humorous. Be confident but never cocky. If you follow these guidelines your status within your organization will grow in the eyes of senior management. You will be known for your ability to think from an enterprise perspective. You will be known for your consistently strong and dependable performance. And ultimately, you will be known for your significant contributions to enterprise value.

To complete a STAR presentation:

- ◆ *S*et the decision frame with supporting background that led to the frame.
- ◆ *T*ell the recommendation as a story with few numbers and analytical results.
- ◆ *A*nswer questions directly and simply using backup data with referenced information sources, and standard PRO Management analytics with additional analytical results for anticipated questions.
- ◆ *R*eview the recommendation and determine what, if anything else, is needed to make a high-quality decision.

A STAR presentation leverages both primacy and recency effects in human cognition by starting with summary results and recommendations and ending with summary results and recommendations. If your decision frame doesn't connect with senior management, the meeting is virtually over and you will need to reframe and redo the PRO assessment or senior management may simply not respond and you are done altogether for the PRO item. Don't battle senior management over decision frames. And don't get defensive over an ill-fated decision frame. According to Oren Klaff: "When you are responding ineffectively to things the other person is saying and doing, that person owns the frame, and you are being frame-controlled … Strong frames are impervious to rational arguments. Weak arguments, made up of logical discussions and facts just bounce off of strong frames."[17] All seasoned executives and managers know the importance of learning "how the saying must be said". PRO managers must learn this too.

---

17 Ibid, pages 26 and 27.

Concluding Remarks

As I said in the beginning, decision making is the fundamental responsibility of executives and managers. Decision making must be considered—more specifically primed—from a risk neutral (expected value) long-term enterprise perspective first, then all other perspectives must follow. Unfortunately, by nature we are not risk neutral decision makers but rather we are *risk seeking in the realm of losses* and *risk averse in the realm of gains*, both of which are value-destroying behaviors from the perspective of enterprise value.[18]

In your personal and professional life you make decisions about only three things:

♦ How to resolve problems,

♦ How to mitigate risks, and

♦ How to capture opportunities.

You own a continuously evolving portfolio of problems, risks, and opportunities. The PRO Dilemma we constantly face: which problems, risks, and opportunities should you pursue at this point in time? To be an excellent decision maker, you must become a master of resolving the PRO Dilemma by efficiently answering and executing the five questions of PRO Enterprise Management:

1. What are your PRO items?

2. Which erode the most value if not pursued?

3. Which, if pursued, create or protect the most value?

4. Which should/will you pursue at this point in time?

5. What are the implications to your plan and budget?

To best leverage our innate cognitive strengths and to minimize the impact of our numerous cognitive short-comings and biases, we need analytics—but not just any logically sound analytics. We need *PRO* Management analytics.

I hope this book informed and inspired you to become a *PRO* Executive and transform your organization into a *PRO* Enterprise.

---

18 In the realm of losses, we try to claw our way back to status quo and in doing so, we exhibit risk-seeking behavior. We make/take risk-seeking bets. On the other hand, in the realm of gains, we exhibit risk-averse behavior. This was demonstrated by the Kahneman and Tversky study that we included as the thought experiment at the beginning of Chapter 10.

Appendix 1: A Five-Step 10–50–90 Value Range Assessment

The five-step method for estimating a continuous value quantity provided in this section combines the probability distribution estimation concepts in Chapter 4, the heuristics and biases concepts from Chapter 8, and the concepts concerning the estimation of extreme values discussed in Chapter 9. This methodology uses a three-point range assessment as opposed to the five-point fractile range assessment discussed in Chapter 9.

As discussed in Chapter 4, a three-point range assessment sufficiently characterizes (with some modest assumptions about the shape of the probability distribution) the underlying uncertainty associated with the targeted continuous value quantity. The range assessments will be discussed within the context of a problem, risk, or opportunity.

1. Frame the Assessment

a. Clearly define the value to be assessed.

  i. There should be no ambiguities regarding its definition including timing.

  ii. The definition of the value must pass the Clarity Test.

b. Consider influences, both internal and external to the organization, that may significantly impact the value to be assessed. This is also referred to as taking an "inside view" and an "outside view" of the underlying situation.

c. Consider the underlying similarities and differences between the current problem, risk, or opportunity and past experiences.

  i. Common biases resulting from the Availability and Representativeness heuristics can result in a focus on similarities while neglecting differences.

d. Perform the assessment in units of measures that are most natural for the subject matter expert's thought processes.

  i. This avoids errors resulting from mentally making transformations and calculations.

  ii. Any calculations or conversions to get to the targeted value should be done analytically and apart from the subjective assessment.

2. Leverage Insights from Information Systems and Predictive Analytics:

   a. Information systems and predictive analytics play a critical role in identifying problems, risks, and opportunities while also helping to inform continuous value range assessments through "what if" type analyses.

   b. It is not uncommon for information systems to use units of measures that are inconsistent with the framing established in Step 1. As mentioned above, it is critical that the frame enables the subject matter expert to leverage and capture their thinking and beliefs in the assessment.

   c. Adjust the assessment frame as required.

3. Estimate the 90th and 10th Percentiles (the tails):

   a. Start with the 90th percentile (the most extreme scenario). Ask the subject matter expert to consider a "surprisingly" large or high impact scenario given that the problem exists, the risk occurs, or the opportunity is pursued. Again, use the unit of measure outlined in Step 1 that matches the subject matter expert's experience and intuition.

   b. Think through the chain of circumstances that would lead to a surprisingly high impact.

      i. What would need to be true to result in a surprisingly high value given that the problem exists, the risk occurs, or the opportunity is pursued? As individuals think in terms of narratives and scenarios, this step is an attempt to invoke the subject matter expert's System 2 to visualize and simulate the contents of a surprisingly high value scenario.

      ii. Fill in the blank for the following statement: "Given that the problem exists, the risk occurs, or the opportunity is pursued, you would be surprised if the impact resulting from this scenario was as high as _____?" Remember, there is only a 1 in 10 chance that the actual impact will be greater than the number you are providing.

   c. Think through the chain of circumstances that would lead to a surprisingly low impact.

      i. What would need to be true for a surprisingly low value given that the problem exists, the risk occurs, or the opportunity is pursued? Once again, this step is an attempt to invoke the subject matter expert's System 2 to visualize and simulate the contents of a surprisingly low impact scenario.

      ii. Fill in the blank for the following statement: "Given that the problem exists, the risk occurs, or the opportunity is pursued, you would be surprised if the impact resulting from this scenario was as low as _____?" Remember, there is only a 1 in 10 chance that the actual impact will be less than the number you are providing.

d. Starting with the tails of the distribution, as opposed to the median, will minimize the bias resulting from the Adjustment and Anchoring heuristic that tends to create too narrow of a range.

4. Estimate the 50th Percentile (Median):

a. Think through the chain of circumstances that would lead to a median or 50/50 impact.

   i. What would need to be true for a median value impact given that the problem exists, the risk occurs, or the opportunity is pursued? And again, this step is an attempt to invoke the subject matter expert's System 2 to visualize and simulate the contents of a median or 50/50 impact scenario.

b. What estimate of impact do you believe is equally likely that the actual impact will be greater than or less than the estimate assuming that the problem exists, the risk occurs, or the opportunity is pursued?

c. Given the problem exists, the risk occurs, or the opportunity is pursued, what value estimate do you believe has a 50/50 chance that the actual impact will either be greater than or less than that number?

5. Review and Confirm the Range Assessment:

a. Do the 10–50–90 values reflect the subject matter expert's comprehensive state of understanding from information systems and predictive analytics as well as the subject matter expert's personal insights? If not, consider revising the assessments.

b. Do the 10–50–90 values reflect influences internal and external to the organization that may significantly impact the assessed value? If not, consider revising the assessments.

c. Do the 10–50–90 values reflect both the underlying similarities and differences between the current problem, risk, or opportunity and past experiences? If not, consider revising the assessments.

"Quality is the presence of that which satisfies users, customers, and other stakeholders, and the absence of that which dissatisfies them. A quality system is fit for the users' purposes, provides the needed features, and contains few, if any, important bugs."[1]
– Joseph M. Juran, Pioneering Guru in Quality Planning and Management'

Appendix 2: Managing Quality and Risk

Extending Quality Management and Risk Management

Joseph Juran expanded the philosophies and practices of quality from its statistical origins of quality control to what is now known as *Total Quality Management.* In Juran's *Quality Control Handbook,* he contends that the word "quality" has two different meanings:[2]

- ◆ *"Quality* means those features of products which meet customer needs and thereby provide customer satisfaction. In this sense, the meaning of quality is oriented to income. The purpose of such higher quality is to provide greater customer satisfaction and, one hopes, to increase income. However, providing more and/or better quality features usually requires an investment and hence usually involves increases in costs. Higher quality in this sense usually *costs more."*

- ◆ *"Quality* means freedom from deficiencies—freedom from errors that require doing work over again (rework) or that results in field failures, customer dissatisfaction, customer claims and so on. In this sense, the meaning of quality is oriented to costs, and higher quality usually *costs less."*

---

1   J. M. Juran, *Juran on Planning for Quality* (New York: Free Press), 1988.

2   Joseph Juran and A. Blanton Godfrey, *Juran's Quality Handbook* (New York: McGraw Hill), 1999.

In Juran's quality definitions we understand his pragmatic view that quality impacts the revenue and costs of an enterprise in both positive and negative ways. In this Appendix we will see the natural link between Juran's definitions of quality and PRO Enterprise Management.

Juran's Quality Management and PRO Enterprise Management

The enterprise impacts of quality based on Juran's two perspectives and definitions are provided in Table A2.1. Upon review of Table A2-1, the link to PRO Enterprise Management assessments should be obvious—additional potential revenue with trade-offs in additional costs versus reduced costs. The pursuit of quality is always in the face of some combination of problems, risks, and opportunities that may be either deemed as must-have investments (for example, compliance) or should be evaluated to determine investment productivity so as to enable quality investments to compete with other investments in the organization's PRO portfolio.

Definition of Quality #1	Definition of Quality #2
Product features that meet customer needs resulting in customer satisfaction. Higher quality enables the enterprise to:	Freedom from deficiencies thereby reducing customer dissatisfaction. Higher quality enables the enterprise to:
• Make products saleable • Improve brand reputation • Increase product sales volume • Secure premium pricing • Meet or beat competition • Increase market share The primary effect is on revenue. Higher quality usually costs more.	• Reduce error rates • Reduce rework and waste • Reduce field failures and warranty charges • Reduce inspection and test cost • Shorten time to market • Increase yields and capacities • Improve delivery performance The primary effect is on cost. Higher quality usually costs less.

Table A2.1: Juran's Two Definitions of Quality in Relation to Customer Satisfaction and Enterprise Impacts to Revenue and Cost

Additional Perspectives on Quality

Key Point – Quality is...

"A subjective term for which each person or sector has its own definition. In technical usage, quality can have two meanings: 1. the characteristics of a product or service that bear on its ability to satisfy stated or implied needs; 2. a product or service free of deficiencies."[3]

Key Point – Quality is...

"...a measure of excellence or a state of being free from defects, deficiencies and significant variations. It is brought about by strict and consistent commitment to certain standards that achieve uniformity of a product in order to satisfy specific customer or user requirements."[4]

Quality management consists of four major components:

◆ Quality planning,
◆ Quality control,
◆ Quality assurance, and
◆ Quality improvement.

Quality management is focused not only on quality of products and services, but also on the means to achieve it. Consistency in quality is achieved through control of processes and quality assurance.

The International Organization for Standardization (ISO) created the Quality Management System (QMS) standards in 1987, which include a series of standards for different types of industries distinguished by the type of activity or process such as designing, production, or service delivery. ISO reviews these standards every few years and provides updated versions. The last major revision was in 2008 and the series was called the ISO 9000:2000 series. The ISO 9002 and 9003 standards were combined into one single standard: ISO 9001:2000. The ISO 9004:2009 gives guidelines for performance improvement over and above the basic standard (ISO 9001:2000) and it also provides a measurement framework for improved quality management, similar to and based upon the measurement framework for process assessment. The Quality Management System standards created by ISO are meant to certify the processes and the system of an organization, not the product or service itself.

---

3   https://asq.org/quality-resources/quality-glossary/q.

4   http://www.BusinessDictionary.com.

Quality is about achieving objectives through consistent compliance to measurable and verifiable standards and processes. Quality objectives include: zero defects, safety, security, reliability, control of process variance, fit-for-purpose, and ultimately customer satisfaction. Quality Risk Management (QRM) is a relatively recent addition to the evolution of corporate risk management and represents yet another isolated attempt at specialized risk management in the enterprise. I will not go into detail about current approaches and tools associated with QRM, but I will attempt to build a bridge from current QRM practices to a consistent enterprise perspective. More specifically, the intent here is not to replace existing and effective QRM practices and tools but to provide a means to integrate QRM practices, methods, and results into a broader enterprise perspective of risk management and corporate decision making—a PRO Enterprise Management perspective.

The Natural Link: Quality Management and Risk Management

Quality and quality management are inherently linked to risk management. Fundamentally, risk management is management of uncertainty and its consequences. If we consider the fundamental focus of quality, we can easily relate it to risk, including:

- ◆ Risk of defects,
- ◆ Safety risk,
- ◆ Security risk,
- ◆ Reliability risk,
- ◆ Risk in process variance,
- ◆ Risk of poor fit-for-purpose, and
- ◆ Risk of customer dissatisfaction.

Whereas quality is about achieving objectives, risk is about the consequences of not achieving objectives. Therefore, from an enterprise perspective, quality management and risk management are inextricable. The link between quality management systems and risk management was recognized as standards organizations shifted focus to risk management.

In 2009, ISO provided a standard on risk management, ISO 31000:2009 Risk Management – Principles and Guidelines. This standard provides principles and guidelines on risk management to be applied throughout the life of an organization, and to a wide range of activities, including:

♦ Strategies and decisions,

♦ Operations,

♦ Processes,

♦ Functions,

♦ Projects,

♦ Products and services, and

♦ Assets.

The risk management standard is intended for any type of risk, whatever its nature, including positive or negative consequences. Additionally, ISO has since released standards by industry that are risk-based including:

♦ ISO 22000 for food safety;

♦ ISO 27000 for IT security, and

♦ ISO 28000 for supply chain security.

ISO 31000:2009 is currently being revised for several purposes including the need by risk practitioners, especially in the G20 economies, for a high-level document that addresses the way risk should be managed in multinational organizations and national governments, as well as how risk management should be incorporated into the governance and management systems of organizations.

In the biopharmaceutical industry, the FDA published ICH Q9[5] in 2006, which provides a framework for implementing QRM as a comprehensive program throughout a product's lifecycle. In 2009, the FDA published ICH Q10,[6] which describes QRM as an enabler that should be integrated throughout a quality system. ISO 14971:2007 is focused on risk management for medical devices. QRM in the biopharmaceutical industry understandably has a great emphasis on product quality and patient safety, the latter of which continues to be a significant challenge in risk assessments.

There is a fairly standard set of QRM risk assessment tools that are used throughout many industries including:

---

5   ICH Q9: Quality Risk Management. Fed. Reg. 71(106) 2006: 32105-32106.

6   ICH Q10: Pharmaceutical Quality System. Fed. Reg. 74(66) 2009: 15990-15991.

- Failure Mode and Effects Analysis (FMEA),
- Failure Mode and Effects and Criticality Analysis (FMECA),
- Fault Tree Analysis (FTA),
- Hazard Analysis and Critical Control Points (HACCP),
- Hazard and Operability Analysis (HAZOP),
- Process Hazard Analysis (PHA),
- Risk Matrices, and
- Various statistical tools.

Essentially, quality can be viewed as a risk management function by shifting from a mostly reactive approach of measuring and controlling variances, to proactively identifying, assessing, prioritizing, and minimizing or eliminating potential sources of failure.

The inextricable link between quality management and risk management is causing some to rethink their relationship in practice and their bridge to an enterprise perspective. Greg Hutchins, an expert and author of several books on ISO 9000, believes the future of quality *is* risk management.[7]

David X. Martin, an internationally recognized expert on risk management and a senior advisor at the global management consulting firm, Oliver Wyman, claims, "The principles of risk management provide a solid framework for managing quality too ... If quality is to receive not only a seat, but also a voice at the proverbial table of management, it needs to address not only 'risks to quality,' but also 'risks to the corporation.' Quality professionals already have the skills to intelligently identify and mitigate risk, but they need to use those skills in a more strategic manner."[8]

The message is becoming clear: the consequences of quality risk, as with all sources of corporate risk, should be considered from an enterprise perspective—a PRO Enterprise Management perspective.

---

7   Greg Hutchins, "Risk Management-The Future of Quality," *Quality Digest*, https://www.qualitydigest.com/currentmag/articles/06_article.shtml.

8   David X Martin, "Risk and the Future of Quality," *The Journal of Quality and Participation*, October, 2012, www.asq.org/pub/jqp.

"A man with one watch knows what time it is.
A man with two watches is never sure."
– Segal's Law (source unknown)

Appendix 3: PRO Management Compared to Other Methods

Other than automated decision-making systems, *analytics* in corporations and government entities are used to inform and prime decision-making processes—decisions made by people. The paradox of business modeling is that complex, "black-box" business models are often "tweaked" when their results conflict with executives' underlying beliefs until the modeling results are more closely aligned with the executives' thinking. The resource-intensive modeling efforts are therefore relegated to the role of feeding executives' (and others') innate confirmation bias. However, the complexity of many business and governmental decisions far outstrips our ability to use intuition alone to determine a best alternative. The only way past this paradox is to *leverage* our innate and learned thinking strengths and to *minimize* our innate and learned thinking weaknesses and biases with analytical methods that account for both—a fundamental design principle of PRO Enterprise Management methods and analytics.

PRO Enterprise Management provides a consistent basis of comparison on the enterprise value and enterprise return on investment for expenditures on problems, risks, and opportunities throughout an organization. For corporations, the primary enterprise value measure used is the expected net present value of discounted free cash flow over an appropriate time horizon, arguably the best (or at least one of the best) surrogate measures of long-term enterprise value. Other measures can be added but should be measured and presented separately so that there are (at most) two or three measures explicitly considered (including their trade-offs) for priming decision making from an enterprise perspective. Other non-enterprise measures can be added specific to the domain of the decision as desired or required as secondary considerations.

It is important to prime decision-making recommendations from an enterprise-value perspective. Present the enterprise perspective first, then present other supporting measures to complete the work of informing the decision makers. This forces the decision frame to begin with what is best for the enterprise rather than considering the enterprise as an after-thought, or not at all. If the decision is to do something that is not best for the enterprise, it should be noted as part of the decision record and coupled with the rationale for choosing an option that is not in the best interest for the enterprise.

With these foundational thoughts on corporate decision making, let's review the strengths and weaknesses of other analytic approaches in use today.

Decision Analysis (DA)

In 1964, Ronald A. Howard, professor of Management Science and Engineering at Stanford University, named an emerging field and academic discipline *decision analysis*. Decision analysis (DA) is comprised of philosophy, theory, methodology, analytical structures, tools, and professional practices that enable systematic structuring and analysis of decisions. Though decision analysis is applied in corporations and governmental entities, it is also applicable to personal decision making. Decision trees and influence diagrams are common tools used to structure the underlying uncertainty associated with a decision or set of decisions and the outcome metrics can be multi-attribute or a single measure (such as expected net present value of discounted free cash flow). In professional practice, major corporations use decision analysis in a variety of capital-intensive industries (e.g., biopharmaceutical industry for R&D investments and oil & gas industry for upstream and downstream projects) to make capital investment decisions.

While decision analysis is used in corporations, it is utilized far less than was envisioned by its pioneers and practitioners, including myself. My interest in developing PRO Enterprise Management was partially motivated by the lack of broad application of decision analysis in corporations. Gary Klein, cognitive psychologist, claims that 90 percent of the *critical* decisions we make are based on our intuition—even for senior executives of corporations.[1] He bases his claim on numerous interviews with senior executives of corporations.

---

1   Gary Klein, *The Power of Intuition: How to Use Your Gut Feelings to Make Better Decisions at Work* (New York: A Currency Book Published by Doubleday, 2003).

Chip Heath, professor of organizational behavior at Stanford University, during an interview with McKinsey & Company stated, "Early in the history of decision making, people were optimistic about a better process called decision analysis. But nobody ever used it, because very few people have the math chops to fold back probabilities in a three-layer decision tree."[2] While I don't believe it is an issue of "math chops," these thoughts are consistent with my experience as articulated in the Chapter 1 discussion on the "Great Corporate Decision Analytics Gap." The bottom line is, for several often-debated reasons, executives are not inclined to dispose themselves to the power of decision analysis as currently practiced—even for the most critical corporate decisions they face.

Multiple-Criteria Decision Making (MCDM)

Multiple-Criteria Decision making (MCDM), also known as Multiple-Criteria Decision Analysis (MCDA), represents a field of operations research that explicitly accounts for multiple criteria in the analysis of a decision or set of decisions. The multiple criteria are often conflicting, such as price versus sales volume, or cost versus safety, or cost versus fit-for-purpose. The premise is that there is no optimal solution or alternative to a problem or decision and so the decision maker's preferences considering all criteria and their trade-offs are used to differentiate among solutions or alternatives.

Rather than explicitly model how a set of multiple criteria translates into a single enterprise measure (as prescribed in PRO Enterprise Management), MCDM assesses or measures each of the criteria or attributes and then either:

♦ Uses a utility function accounting for the decision maker's preferences with respect to the multiple criteria and their trade-offs to determine a single utility score to be used to compare, contrast, and prioritize solutions or decision alternatives based on a rank ordering, or,

♦ Does not mathematically combine the multiple criteria and simply presents the decision maker with the multiple criteria scores, thus requiring the decision maker to make the preference trade-offs to come to an ultimate decision.

---

2   Dan Lovallo and Olivier Sibony, "Making great decisions: Stanford's Chip Heath and McKinsey's Olivier Sibony discuss new research, fresh frameworks, and practical tools for decision makers," *The McKinsey Quarterly*, April 2003. http://www.mckinsey.com/insights/strategy/ making_great_decisions.

There are many forms of MCDM analyses that have been developed since the 1960s and they can be split between approaches that capture the decision maker's criteria preferences before assessment and analysis, and approaches that capture criteria preferences during the assessment and analysis.

An approach to MCDM is Multi-Attribute Utility Theory (MAUT), a structured methodology designed to handle tradeoffs among multiple objectives. An early application of MAUT involved a study of alternative locations for a new airport in Mexico City in the early 1970s (Ralph Keeney).[3] The factors that were considered included cost, safety, the capacity of the airport facilities, noise levels, social disruption, and access times. Utility theory is a systematic approach for quantifying an individual's preferences. It is used to rescale a numerical value on some measure of interest onto a 0-to-1 scale with zero representing the worst preference and 1 the best. This enables direct comparison of many distinct and diverse measures. The output is a rank-ordered evaluation of alternatives that accounts for the decision makers' preferences.

The early applications of MAUT focused on public sector decisions and public policy issues. These decisions have multiple objectives and multiple constituencies that are affected by the decision. The U.S. federal government requires that design decisions of new weapons systems account for tradeoffs of cost, weight, durability, lethality, and survivability and that these trade-offs must be made explicit and analyzed by an MCDM method. MAUT is one such method commonly used for these applications as well as the Analytic Hierarchy Process (AHP) that will be discussed in a subsequent section of this Appendix.

While these methods are well developed and have been used in hundreds of applications, there is a critical drawback in comparison to PRO Enterprise Management methods and analysis. In general, MCDM methods lack the ability to compare different analyses' results on a consistent, enterprise-wide basis. Each analysis only allows comparison of alternatives within the set of alternatives under a single investigation. Consequently there is no way to determine return-on-investment based on enterprise-value to be compared with other recommendations resulting from other MCDM-based analyses. Ultimately, these methods alone are unable to resolve the PRO Dilemma.

---

3   Ralph L. Keeney, "A Decision Analysis with Multiple Objectives: The Mexico City Airport," *The Bell Journal of Economics and Management Science*, Vol. 4, No. 1 (Spring 1973), pages 101-117.

In lieu of the ability to analyze preference trade-offs among multiple criteria, PRO Enterprise Management attempts to minimize the set of value criteria to a single priming metric, expected net present value of discounted free cash flow, or at most two to three priming metrics. These metrics are analyzed separately with the decision maker(s) incorporating their preference trade-offs through debate and discussion informed by the pair or triplet of output metrics ultimately culminating in decision making. When impacts to human health or safety are involved, a second decision criterion, Quality-Adjusted Life Years (QALYs)[4] has proven to be a good second measure in PRO Enterprise Management.

Analytic Hierarchy Process (AHP)

One of the most popular MCDM methods is the Analytic Hierarchy Process (AHP) developed by Thomas L. Saaty in the 1970s. AHP is mathematically sound and attempts to address the mental strengths and limitations of human judgment in articulating preferences. AHP is a successful integration of mathematics and cognitive psychology for analyzing corporate and public policy decision making. Part of AHP's success may be due to its procedural design of using hierarchies to decompose complexity and focusing on pairwise comparisons as part of its assessment process—both of which leverage strengths of human thinking, as detailed in Chapter 6.

The downside of the Analytic Hierarchy Process (AHP) is the same as with other MCDM approaches. AHP lacks the ability to consistently compare different analyses' results on an enterprise value basis. Each AHP analysis only allows comparison of alternatives within the set of alternatives under a single investigation. Consequently, there is no way to determine a return on investment based on enterprise value to be compared with other recommendations resulting from other AHP-based analyses. AHP analyses alone are unable to resolve the PRO Dilemma. From a PRO Enterprise Management perspective, employing analysis methods that enable a consistent basis of comparison of resolving problems, mitigating risks, and capturing opportunities on an enterprise-value perspective enables answering the five PRO Enterprise Management questions, which resolves the PRO Dilemma.

---

4   Sarah J. Whitehead and Shehzad Ali, "Health outcomes in economic evaluation: the QALY and utilities," *British Medical Bulletin*, Vol. 96, Issue 1, 1 December 2010, pages 5-21.

Monte Carlo Methods

Monte Carlo methods are being used more and more in corporations. There is no standard "Monte Carlo Method." The term simply refers to any kind of simulation that uses randomly generated numbers to estimate an output parameter and its underlying probability distribution. These methods are useful for obtaining numerical solutions to problems that are too complicated to solve analytically.

The Monte Carlo method was eventually named by Stainslaw Ulam, a mathematician, in 1946. He named it after the town where his uncle gambled, reflecting the underlying importance of accounting for uncertainty. In general, the Monte Carlo method (or Monte Carlo simulation) can be used to describe any analytical technique that approximates solutions to quantitative problems via statistical sampling. With respect to corporate decision making, Monte Carlo methods are specifically used to describe a method for propagating (translating) uncertainties in model inputs (i.e., costs, product demand, likelihood of an earthquake) into uncertainties in model outputs (e.g., net present value of discounted free cash flow).

In practice, a static, deterministic model is constructed with input parameters required to calculate the model's output parameter(s). Any input parameters with uncertainty that drive significant uncertainty in the output parameter(s) must be represented and modeled as a probability distribution. Since the inputs are uncertain, the output parameter(s) is/are uncertain as well and must be represented as a probability distribution(s). During the Monte Carlo simulation, the static, fixed input parameters are left at their fixed values while the uncertain input parameters are sampled based on their underlying probability distributions. During each simulated scenario, the values of the model output parameters are recorded. The number of simulated scenarios is typically in the thousands. This results in a large number of separate and independent output results, each representing a possible future state of the output parameter. The results of the independent sample outputs are assembled into a probability distribution of possible outcomes, typically represented as a histogram and/or cumulative probability distribution.

Considerations of probabilistic dependence (correlation) of input parameters must be understood and built into either the model or accounted for during the Monte Carlo simulation input parameter sampling. Monte Carlo methods can be used as a PRO

Enterprise Management method to support PRO item assessments as a second approach to the standard "direct assessment" methods described throughout this book.

Figure A3.1 provides an overview comparison of a PRO item assessment and decision performed through a Monte Carlo simulation versus the PRO item standard "direct assessment" approach. As indicated in Figure A3.1, the direct assessment approach can minimize or eliminate the rework sometimes required in Monte Carlo modeling efforts to "tune the model" when unexpected results show up in the scenarios associated with the tails of the output distribution.

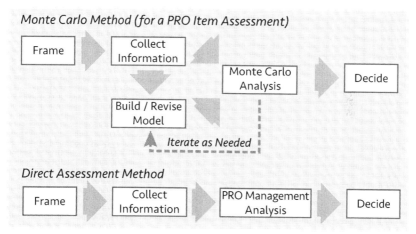

Figure A3.1: Comparison of a Monte Carlo-based PRO Item Assessment versus a Direct Assessment

When performing PRO item assessments, there are advantages and disadvantages to a Monte Carlo-based approach and standard direct assessments. Table A3.1 provides a summary of the advantages and disadvantages for both approaches. Both approaches can be used successfully in organizations as long as explicit care is taken to ensure a consistent basis is used across all results. In many situations, the standard direct assessment can be completed more quickly with less effort.

Monte Carlo-based Assessment	Direct Assessment
Advantages • Can create multiple output distributions • Provides full estimate of output distribution (expected values and all percentiles) • Can model complex relationships among input variables • No limitations on what can be modeled • Can be designed to ensure a level-playing-field of comparison across all situations and analyses	*Advantages* • Typically less effort to get to insights and conclusions required for decision making • Can increase granularity and complexity dynamically to the degree required to ensure decision quality • Can model complex relationships (but may require construction of a template) • No model building required • Effort focuses discussion on most important aspects of analysis, "what drives the tails of the output distribution" • Consistency across all situations and analyses • Easy to explain results and conclusions and easy to modify to support exploratory "What if" questions
Disadvantages • Separate, independently made models throughout corporation lacking standards on outputs (no consistency across model results) • Requires significant skill to do well, often residing in only a few individuals (wide range of model quality) • Can be time consuming to create models especially if building from scratch • Must know underlying distributions of input variables and their dependencies (correlations) • Model level of detail and frame decomposition often goes beyond level of detail of insight and knowledge • Can create results that are artifacts of modeling assumptions and input distributions (non-existent scenarios) • Executives mistrust results until results match intuition • Can be laborious to modify to support executives' exploratory "What if" questions	*Disadvantages* • Only output variable is NPV of free cash flow (and EBITDA, Quality-Adjusted Life Years) • Provides expected value, and 10th and 90th percentiles of output distribution (but not 1st, 5th, 95th nor 99th percentile) • Some limitations on what can be modeled

Table A3.1: Advantages and Disadvantages of Monte Carlo-based and Direct Assessments of PRO Items

Real Options Analysis (ROA)

Another decision tree-based approach to analyze corporate capital investment decisions is real options analysis (ROA), also referred to as real options valuation (ROV). A *real option* is the right—but not the obligation—to pursue certain business initiatives or actions such as deferring, expanding, contracting, abandoning, staging, switching, or growing. Real options analysis is an adaptation of financial options techniques used in financial investments to "real-life" decisions associated with tangible assets such as capital equipment.

Real Option	Description	Examples
Defer	Wait before taking an action until key uncertainties are resolved or timing is expected to be more favorable.	Deferring scheduled replacement of equipment until corporation decides on manufacturing strategy.
Expand or Contract	Increase or decrease the scale of an operation in response to future demand.	A company entering a new geographic market may build a distribution center that it can expand easily if market demand materializes.
Abandon / Terminate	Discontinue an operation or agreement.	A company abandons a licensing agreement due to poor performance.
Investment in Stages	Commit to investment in stages resulting in a series of abandonment options.	A company's future R&D investment often depends on specific performance targets achieved in the lab. The option to abandon research projects is valuable because the company can make investments in stages rather than all up-front.
Switch Mix of Inputs or Outputs	Change the mix of inputs or outputs of a production process in response to changes in market demand or profitability.	A manufacturing facility's ability to quickly and efficiently switch mix of products produced.
Extend/Grow	Expand the scope of activities to capitalize on emerging opportunities	A company leverages its brand name and infrastructure to extend its operations into a variety of new businesses

Table A3.2: Types of Real Options Considered by Corporations and Examples

As an example, a biopharmaceutical company may desire the option to invest sometime in the future in expansion of a contract manufacturing organization's (CMO's) plant for manufacturing the biopharmaceutical company's products, or alternatively, to discontinue outsourcing to the CMO on short notice. These represent a "real call option"[5] and a "real put option,"[6] respectively. The flexibility gained by management in owning a "real option" comes at a cost, the option premium—an upfront, non-recoverable expenditure given to the other entity (or entities) providing the valued flexibility. When both entities are the same company, the option premium becomes the cost to create the flexibility. The power of real options analysis is the ability to determine the enterprise value of having the option—the value of having the flexibility.

Table A3.2 describes the types of real options typically considered coupled with examples.

Using a net present value (NPV) of discounted cash flows evaluation approach usually assumes that management is *passive* with regard to their capital investment once committed. The issue is that, as risk and uncertainty are resolved or are better understood, the value of the opportunity may change, causing management to change their minds. In contrast, a Real Options Valuation (ROV) assumes that management is active and can continuously respond to downstream changes. ROV analyzes each scenario and determines the best action in any of these potential events or circumstances. Assuming management adapts to each negative outcome by decreasing its exposure and to positive scenarios by scaling up, the enterprise benefits from actively managing uncertainty, achieving lower variability in profit than under the upfront total investment commitment assumed in a basic NPV evaluation (*including* a standard PRO Enterprise Management evaluation).

An ROV of a capital investment is typically higher than an NPV valuation or a PRO Enterprise Management evaluation. As downstream flexibility and uncertainty increase, this difference increases. The downside to real options approaches include:

---

5   A real call option represents an agreement that gives a company the right (but not the obligation) to pursue an endeavor at a specified price (cost) within a specific time period.

6   A real put option represents an agreement giving a company the right, but not the obligation, to exit an endeavor at a specified price (cost) within a specified time. This is the opposite of a real call option.

♦ They can be complex to model, especially with compounded real options (options on options), and

♦ They assume that management will act on favorable options when they arise without delay—as the option value dictates—which, for a variety of reasons, including corporate culture, may not be the case.

Real options only work if executives and managers can truly commit to canceling projects if the numbers look bad after the initial investment.

The gravity of psychological, political, and budgeting realities works against that discipline. This is not a downside of the analytical technique per se, though it begs the question on whether the level of effort is worth it. The thinking required to structure a real options analysis provides important insight into capital investment decisions.

However, the level of effort to perform real options analysis must be relegated to the most impactful capital investment decisions. It is too rigorous and resource intensive to be applied broadly across a corporation. Importantly, if real options analysis is performed, it can be measured in terms of expected net present value of discounted free cash flow and investment productivity as in PRO Enterprise Management. Consequently, a real options analysis of a capital investment can be positioned on a consistent basis with problems, risks, and opportunities (and compete for resources with other PRO items).

Game Theory

Game theory is a branch of applied mathematics that deals with the analysis of games—situations involving conflict, competition, and cooperation between intelligent rational decision makers (also referred to as "players"). Originally, it addressed zero-sum games, in which one player's gains result in losses for the other players. Modern game theory emerged with the book, *The Theory of Games and Economic Behavior* by John von Neumann and Oskar Morgenstern in 1944, which considered cooperative games of several players. [The second edition[7] of this book in 1947 provided a set of axioms for choice behavior that leads to maximization of expected utility. Utility functions satisfying this set of axioms are referred to as "von Neumann-Morgenstern utility functions." The axioms provided a

---

7   John von Neumann and Oskar Morgenstern, *Theory of Games and Economic Behavior* (Princeton, N.J.: Princeton University Press, 1947).

foundation for the analysis of decision making under uncertainty and decision analysis (DA). It should be noted that while von Neumann and Morgenstern are credited with naming this class of utility functions, Frank P. Ramsey[8] first introduced the axioms of expected utility and the notion of subjective probability in 1931.

According to Paul Papayoanou, a leading practitioner of the application of game theory to corporate decision making, "The applicability of game theory to situations beyond those with pure rivalry (and thus to a broad set of business issues) is due to John Nash's equilibrium concept. The contribution, which won Nash the Nobel Prize in Economics in 1994, enabled scholars to use game theory for analyzing a wide array of problems involving dilemmas of competition and cooperation rather than just win-lose situations."[9] In game theory, decisions made by players are interrelated as players anticipate each other's moves. Each player must decide whether to compete or cooperate in the face of strategies and reactions of other players contemplating the same dilemma, all of which affect the outcomes of all players. A solution to a game describes the optimal decisions of the players and the outcomes from each of the player's perspectives.

In the world of corporate strategy, game theory, (or "strategic gaming" as named by Papayoanou) has been applied in many industries for a variety of strategic decisions including:[10]

- ◆ Alliance and joint venture strategy,
- ◆ Growth strategy,
- ◆ Investment and capacity expansion decisions,
- ◆ Pricing,
- ◆ Market entry decisions,
- ◆ Product launch timing,
- ◆ Negotiations,
- ◆ Licensing issues,
- ◆ Political risk assessment and governmental regulations, and
- ◆ Auction design and bidding strategies.

---

8   Frank P. Ramsey, "Truth and Probability," In R.B. Briathwaite (ed.) *The Foundations of Mathematics and Other Logical Essays*, New York: Harcourt Brace, 1931.

9   Paul Papayoanou, *Game Theory for Business: A Primer in Strategic Gaming* (Sugar Land, Texas: Probabilistic Publishing, 2010), page 5.

10   Ibid, page 2.

The value measures used for outcomes in game theory can be varied, including the expected net present value of discounted free cash flow and investment productivity. Consequently, game theory analyses of capital investments can be positioned on a consistent basis with problems, risks, and opportunities (and compete for resources with other PRO items).

Risk Matrices and Risk Heat Maps

One of the most broadly used risk assessment tools is called a risk matrix or risk heat map. In this approach, individual risks are assessed on two ordinal scales:

♦ Likelihood of risk occurrence, and

♦ Degree of consequence or harm given the risk occurs. [Please see Appendix 5 for a detailed discussion of risk matrices and risk heat maps.]

There are many shortcomings in using risk matrices. While these methods have been used in hundreds of applications, the approach lacks the ability to compare different analyses' results on an enterprise-value consistent basis of comparison. Each risk analysis only allows comparison of risks within the set of risks under a single investigation. Consequently there is no means to determine a return on investment based on enterprise value to compare with other recommendations resulting from other risk matrix-based analyses. Ultimately, these methods alone are unable to resolve the *PRO Dilemma*.

Summary, Other Methods and Practices

Most Multi-Criteria Decision making (MCDM) methods, including the Analytic Hierarchy Process (AHP), cannot be used as stand-alone analytical methods within a PRO Enterprise Management framework. Risk Matrices (also known as Risk Heat Maps) represent another class of analytics that cannot be used as a stand-alone approach within a PRO Enterprise Management framework.

On the other hand, Decision Analysis (DA), Monte Carlo Methods, Real Options Analysis (ROA), and Game Theory analytics can be easily integrated into a PRO Enterprise Management framework, enabling consistent comparisons on an enterprise-value basis.

"What I've seen a lot with the proliferation of data and data warehouses and business intelligence systems is that the tie to actual decision making has been lost." [1]
– Thomas H. Davenport, Author and Pioneer of concept
'Competing on Analytics'

Appendix 4: Information Systems and Data Analytics

How Information Systems and Data Analytics Should Inform Corporate Decision Making

In a 2010 interview with Michael S. Hopkins, editor-in-chief of MIT Sloan Management Review, Thomas H. Davenport provided a telling perspective on the state of corporate decision making: "I advocate that a good first step for executives is to identify what their company's top five strategic decisions and their top five operational decisions are. I usually do informal surveys when I'm speaking about this topic and I'll say, 'Raise your hand if you have a sense for that.' Maybe one in five hundred executives will say, 'Yeah, we know what our key decisions are.' It's quite astounding. I argue that they have to do some sort of inventory of the decisions that they care about and what kind of information is used to make them and how often do they take place and who's supposed to make them—the whole decisions roles issue."[2]

Wouldn't formalizing the five questions of PRO Management align these executives with Davenport's insights and recommendations? Executives and managers are often overwhelmed with data, yet feel ill-informed for decision making. The lack of decision management *is* "astounding." Executives currently have no standard by which to implement Davenport's identified decision-making process

---

1   Thomas H. Davenport interviewed by Michael S. Hopkins, "Are You Ready to Reengineer Your Decision Making," *MIT Sloan Management Review*, October 1, 2010. http://sloanreview.mit.edu/article/are-you-ready-to-reengineer-your-decision-making/.

2   Ibid, page 3.

void at not only the executive-level, but at most other levels and functions within their corporations.

Let's extend Davenport's senior executive query from above to any one executive or management role in a corporation or governmental entity and determine how well your current information systems and data analytics can support answering the five questions of PRO Management from Chapter 13:

1. What are your PRO items?

2. Which erode the most value if not pursued?

3. Which, if pursued, create or protect the most value?

4. Which should/will you pursue at this point in time?

5. What are the implications to your plan and budget?

If we think of the capability to answer the five questions of PRO Management on an enterprise-wide basis as part of the system-level requirements of enterprise information systems and data analytics, we could more directly drive future systems and analytics towards their ultimate goal—improving decision making throughout the enterprise. Short of this, information systems and data analytics will continue to be focused on siloed solutions for siloed issues.

The Three Classes of Data Analytics

Information supports two primary enterprise needs: reporting, and informing decision making. There are three classes of data analytics to fulfill these needs:

- ◆ *Reporting analytics* that are required for regulatory compliance and are used to summarize past performance data (what you find in a multitude of management dashboards),

- ◆ *Predictive analytics* that use past data and models to predict the future under the assumption that the past is an accurate prediction of the future (which is valid in many situations), and

- ◆ *Prescriptive analytics* that recommend what you should do.

PRO Enterprise Management is intended to leverage all three classes of data analytics by filling the gap between data analytics and decision making.

The Gap between Data Analytics and Decision Making

Without a generalized and standardized decision analytic structure to target, data analytics are relegated to specialized, one-off classes of decisions at best. Companies are making investments in data, data scientists, data warehouses, and business intelligence systems but, as Davenport points out, "the tie to actual decision making has been lost," or perhaps was never really considered in a comprehensive and concerted way. There are several root causes for the gaps between current data analytics and decision making:

♦ Data represents information about the past, which sometimes represents a possible future—decision making is only about the future.

♦ Data analytics has focused on generating insights without a context for a specific decision or class of decisions, leaving decision makers with the task of translating insights into high quality decisions.

♦ Data analytics reports are often large presentations that are full of pages of graphs and summary insights without any bridge to specific decisions, leaving executives and managers with a "So, what now?" response.

♦ Data analytics reporting cycles are often disconnected with real-time decision making, resulting in "shelved" reports long forgotten at the time of decision making.

In a research report published in 2013 by the MIT Sloan Management Review in collaboration with SAS Institute, they identified six ways data analytics can be used for competitive advantage and innovation, including:[3]

♦ Reduce enterprise costs,

♦ Improve resource allocations,

♦ Increase customer understanding,

♦ Make real-time decisions,

♦ Identify new markets, and

♦ Accelerate development of new products/services.

---

3   David Kiron, Renee Boucher Ferguson, and Pamela Kirk Prentice, "From Value to Vision: Reimagining the Possible with Data Analytics—What makes companies that are great at analytics different from everyone else," *MIT Sloan Management Review*, Spring 2013. http://sloanreview.mit.edu/reports/analytics-innovation/.

All of these represent *opportunities* from a PRO management perspective. Data analytics should span the corporate decision-making space of problems, risks, and opportunities—not just opportunities. Decision making is about the future. Data is about the past and may provide insight about the future. To completely leverage available insights about the future we must systematically integrate data, predictive and prescriptive models, and subject matter expertise. Information systems and data analytics providers must close the gap between data and decision making across the enterprise (or face the fate of just being the latest failed information systems fad).

The Information Value Chain

The call for "data-driven" decision making is a familiar marketing slant for data analytics providers. However, data is not the complete source of insight for decision making (with the exception of automated decision-making processes). In Chapter 9, we introduced the concept of a decision maker's or subject matter expert's "state of understanding" for a situation and in the broader context, a PRO item. Figure A4.1 displays the "information value chain" from a PRO Management perspective. Of critical importance is that the value chain begins with a PRO item's—or class of PRO item's—decision frame. If data is to be used to inform a decision or class of decisions, we must start with the decision frame to identify the information requirements of the decision.

The "state of understanding" of an individual or system used to inform PRO item numerical assessments is a perspective based on data, or subject matter expertise, or the combination of the two. As discussed in Chapter 6, the personal beliefs that individuals bring to bear in decision making come as an intertwined set of knowledge-based and faith-based beliefs. PRO Management analytics then provide the standardized enterprise value-based outputs that inform decision making.

Building the Link from Data Analytics to Decision Making

Decision making efficiency and efficacy require good decision-framing processes, which has proven to be difficult to automate for the vast majority of decisions in organizations. However, the more data analytics can support the definition of decision frames and subsequently support the numerical population of these frames, the greater the benefits from data analytics will be. More specifically, data analytics providers should work toward systems that support and improve:

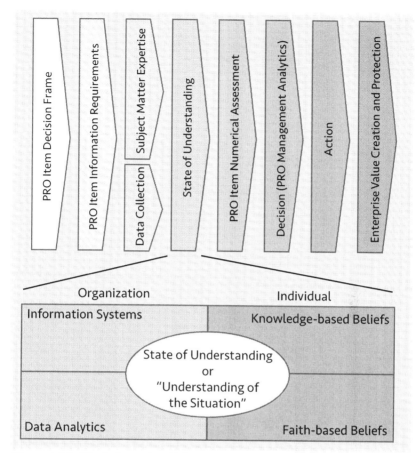

Figure A4.1: The Information Value Chain from a PRO Management Perspective

- ◆ PRO item identification,
- ◆ Specification of the "tipping point of a material consequence" using backward chaining logic (e.g., inability to supply patients to lost sales to safety stock is consumed to production line down for 3 months or more),
- ◆ Assessment of probability of occurrence of the tipping point,
- ◆ Identification of the types of consequences (impacts) given tipping point occurrence,
- ◆ 10–50–90 scenario descriptions of consequences given tipping point occurrence, and
- ◆ 10–50–90 numerical assessments of consequences given tipping point occurrence.

Antecedent: Tipping Point of a Material Consequence

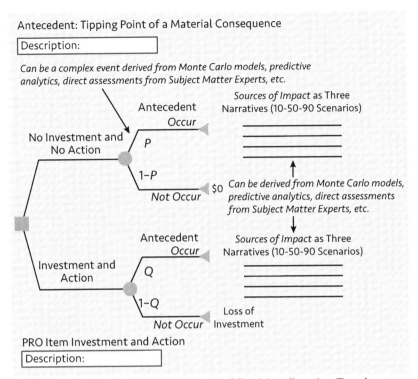

Figure A4.2: A PRO Item Narrative-Based Decision-Framing Template Indicating Areas Data Analytics Can Inform

A critical component connecting data analytics to human thought is the use of narratives or stories as discussed in Chapter 6. Thomas Davenport provides another telling statement this time on the current use of data analytics: "Scratch a highly analytical company and you find highly analytical people in large numbers. That's a big problem, actually, because there are not enough of those people around who can tell good stories with data and explain what's happening in common sense terms."[4] In Chapter 11, we provided an example of a narrative-based decision-framing template that is provided again here in Figure A4.2. Noted in Figure A4.2 are the areas in which predictive analytics and models can contribute to decision framing.

Figure A4.3 provides an overview of the information flow in PRO Management decision making and the role of data analytics in achieving decision quality. Automated decision systems will not include elements associated with the "Individual" perspective in Figure A4.3. Decisions that have no relevant, reliable information

4   Ibid, page 6.

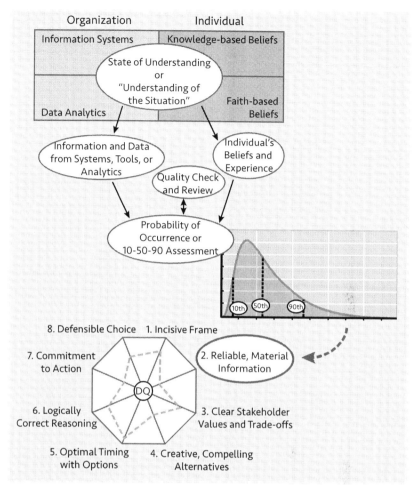

Figure A4.3: Flow of Information from "State of Understanding" to Decision Quality

within information systems will not include elements associated with the "Organization" perspective in Figure A4.3 . Most decisions should leverage and integrate both perspectives to ensure the best state of understanding is achieved. However, it should be noted that any one element of the four contributors to a state of understanding regarding a PRO item can be erroneous or misleading. Data can be wrong or misleading or inappropriate. Predictive models can be based on false assumptions or have faulty logic. As we've learned, expert thinking, opinion and intuition have many shortcomings when it comes to their predictive accuracy.

For any given area (such as R&D investments, or project risk assessments, or procurement sourcing, or marketing and sales initiatives, or quality risk management, or classes of ERM risks, or capital projects), there are typically no more than three to five decision frames (templates) that span the various PRO items associated with the area. And once these frames (templates) have been identified and applied a few times, we can standardize the decision frames (templates) including their information requirements and build these into the associated business process. Figure A4.4 suggests a conceptual architecture of the relationships among databases, information system/data analytics, PRO Enterprise Management assessment templates, and a PRO Enterprise Management analytics platform (such as PRO-Prospector—an existing web-based PRO Enterprise Management software application).

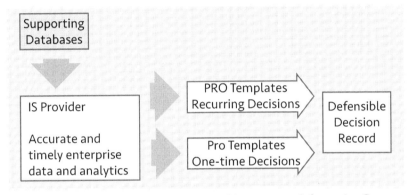

Figure A4.4: Conceptual PRO Enterprise Management Information System Architecture

The Role of "Big Data"

A 2012 survey of senior executives at Fortune 500 companies indicated that 85% of the companies had launched "Big Data" initiatives.[5] Most managers consider the movement to leveraging Big Data as still in its infancy. Analytics are still limited, with much effort focused on collecting and processing data. The analytics generate great looking graphs and visuals, but how well do they inform decision making? From a PRO Enterprise Management perspective, how well does Big Data inform the five questions of PRO Management? How can we leverage the emergence of the many Big Data initiatives currently in vogue?

---

5   Randy Bean interviewed David Kiron, "Organizational Alignment is Key to Big Data Success," *MIT Sloan Management Review*, January 28, 2013. http://sloanreview.mit.edu/article/organizational-alignment-is-key-to-big-data-success/.

Fundamentally, Big Data is about pattern recognition, sifting through large amounts of data and identifying patterns. As discussed in Chapter 6, the human brain performs three functions that are critical to human contemplation and decision making including:

♦ Generating and retaining beliefs,

♦ Perceiving,recognizing, generating, and storing patterns, and,

♦ Predicting and anticipating, which results in expectations.

Big Data pattern recognition capabilities can support PRO Enterprise Management in a multitude of ways, including:

♦ Identifying problems, risks, and opportunities,

♦ Assessing probabilities of occurrence, and

♦ Identifying types of potential consequences (impacts) coupled with the numerical assessments of these consequences.

IBM's Watson computer system is an example of Big Data real-time prediction capabilities integrated with a large number of database resources. A Watson predictive-analytics innovation is the ability to understand natural language to enable hypotheses generation. It uses a machine-learning approach based on successes and failures to improve future responses. The result is the ability to process large numbers of unstructured natural language documents to answer natural language questions—something that could improve both decision framing and PRO item numerical assessments.

We need a standardized framework for which information systems and data analytics can inform decision making. PRO Enterprise Management structures represent a starting point—a reference point that attempts to get information systems and data analytics providers the information requirements of corporate decision making. In the simplest of terms regarding the data output requirements of information systems and data analytics intended to inform corporate decision making, their data output must inform enterprise-wide PRO item assessments that in turn enable answering the five questions of PRO Management from an enterprise value-based perspective, which ultimately resolves the PRO Dilemma for managers and executives throughout the enterprise.

Appendix 5: Beyond Risk Alchemy

Why Risk Matrices Are a Dangerous Brew

Astonishingly, in the pharmaceuticals and biotech industry where corporate pride and ultimate corporate survival are derived from excellence in the pursuit of breakthroughs in science for the well-being of individuals, these same corporations measure and manage *risk* with methods and tools that are acknowledged as unscientific and flawed. This results in:

♦ Misinforming decision making (ultimately undermining their mission and value protection efforts), and more worrisome,

♦ Potentially mismanaging risk to their customers and patients.

I am referring to the ubiquitous *risk matrices* found in operations, quality, and compliance organizations that unfortunately are condoned by regulatory agencies such as the U.S. Food and Drug Administration and the European Medicines Agency, and other governmental departments and agencies such as the Department of Health and Human Services, the Department of Defense, the Department of Transportation, and many more. These often home-grown creations have been criticized by risk analysis experts[1] for years for their faulty mathematics and resultant misleading conclusions. But these criticisms have been muffled and out-marketed by consultants and software providers peddling alchemy. Providers and practitioners of risk matrices defend their use with statements like, "they are simple to use and everyone uses them."

The same could be said for the consumption of fast foods, though a steady diet of fast foods is known to be unhealthful. Or statements like, "they promote a good risk-based conversation that all stakeholders can be involved in," which is a valid point but wouldn't we rather have a good risk-based conversation that enables well-informed decision making rather than ill-informed decision making? Or statements like "risk matrices are rigorous and accurate enough to identify the top three or four risks that require mitigation investment and action." That is not necessarily true.

---

1   L.A. Cox, "What's Wrong with Risk Matrices?" *Risk Analysis* 28(2), 2008, pages. 497-512.

Severity	
Score	Scenarios
9 (Severe)	* Impact to critical quality attributes * Fatality * Environmental harm * Business delayed > 4 months * Financial impact > $50M * Product recall or withholding product approval
7 (Major)	* Impact to non-critical quality attributes * Hospitalization * Potential environmental harm * Business delayed 1-4 months * Financial impact $10M to $50M * Warning letter
5 (Moderate)	* Quality attributes impacted but does not impact product quality * OSHA recordable incident * Environmental regulatory non-compliance * Business delayed 2 weeks to 1 month * Financial impact $1M to $10M * Product recall or withholding product approval
3 (Minor)	* Non-conformance; no safety impact * First aid injury * Environmental system non-conformance * Business delayed 1 day to 1 week * Financial impact $500K to $1M * Potential regulatory observation
1 (Insignificant)	* Quality attributes impacted but does not impact product quality * No injury or health impact * Environmental impact or non-compliance * Business delayed < 1 day * Financial impact <$500K * No compliance impact
Likelihood	
9 Frequent	* Failure is almost inevitable. * Consistent failures observed.
7 Likely	* Failure will occur in most circumstances. * Repeated failures observed.
5 Occasional	* Failure is probable at some time and has been observed.
3 Unlikely	* Failure could occur at some time. * Only isolated incidents observed.
1 Remote	* Failure is extremely unlikely. * No history of failure.

Table A5.1: Example of Ordinal Severity and Likelihood Scales Used in Risk Matrices

So risk matrices might help occasionally, but they should be avoided as a stand-alone risk management practice in any industry or organization.

Table A5.1 provides an example of the scales used in a risk matrix and Table A5.2 provides an example of a risk matrix with an embedded Risk Priority Number (RPN) scheme.

RPN = Likelihood x Severity		Severity				
		1	**3**	**5**	**7**	**9**
		Insignificant	Minor	Moderate	Major	Severe
9	Frequent	9	27	45	63	81
7	Likely	7	21	35	49	63
5	Occasional	5	15	25	35	45
3	Unlikely	3	9	15	21	27
1	Remote	1	3	5	7	9

(Likelihood)

Table A5.2: Example of a Risk Matrix with Embedded Risk Priority Number (RPN) Scheme

Advocates of risk matrices freely admit their short comings, of which we will see are many. Consequently, advocates claim that risk matrices should not be used in isolation, but considered as a risk analysis tool to be used in conjunction with other tools (such as a hierarchy of controls, cost-benefit analysis).

Unfortunately, in an era of shrinking staff sizes and bulging work-loads, risk managers and analysts don't have the time to perform multiple analyses of risks. So in practice, far too often, the risk matrix assessment is the primary (if not sole) analysis performed in support of making resource allocation decisions across a portfolio of risks. They provide a "low-side" compliant solution when risk management is required. The need is great for a straight-forward, efficient, effective, truly decision-informing, single form of risk analysis that can be applied throughout a corporation, establishing a consistent basis for decision making. And the good news is that such risk analysis methods exist (though their use is still emerging in practice).

Important to remember is that risk management is a decision-making process. In fact, knowledge about risk is only informative, meaningful, and useful if it supports making a decision. In short, any risk management process should be able to answer five questions:

(1) What are the risks?

(2) Which risks potentially erode the most value if not mitigated?

(3) Which risks, if mitigated, protect the most value?

(4) Which risks should mitigation resources be allocated to at this point in time?

(5) Given the expenditure of the risk mitigation resources, what is the residual risk liability and what is the impact to the associated plan and budget?

The arguments against the use of risk matrices are mathematical in nature and are not readily understood by many business professionals or are at least not interesting enough for them to consider. In lieu of restating those technical and mathematically sound arguments, here are my top ten reasons why risk matrices should be avoided and replaced with improved decision-informing risk analysis methods.

Top Ten Reasons to Avoid Risk Matrices

1. You Can't Use Multiplication and Addition on Ordinal Scales

Risk matrices employ "ordinal" scales such as severity scores of 1, 3, 5, 7, and 9 and likelihood scores of 1, 3, 5, 7, and 9 (See Table A5.1). Ordinal scales just "order" things. The score does not offer any information on the degree of difference in severity. A "5" is more severe than a "3" and a "9" is more severe than a "7." So the severity scale could be 1, 2, 3, 4, 5 or 1, 10, 100, 1000, 10000. Or the severity scores could be language such as "not that bad" to "kind of bad" to "extremely bad." Using numbers gives the "illusion of rigor" where there is little or none.

For ordinal scales, the mathematical operations of multiplication and addition are not defined. That is, multiplying two ordinal scale scores means absolutely nothing. It is meaningless. In a race we could have a first-place winner and a third-place contestant. Multiplying 1 by 3 in this case means nothing—obvious nonsense. Risk Priority Number (RPN) scores are calculated as a severity score multiplied by a likelihood score. That is, an ordinal-scale value multiplied by second ordinal-scale value resulting in a product value that is not defined. It is meaningless. In fact, some experts in the field of risk management call these approaches "worse than useless"[2] because they can be very misleading for decision making.

Some risk matrix approaches avoid the RPN scoring conundrum by just filling in the cells of the 5 x 5 matrix with terms like "Critical" in the upper-right cell associated with a severity score of "9" and a likelihood score of "9" as if this language truly added some additional insight. We didn't need a risk matrix to inform us that a risk of this nature would be "critical." When two values from scales are used as terms in multiplication or addition, the only way this has meaning is if the values include information on the degree of difference between the numbers. So users of ordinal scales unknowingly invoke this false assumption invalidating all subsequent insights resulting from the ill-defined mathematics.

Ordinal scale methods for risk management are inadequate replacements for more rigorous risk assessment methods that require similar levels of effort offering far more clarity in language and generating true decision-making insights.

2. Compression within Categories

The "Severe" category has the most within-category compression. As per Table A5.1, a "Financial Impact" of $51M to potentially multi-billion dollar impacts all are scored as "9." One fatality to many fatalities all are scored as "9." Consequently, widely differing degree impacts are treated as equivalent. This is a big problem that makes the overall portfolio of risks resemble a beehive when graphed with many risks seemingly clustered when in fact the risks would be widely spread on likelihood versus impact measures that truly account for degree.

---

2   Ibid. page 500.

3. Compression across Categories

As per Table A5.1, a "Financial Impact" of $500K is scored as "3." A "Financial Impact" of $150M is scored as "9." An impact of $150M is not three times as severe as a $500K impact; it is 300 times as severe. A second degree burn on an employee's hand would be scored as a "3." A fatality is scored as a "9." Obviously, a fatality is not three times more severe than a second degree hand burn. A fatality (scored as "9") is 29% more severe than an individual being hospitalized (scored as "7")? I don't think so! And even the term "hospitalized" is problematic. An individual being hospitalized, treated, and released in the same day to return to a normal life is scored as equivalent to an individual being hospitalized for three-months and disabled for life. Obviously, the notion of human impact is woefully inadequate in these matrices.

4. Implied Equivalence within Categories

Pick any Severity category. As an example, let's pick the "Moderate" category in Table A5.1. There are six "implied equivalent severity" issues for "Moderate" severity. As an example, an "OSHA recordable incident" is equivalent in severity as a one-month business delay. There is a broad range of types of month-long business delays from delaying the launch of a product (a material consequence) to delaying the shipment of a raw material that has a six month safety stock (an insignificant consequence). In either case, it is deemed equivalent to an "OSHA recordable incident."

More problematic is the implied equivalence of human impacts to business/economic impacts. According to Table A5.1, for the "Severe" severity category, a fatality is equivalent to a $50.1M financial impact. According to the "Minor" severity category, putting a band-aid on a cut finger is equivalent in severity to a potential regulatory observation. This can get corporations in legal trouble and should be avoided.

5. Occurrence of Multiple Issues within a Category

Pick any Severity category. As an example, let's pick the "Major" category in Table A5.1. There are six issues that result in a severity score of "7" ranging from "Impact to non-critical quality attributes" to "Hospitalization" to "Potential harm to the environment" to "Warning letter" plus two more. If any one of these six issues occur, the severity score is "7", and is considered a "Major" impact. But what if two-out-of-six occur, or three-out-of-six occur, or even all six occur? Given six issues are defined in a category (as in Table A5.1), there are 63 distinct scenarios that can be defined by considering all of the combinations of the six issues. Regardless of whether only a single issue occurs or all six issues occur, the severity of the risk is scored as a "7."

Things get even more troublesome when we look across severity categories. As an example, if all six issues occur in the "Moderate" severity category, then the severity score is "5." However, a single instance of an issue resulting in "potential harm to the environment" is considered a more severe impact and is scored as a "7" in Table A5.1.

6. Double Counting, Triple Counting, and More

Each severity category has a "financial impact" issue. Even intangible issues (such as reputational risk) have an inferred financial impact, in this case, potential loss of future sales. Moreover, every issue in every severity category results in a financial impact—even a fatality. Is the "financial impact" range of values in each category intended to account for all of the financial impacts resulting from the issues being included such as human impacts, environmental impacts, business disruption, product recalls, and regulatory issues? In practice, teams are very inconsistent in their interpretations of what is considered in the financial impact measure of these scoring systems. And furthermore, what is the definition of financial impact? Lost sales? Additional costs? Impact to free cash flow? Under-counting and double-counting financial impact with risk matrix methods is rampant and ubiquitous.

7. Lack of Accounting for Time

The overall risk matrix approach in practice is often void of the concept of time. The "likelihood" of a risk occurring must be with respect to some defined window of time. Consider the Likelihood categories and the language used in Table A5.1. "Failure is probable at some time," or "Failure is almost inevitable." With respect to what time window? Next month? This year? The next 10 years? This ambiguity muddies the ability to compare and contrast Likelihood scores.

8. Single Occurrence Risk Versus Recurring (or Annual) Risk

Related to the concern of the "lack of accounting for time" is the issue of single occurrence risk versus recurring risks or annual risks. As an example, equipment failure risk has an annualized rate of occurrence or failure rate per a number of hours of service. If there are five pieces of such equipment and any one failing has a material consequence, then how does that get interpreted in the likelihood categories? What about three failures within a year? Or two failures in the next two months? Does the mitigation action mitigate a single failure or all future failures? The degree of ambiguity is great and casts grave doubt on the insight garnered from such a simplistic matrix-based assessment.

9. Mixing Human Impacts with Financial Impacts

No manager nor executive or, for that matter, *nobody* is willing to make explicit corporate value-based trade-offs on financial impacts versus life and death. Yet, that is exactly what is done in the "Severe" category of the severity scale. People don't process financial impacts and human impacts together, inter-twined in their thinking. They are separate and should be dealt with separately if human impacts including death are to be explicitly dealt with.

That said, cash flow measures will indirectly account for impacts to humans in the form of legal fees, fines, and loss of sales, etc. So a cash flow measure can be used as a surrogate measure possibly considered as a "sufficient statistic" indirectly accounting for human impacts.

However, if human impacts are to be directly and explicitly addressed in a risk assessment then they should be dealt with separately as a second severity scale. Unfortunately, this is rarely done in practice. An example of a preferred human impact scale is "Quality-Adjusted Life-Years" (QALYs)[3] that accounts for the number of individuals impacted and the degree these individuals are impacted over time. Incidentally, if you are planning to update your risk matrix, there are fates worse than death on the human impact scale.

10. Can't Answer the Five Questions of Risk Management

All risk management processes should be defined as decision-making processes as knowledge about risk is only informative, meaningful, and useful if it supports making a decision. The principal requirements of all risk management processes is to answer five questions noted previously.

Employing risk matrices can result in a satisfactory answer to the first question, and, if done with extreme care and consistency after eliminating the ambiguities presented herein, an acceptable

---

3   Milton C. Weinstein, George Torrance, and Alistair McGuire, "QALYs: The Basics," *Value in Health*, Vol. 12, Supplement 1, 2009, pages 55-59.

answer to the second question. But risk matrices cannot adequately answer the third and fourth questions. In fact, risk matrices can be erroneous and misleading when applied to the third and fourth questions. Depending on the application, a risk matrix-based approach to risk management may or may not be able to answer the fifth question. Let's demonstrate all of this with an example risk portfolio.

Comparison of Risk Assessment Approaches

Risk Matrix Method versus PRO Management Method

For a pharmaceutical company, a portfolio of ten risks has been selected that spans research and development, commercialization, and manufacturing operations. The following is a brief description of each of the risks and a description of a proposed risk mitigation action and estimated cost of the action.

1. Clinical Trial Data Quality Concerns (CTDQ)

A colon cancer pivotal study is ongoing with enrollment complete. The last patient visit is scheduled for Sep 30, 2018; the final report is scheduled for Dec 15, 2018, and the Market Authorization submissions for Feb 15, 2019 with approvals 12 months later resulting in targeted peak sales of $2B by 2024. The quality and interpretability of the patient data (compliance risk) has a chance of affecting the regulatory review timeline to approval and has a chance of even preventing approval. To prevent this quality risk, the Contract Research Organization (CRO) has indicated it needs an additional $5M in resource expenses while management in the sponsor pharmaceutical company believes that the CRO created the risk by not staffing as originally planned and funded.

2. Clinical Trial Enrollment Schedule Delay (CLTE)

A breast cancer pivotal study is scheduled to start enrollment in July 2018 and complete enrollment in June 2019 with 1,000 patients. Several individuals involved in managing the CRO relationship have raised concerns about the aggressiveness of the schedule and claim there is a 50% chance of enrollment being delayed by six months. The CRO predicts that it would cost an additional $8M on this $100M study to keep the timeline on track. Planned market authorization applications for the US and EU are June 2020 with approvals 12 months later and peak sales of $1B by 2026.

3. Single-Source Stock Out Concern (SSSO)

A product that is becoming a higher value product in the company's product portfolio is currently sole-sourced. Should the company invest in establishing a second manufacturing source to reduce the chance of product supply interruption? The cost of establishing a backup supplier is about $5M with additional annual costs of about $1M per year to maintain the manufacturing option.

4. Free Goods for Indigents (FGIN)

For many years the company has been running a program that donates free pharmaceutical products to indigent patients. It has been determined that there is insufficient policy, procedures, and documentation for these free goods distribution to ensure there is no off-label use. It would cost about $16K to establish an appropriate policy, procedures, and documentation.

5. Stockout Resulting from Delayed Tech Transfer (SOTT)

Concern is rising over the Contract Manufacturing Organization's (CMO's) ability to complete the tech transfer on schedule. A six-month safety stock is already built into the overall tech transfer plan and budget. Recent increases in the demand for the product coupled with a delayed tech transfer could result in a stock out. Some customers would be lost during the stock out as physicians change over to a competitor's product. To mitigate the risk of a stock out, the tech transfer team is recommending to hire a well-respected outside contractor as a "man-in-the-plant" and build up another four months of safety stock. The tech transfer team is also recommending that executive management step up their communications and concerns with the management of the CMO. The total cost of these risk mitigation efforts is about $650K.

6. Quality System Risk Assessment and Upgrade (QSRA)

A well-respected consulting firm has worked with the quality organization to perform a quick, pro bono risk assessment of the company's quality systems and has made a recommendation on a project to do a thorough examination of the quality systems followed by a "change program" to improve quality and minimize the chances of future regulatory issues and actions. The total cost of the proposed program is $5.1M over two to three years.

7. Change in Demand Contract Impacts (CDCI)

A contract with a CMO lacks a documented process to address changes in demand or changes in production capabilities. Potential for changes in demand are emerging and there are two years remaining with the existing contract until renegotiation. An early renegotiation of the contract will cost an additional $700K.

8. Customer Care Service Complaints (CCSC)

Customer complaints are increasing about the quality of service from the call center and the supporting web-based system. Concern is rising over how this might negatively impact future sales. A system upgrade is scheduled in two years that should improve the quality of service and reduce the cost of running the call center and supporting systems. Should the Customer Care Center (Call Center and Web-Site) be revamped this or next year or is it okay to wait before pursuing this upgrade? The incremental cost of revamping the Customer Care Center earlier than planned is about $1.0M.

9. Unreported ADEs and Inconsistent NDA Database (UADE)

For an ongoing clinical trial, medical coding responsibility was given to MDs and other clinical scientists. Unfortunately, no standardized coding guidelines were documented for terms. Concern is rising that the lack of standards could result in delayed product approval due to inconsistencies in coding. The risk is receiving a Not-Approvable Letter at time of NDA filing. The recommendation is to immediately hire a CRO to redo the safety database at a cost of $10M. Also recommended is the creation of a centralized coding group by hiring a lead of medical coding and three coding specialists. The annual cost to the company is about $600K per year for the new staff.

10. Security System Upgrades (SSUP)

Recent system penetration testing revealed several vulnerabilities including:

- ◆ Error messages information that can reveal system backdoors, and
- ◆ Some old test APIs that, under certain circumstances, could allow a direct path into the main financial system.

The question is whether to mitigate these vulnerabilities now or wait until there is a breach of customer data. A breach of customer data will create costs of breach discovery and recovery with some loss of customers that once lost will not return. If there is a breach of customer data, the company would most likely pursue the security system upgrades it is currently considering as a project. The cost of the security system upgrade is about $3.5M.

Table A5.3 provides an example of a completed risk matrix including both the "Before Investment and Mitigation Action" scoring as well as the "After Investment and Mitigation Action" scoring.

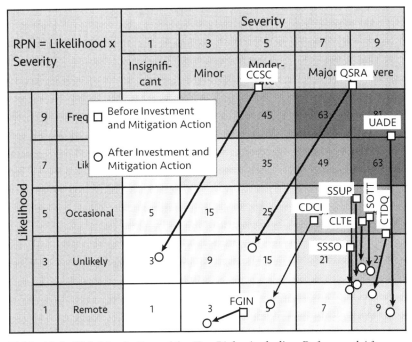

Table A5.3: Risk Matrix Scored for Ten Risks, including Before and After Mitigation Investment and Action

The immediate question that arises is how do you prioritize or choose which risks to mitigate based on the information provided in risk matrices coupled with estimates of the cost of mitigation?

♦ Prioritize by RPN score before investment and action?
♦ Prioritize by the reduction in the RPN score?
♦ Create some pseudo cost/benefit or return on investment score?
♦ Have a conversation and vote on the priorities?
♦ A combination of some or all of the above?

Table A5.4 suggests a prioritization of the risks based on reduction in RPN score as determined by examination of the risk matrix in Table

A5.3. So a starting position in a discussion on how much to invest in risk mitigation actions might be to fund all risks with an "RPN Reduction" of 30 or more for a total investment of about $26.3M. Of course, no one would claim that the final decisions on which risks to invest in should be based solely on any one analysis. However the analysis does provide the starting point for the discussion and consequently provides a "priming effect" to the decision process—an anchor and reference point in which arguments must be made on why the prioritization offered is incorrect. And we know that confirmation comes more readily than disagreement, especially in a group setting.

Priority Based on RPN Reduction	Risk	Reduction in RPN	Cost of Mitigation ($M)	Cumulative Cost ($M)	Cumulative RPN Reduction
1	QSRA	66	5.1	5.1	66
2	UADE	54	16.0	21.1	120
3	CCSC	42	1.0	22.1	162
4	SSUP	36	3.5	25.6	198
5	CDCI	30	07	26.3	228
6	SOTT	18	0.65	26.95	246
7	CLTE	18	8.0	34.95	264
8	CLDQ	18	5.0	39.95	282
9	SSSO	18	13.5	53.45	300
10	FGIN	2	0.02	53.47	302

Table A5.4: Risk Mitigation Action and Investment Prioritized by RPN Reduction

As an alternative to the risk matrix-based approach, let's consider a second approach based on PRO Enterprise Management.

PRO Enterprise Management is designed to do one thing—answer the five questions of PRO Enterprise Management, which are a generalization of the five questions of risk management. It is based on a narrative approach initially focusing on the "tipping point of a material consequence," the antecedent of a risk, and then the range of potential consequences accounting for all sources and magnitudes of value and cost to the corporation over an agreed-to time horizon. Arguably, all sources of value and cost to a corporation impact cash flow at some point in time, even so called intangibles like reputation, brand equity, patents, and copyrights.

Consequently, the net present value (NPV) of impacts to cash flow is the primary measure used in PRO Enterprise Management. And when human impacts are to be explicitly discussed and considered, a second and separate measure is used, Quality-Adjusted Life-Years (QALYs). Critical to the practicality of the PRO Enterprise Management approach, is that it can be performed in as little as 15 minutes in a facilitated discussion or can be built-out to a higher level of complexity and detail but only if required at the request of the decision-maker or another key stakeholder.

A key measure in PRO Enterprise Management is *investment productivity* (see Chapters 12 and 13), a type of return on investment measure that accounts for the uncertainty in the risk assessment as well as the time value of money to the corporation. It has a very simple interpretation. An investment productivity of 3.0 for a risk mitigation action means that each $1 of mitigation investment protects $3 of corporate value as measured in today's dollars. Table A5.5 provides the priority of risk mitigation investments for the ten risks based on *investment productivity*.

Priority Based on Investment Productivity	Risk	Investment Productivity	Cost of Mitigation ($M)	Cumula- tive Cost ($M)	Cumulative Protected Value ($M)
1	SOTT	167.0	0.65	0.65	106.2
2	CLDQ	62.3	5.0	5.65	417.6
3	UADE	20.7	16.0	21.65	721.0
4	CLTE	12.82	8.0	29.65	820.7
5	SSUP	7.95	3.5	33.15	842.4
6	CCSC	6.71	1.0	34.15	848.9
7	QSRA	3.44	5.1	39.25	866.4
8	CDCI	2.97	0.7	39.95	868.4
9	SSSO	(0.02)	13.5	53.45	868.2
10	FGIN	(0.29)	0.02	53.47	868.2

Table A5.5: Risk Mitigation Action and Investment Prioritized by PRO Enterprise Management Investment Productivity

Notice the broad range of investment productivity values in Table A5.5, ranging from about 167 down to negative values, which represents a typical spread across a portfolio of risks for a pharmaceutical or biotech company. Through a straightforward analysis consistent with the level of effort required by a well-scored risk matrix, we can discover, for example, that investment in a risk such as "Quality System Risk Assessment and Upgrade" (QSRA) has an investment productivity of about three to four. This tells us that it is not negative nor is it over five as compared to other risk investments that are negative or ten to fifty times more productive. Risk matrices are unable to provide this critical decision-making insight.

According to Table A5.4, the risk matrix-based analysis based on an RPN reduction prioritization would suggest the Top Four risks to pursue at this point in time would include:

(1) Quality System Risk Assessment & Upgrade (QSRA),

(2) Unreported ADEs and Inconsistent NDA Database (UADE),

(3) Customer Care Service Complaints (CCSC), and

(4) Security System Upgrades (SSUP).

The total RPN reduction of 198 points costs about $26M.

The PRO Enterprise Management-based approach suggests a very different Top Four risks to pursue list including:

(1) Stock Out Resulting from Delayed Tech Transfer (SOTT),

(2) Clinical Trial Data Quality Concerns (CLDQ),

(3) Unreported ADEs and Inconsistent NDA Database (UADE), and,

(4) Clinical Trial Enrollment Schedule Delay (CLTE).

This results in total reduction in risk of about an expected $820M in net present value (NPV) at a cost of about $30M.

As with any form of decision analysis, the analysis does not provide the decision, it merely informs the decision makers and the decision process. Arguably, Table A5.5 represents an improved value-based starting point for a discussion on which risks to allocate investment and action at this point in time. In this case, the decision makers recognized the lack of investment return in securing a second source for the SSSO risk, but they nonetheless decided to pursue the second manufacturing source as a "must have" spend. Additionally, the decision makers believed that establishing a policy, procedures, and documentation for the "Free Goods for Indigents" (FGIN) risk was an appropriate and inexpensive risk mitigation action to take at this time. So the decision was to include these two "must have" spends plus all of the risks with an investment productivity of greater than ten as depicted by the investment productivity curve in Figure A5.1.

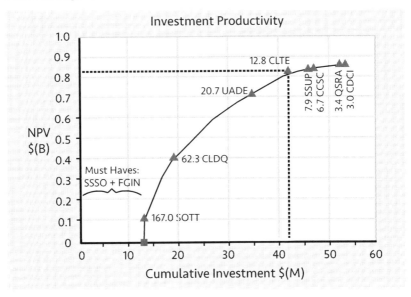

Figure A5.1: Decision to Fund Risk Mitigations, Including "Must-Haves" and Top Four Risks Based on Investment Productivity

The total investment in risk mitigation at this point in time totals about \$43.2M and protects an expected \$820M in today's corporate value. The investment productivity on the set of six risks is about 21.

Using the PRO Enterprise Management standard of risk measurement, the risk matrix-based approach would have protected an expected \$350M in net present value (NPV) for a total investment of about \$40M allocated to the Top Four Risk Matrix risks plus the "Single-Source Stockout Concerns" (SSSO) risk and the "Free Goods for Indigents" (FGIN) risk. The investment productivity on the set of six risk matrix-assessed risks is about ten, which is less than 50% of the productivity of the PRO Enterprise-based investments.

Back to the Five Questions of Risk Management

Without providing all of the details and graphs, here are the answers to the five questions of risk management based on the PRO Enterprise Management-based risk analysis:

(1) What are the risks? (As listed in previous section)

(2) Which risks potentially erode the most value if not mitigated?

The Top Four greatest risks include: (1) "Unreported ADEs and Inconsistent NDA Database" (UADE), (2) "Clinical Trial Data Quality Concerns" (CTDQ), (3) "Stock Out Resulting from Delayed Tech Transfer" (SOTT), and, (4) "Clinical Trial Enrollment Schedule Delay" (CLTE) for a total expected risk liability of about $900M in NPV. The expected risk liability of the total portfolio of ten risks is about $980M in NPV.

(3) Which risks, if mitigated, protect the most value?

The greatest value protection results from investment in "Clinical Trial Data Quality Concerns" (CTDQ) with an expected protected value of about $310M in NPV. In this case, the Top Four risks as measured in terms of value protection from risk mitigation investment are the same as the Top Four most productive risks for investment. That is not always the case. By pursuing the Top Four most productive risks to invest in, the expected total value protected is about $820M in NPV.

(4) Which risks should mitigation resources be allocated to at this point in time?

As per Table A5.5, the recommendation was to fund the Top Four most productive investments, which is equivalent to investing in all risk mitigation actions with an investment productivity greater than or equal to 10.

(5) Given the expenditure of the risk mitigation resources, what is the residual risk liability and what is the impact to the associated plan and budget?

Given the investment decisions as detailed in Figure A5.1. including six risk mitigation actions for a total investment of about $43.2M, the residual risk liability for the set of ten risks is $160M in NPV—about an 84% reduction in expected risk liability.

Concluding Remarks

Risk matrices are an oft-used but inadequate stand-alone approach to risk management and cannot satisfactorily answer the Five Questions of Risk Management. And executives, managers, and risk analysts do not have time to perform and communicate multiple forms of risk analysis to get to the bottom-line question: At this point in time, which risks should resources be allocated to based on best-value to the corporation or customer or patient?

The severity and likelihood scales in risk matrices can be used effectively in very focused applications like a design review of a medical device as part of a failure modes and effects analysis (FMEA). However, the broader the scope of a risk assessment, the more problematic the risk matrix-based scoring system becomes as indicated by the list of ten reasons to avoid their use. This is especially true for cross-functional applications.

Explicitly mixing human impacts with financial/economic impacts, as often done with risk matrices, is problematic from many perspectives. At a neurobiological level, people process human impacts separately and differently from financial/economic impacts and risk analyses should be consistent with this separation. If human impacts including risk of fatality are to be explicitly analyzed, consider using a robust measure such as Quality-Adjusted Life-Years (QALYs) enabling accounting for the degree and number of individuals impacted and the duration that individuals are impacted. A companion PRO Enterprise Management approach exists, though not detailed here, based on QALYs including an investment productivity curve.

It should also be noted that changing the scale threshold values or adding or subtracting levels (categories) of likelihood or severity to a risk matrix will not overcome any of the Top Ten reasons for avoiding them. At the heart of the problem with risk matrices is their foundation in ordinal scales.

If we want risk management resources to compete on a consistent basis with resources for problem management and opportunity management, then we need to determine a defendable return on investment (ROI) measure, such as the investment productivity score, to inform the decisions on which risks currently should be pursued with mitigation investment and action, and which should be tracked and measured going forward to compete for resources in the future. Short of that, you can't manage risk on a best-value basis.

Investment productivity has a nonlinear relationship with respect to the cost of mitigation. People think best in terms of linear relationships and have little proficiency thinking in terms of nonlinear relationships. Consequently, we need mathematics, not risk alchemy methods, to circumvent this inability.

Index

Made in the USA
Coppell, TX
09 May 2021